AF735143

"In an age of 'strong man' politics and increased totalitarianism, being superficially provocative is sometimes mistaken for leadership. But this book reveals that using provocation in real leadership requires intelligence, cunning and, perhaps, most importantly, the ability to think outside the square, in persuading people that change that is uncomfortable for them is a good idea. This book gives a roadmap to using provocation as a tool of both leadership and change: recognizing its boundaries, its risks, and the instruments at hand."

Laura Tingle, *Chief Political Correspondent for the ABC's* 7.30 Report *and author of* Follow the Leader: Democracy and the Rise of the Strongman

"I had the privilege of seeing Michael and Maxime in action when I was their client. Through their wisdom, care, and yes—provocation—I grew as a person and leader, as have so many others. In their book, *Provocation as Leadership*, they are sharing the secrets of their delicate and powerful art. Drawing from a wide range of disciplines and using rich case studies as illustration, *Provocation as Leadership* is a deep exploration of both the anatomy of provocation and requisite conditions for it to create change. The book is full of useful tools and frameworks to enable leaders and consultants to assess how, when, and in what form provocation can lead to change that may have otherwise felt unattainable."

Karen May, *Former Vice President of People Development, Google*

"Exercising leadership is always risky because it involves taking people out of their comfort zone. Maxime Fern and Michael Johnstone remind us in this splendid book that leading means provoking, and that it is necessary to be brave to do so. They provide valuable and well thought out tools—supported by many examples from which to be inspired—to know how to provoke effectively and not to be damaged in the attempt."

Juan Carlos Eichholz, *Professor, Universidad Adolfo Ibanez, Chile, and author of* Adaptive Capacity

"Maxime Fern and Michael Johnstone have delivered a practitioner's dream: a comprehensive field guide to purposeful provocation. Using detailed case studies and relatable stories from their decades of teaching and training, they animate the theory, provide tools to tackle the practice, and offer an honest assessment of the risks and rewards of this approach. While we know our world's most wicked challenges lack easy answers, this book will surely sharpen the mind, steady the hands, and embolden the heart of any intrepid changemaker who seeks to tackle them."

Laura Berlind, *Executive Director, Adaptive Leadership Network, Washington DC*

"This is a timely written book given the lack of leadership in the world today. Maxime and Michael present powerful principles and concepts that address the realities of helping groups, institutions, and complex systems make progress on their toughest challenges. The art of provocation is a vital leadership skill to get attention and stir people to action."

Dean Williams, *President, Thinking Heads Global and author of* Real Leadership

"People experience provocation all the time, especially lately. Rapid technology advances, a global pandemic, evolving understandings about inclusion, high geopolitical tensions, all have many feeling provoked. *Provocation as Leadership* claims 'provocation' as a tool for the greater good and gives examples of how the conscious use of effective provocation can unlock successful change efforts in our families, organizations, and communities. We don't need less provocation in our world. We need better provocation. This book guides the way."

Ed O'Malley, *Former President and CEO of the Kansas Leadership Center*

PROVOCATION AS LEADERSHIP

To create deep change, you have to disturb people, or at least risk doing so. Shaking people out of their comfort zones not only generates the possibility of change but also elicits new information and brings out hidden resources that people need to navigate unfamiliar waters. Nevertheless, provoking without antagonizing or shutting people down and tolerating their pushback are complex challenges, requiring skill and will.

This is the first comprehensive provocation roadmap: why provocation is necessary for effectively leading change, the different forms of provocation, action tools and frameworks, and case studies illustrating how change is achieved through the sustained and careful use of provocation and disturbance, with strategies and tactics for minimizing the risks involved. We illustrate, for example, how two Australian farmers challenged centuries-old farming practice to regenerate their properties and how a large American bank used the death of a revered CEO to reinvigorate the business. We show how a young indigenous school principal tackled entrenched attitudes to turn a failing school around and how a national statistical service acted like a technology start-up to innovate during the Covid-19 pandemic. The case studies address change at the local level, within organizations, as well as on a national scale. We finish with a synthesis of the lessons learned and a set of ideas about building people's capacity to use provocation to live, learn, and thrive.

Provocation as Leadership offers a blueprint for people who, using provocation, want to ignite change and help their organizations, group, or community break through to a better future. This book provides a vehicle to see provocation in its potential for necessary disturbance, to lay bare its anatomy, and give access to its possibilities, including how to enable provocateurs to live another day.

Maxime Fern, M.Ed. and Michael Johnstone, PhD., partners in life and work, trained in Psychology, Systems Family Therapy and Human Geography, developed the art of provocation as therapists and then leadership consultants. Stepping into places where others may be too polite to go, they refined provocation at Harvard's Kennedy School as a framework to help others understand and succeed when change and adaptation is the only option. Both authors live in Australia and Italy.

PROVOCATION AS LEADERSHIP

A Roadmap for Adaptation and Change

Maxime Fern and Michael Johnstone

Routledge
Taylor & Francis Group
LONDON AND NEW YORK

Cover design: Alison Stannard (Bobdog Design) and Lynn Staley
Cover image: © Alberto Gagliardi / Getty Images

First published 2023
by Routledge
4 Park Square, Milton Park, Abingdon, Oxon OX14 4RN

and by Routledge
605 Third Avenue, New York, NY 10158

Routledge is an imprint of the Taylor & Francis Group, an informa business

© 2023 Maxime Fern and Michael Johnstone

The right of Maxime Fern and Michael Johnstone to be identified as authors of this work has been asserted in accordance with sections 77 and 78 of the Copyright, Designs and Patents Act 1988.

All rights reserved. No part of this book may be reprinted or reproduced or utilised in any form or by any electronic, mechanical, or other means, now known or hereafter invented, including photocopying and recording, or in any information storage or retrieval system, without permission in writing from the publishers.

Trademark notice: Product or corporate names may be trademarks or registered trademarks, and are used only for identification and explanation without intent to infringe.

British Library Cataloguing-in-Publication Data
A catalogue record for this book is available from the British Library

Library of Congress Cataloguing-in-Publication Data
Names: Fern, Maxime, author. | Johnstone, Michael (Leadership consultant), author.
Title: Provocation as leadership: a roadmap for adaptation and change / Maxime Fern and Michael Johnstone.
Description: Milton Park, Abingdon, Oxon; New York, NY: Routledge, 2023. | Includes bibliographical references and index. |
Identifiers: LCCN 2022026550 (print) | LCCN 2022026551 (ebook) | ISBN 9781032334721 (hardback) | ISBN 9781032342535 (paperback) | ISBN 9781003321200 (ebook)
Subjects: LCSH: Leadership. | Organizational change.
Classification: LCC HD57.7.F467 2023 (print) | LCC HD57.7 (ebook) | DDC 658.4/092--dc23/eng/20220624
LC record available at https://lccn.loc.gov/2022026550
LC ebook record available at https://lccn.loc.gov/2022026551

ISBN: 978-1-032-33472-1 (hbk)
ISBN: 978-1-032-34253-5 (pbk)
ISBN: 978-1-003-32120-0 (ebk)

DOI: 10.4324/9781003321200

Typeset in Garamond
by MPS Limited, Dehradun

To our parents Luise and Johnny Johnstone & Gladys
and John Fearn.

For all that we are.

CONTENTS

ABOUT THE AUTHORS

Maxime Fern and **Michael Johnstone** are life and working partners, based in Canberra, Australia, where they started their consulting practice (Vantage Point Consulting Pty Ltd.) in 1988. For the past forty years, they have worked together around the globe as leadership consultants, facilitators, and coaches with clients in the public and private sectors, not for profits, and professional service firms. They are known for their different but complementary approaches which have assisted many hundreds of executives expand their skills and mindsets to lead change and adaptation. They were visiting faculty at the Kennedy School of Government, Harvard University for fifteen years, are on the Faculty Advisory Board of the global Adaptive Leadership Network (Washington, D.C.), and are members of the Inaugural Faculty for the Australian Adaptive Leadership Institute. Both authors are Members of the Australian Psychological Society, Chartered Management Consultants and Members of the Australian Institute of Management Consultants.

They have three children and eight grandchildren, and they live in both Canberra and at their home in Lazio, Italy, north of Rome.

Prior to starting Vantage Point, Maxime worked as a development officer for the Australian Public Service, a social heath visitor in a low-income neighborhood, and as a counseling psychologist for the Commonwealth Scientific and Industrial Research Organisation. She is a graduate of the Australian National University (Psychology and Politics) and holds a Master of Educational Counselling from the University of Canberra. In her spare time, Maxime can be found in her gardens, and practicing her Italian on Duolingo.

Michael trained as a youth worker, and has worked as a town and regional planner, social researcher, university lecturer in Human Geography and Sociology, and for while was a dairy farmer on a kibbutz in Israel. He holds a BA from Auckland University, a Master of Social Science (cum laude) from the Hebrew University of Jerusalem, and a Ph.D. from the Australian National University. Michael has lived and worked in New Zealand (his country of origin), the UK,

Malaysia, Italy, and Australia. In his spare time, he likes to read, cook, watch movies, and work out in the gym.

Source: Photo by Teresa Mancini at ByCam Fotografia, Italy.

FOREWORD

This is a book about pissing people off.

People you care about. People you love. On issues that matter to you.

Fern and Johnstone's blazing insight is that the willingness to provoke and the capacity to do so skillfully may be uncomfortable for the provocateur and unsettling for the provoked, but necessary for individuals, organizations, and communities to move away from their adherence to the status quo.

The disturbance of useful provocation can come from one person or from an event. It can consist of a single dramatic moment or persist over some time as an ongoing condition or a continuing interaction.

I was eighteen when I first experienced the benefits of being discombobulated by a master provocateur. I was in college, taking a seminar required of anyone who wanted to be an Honors Major in Political Science. We met in the late afternoon, on the second floor of a small house at the edge of the campus, eight of us seated around an oval-shaped wooden table. The professor was a small, intense man with a round head that seemed too big for his body, framing huge dark brown eyes, which appeared to nearly pop out of their sockets when he glared in your direction. He sat at one end of the oval table, and I was sitting at the other. He asked me something about the reading, an excerpt from Spinoza's *Ethics*. I did what I always did in school, dutifully barfing back to the teacher what I had read the night before, demonstrating that I had done the homework. This game of doing the homework, recalling it in class or in an exam, had worked very well for me. That's what school was about, wasn't it? Study, regurgitate, get a good grade, go on to the next level.

There was a pause. Professor Gaudino leaned over the table, coming as close as he could get to me, those eyes bulging so much I felt they were almost touching mine as he said, "Yes, that's what Spinoza said, but what does that have to do with you, Mr. Linsky?!"

What the hell was he talking about? I experienced myself sinking into the chair, trying to disappear. Everyone was looking at me. We were talking about some 17th-century Dutch philosopher, not about me. The whole idea that anything I was doing at school had any connection to me personally was incomprehensible. I said nothing. Gaudino did not take me off the hook or let any of my classmates do so either. He held the silence long enough to make sure it sunk in. I do not remember anything else about that conversation. My head hurt. So did my gut. What I do remember is that I did not sleep at all that night.

That moment, that impolite provocation, changed my attitude toward my education, and in doing so, changed my life.

Gaudino was an apostle of uncomfortable learning. To him that phrase was a redundancy. There is no deep learning, no real change, without discomfort. He was an equal opportunity provocateur. Each of us in the seminar had a moment like that. So did the college community as a whole, his faculty colleagues, and the college itself.

Gaudino was relentless in his commitment to challenging the spoken and unspoken assumptions of everyone he encountered and every community he was a part of. He was not popular. His impact was extraordinary.

Look, I like to be liked. There are limits to my tolerance for risk. I like some predictability, calm, and orderliness. So did Gaudino. So do Maxime Fern and Michael Johnstone. So do you, I bet. It's a human thing. I've known many curmudgeons along the way, although best as I can tell even the crustiest of them don't leap out of bed in the morning proclaiming how much they are looking forward to a day of disturbance and disorder which might well involve upsetting folks they care about.

It is much easier to upset the enemy, those who you and your people are striving against. I started out as a politician. Politicians understand this well. You see a politician standing in front of an angry crowd of opponents, and you might say to yourself, "Wow, that takes courage. I could never do that." Getting booed by your opponents makes you feel even more self-righteous and puffed up than you were before. It reinforces your identity with your own community. What you almost never see is a politician in front of an angry crowd of his or her own people. That really does take courage.

Whether you a politician or a parent, a president, or a peon, you have probably had the challenge of a time when you knew you had to provoke people to make progress on some difficult issue.

The status quo is not an accident. The way things are is the product of conscious and not so conscious choices about the way people want things to be. Your need to be liked and to have order in your existence conflicts with the need for those people in your life to be jarred out of their comfort and complacency, to, well, be provoked in order to address some underlying issues they would rather avoid.

That is the human and, yes, leadership dilemma Fern and Johnstone probe so skillfully and deeply in these pages. Tolerating the discomfort of people you care about, the willingness yourself to be uncomfortable and maybe disliked, at least in the moment, if not longer, is a huge asset for making progress.

The authors draw on their own training and experience, a cornucopia of research from a swath of related disciplines, and lots of stories of people like you, to powerfully describe how your desire to be liked might get in the way if you are trying to lead change, close the gap between your aspirations and the current reality, or transform the status quo and how you can effectively overcome that reluctance.

What follows in these pages is a roadmap full of checklists and application techniques for when and how to provoke, not as an end in itself, but as a complex tool, to help you and your family, organization, or community move forward. Provocation is always a risk, but if you follow their guidance, you will be able to overcome your own reluctance and use provocation selectively and strategically, customized to the particular context in ways that will maximize your chances of success and minimize the chances that you will create a long term breach with the community you are trying to nurture.

This is a no, it is THE Provocation Encyclopedia. Read it. Treasure it. Be a courageous and skillful provocateur. I learned Provocation 101 from Gaudino. Fern and Johnstone have given us the gift of a Ph.D.

Marty Linsky
New York, NY
April 2022

ACKNOWLEDGEMENTS

This book is based on three main sources—our experience, the inspiration of our teachers and mentors, and interviews with a wide range of people including our clients, friends, and those we met along the way.

The ideas we explore have been brewing for some time and have their origins in our history. We are a life couple who chose to work together and build a business, living a dream of doing work we love with people we admire. The diverse ways we each show up in the world have been a source of productive conflict (ah yes, and at times pain) as well as stimulation and joy. We have provoked each other and, in the heat, annealed a set of ideas and ways of working that we now offer here.

If our relationship (personal and professional) was the spark that started the provocative fire, then our work at Harvard's Kennedy School of Government, with Professors Ron Heifetz and Marty Linsky, was the fan that kept the flame burning. It is true to say that our time with Ronnie and Marty changed our lives and we are enormously grateful for the lessons and guidance they so generously offered. From Ron Heifetz, we gained new ways of thinking about change and progress, including how to see and utilize the complexity that exists in any group, an engaging way of working with people, and the drive to stay focused on the central work at hand. From Marty Linsky we slowly came to accept the reality of the hard edge of change; the essence of alliances and loyalties; the need to examine the ecosystem of relationships; and finally, and most important really, an enduring friendship.

While teaching at the Kennedy School, we were supported and encouraged by the faculty team of Dr. Lee Warren, Nancy Houfek, Professor Bob Kegan, and more recently Dr. Lisa Lahey. Lee played a significant role in our fifteen-year involvement at Harvard as she encouraged us to become members of the faculty team and was an endless source of support, and love. Nancy Houfek generously taught us to tell great stories and how to bring grace and joy to the work of leadership. Bob Kegan and Lisa Lahey introduced us to their breakthrough work on Immunity to Change and their understanding of the centrality of provocation continues to inspire us.

In our early careers, we trained and worked with many outstanding teachers and mentors who added layer upon layer of understanding, skill and simply ways of looking at the world of people and how we all change and learn. John Barnaby (Transactional Analysis), Phil Boaz (NLP), Brendon Reddy (Team Dynamics at the National Training Labs), John and Joyce Weir (Self Differentiation and Percept Language),

Michael White (Narrative and Systems Family Therapy), Dr. Max Clayton (Psychodrama and Action Methods), and Frank Farrelly (Provocative Therapy).

The stories, examples, and anecdotes we tell throughout the book are mainly drawn from our experience, both personal and professional. Here we have many hundreds of people to thank and recognize. These include all of the managers, executives, and leadership development professionals who were participants in a program or consulting assignments we facilitated. You all were our teachers, and we are wiser because of you. We acknowledge in particular those of you who contributed to the *Art and Practice of Leadership Development* at Harvard University's Kennedy School of Government between 2000 and 2016; and participants from leadership activities we designed and delivered around the world for companies like Google (2010–2016), and for the Australian Public Service Commission (2000–2022).

The case studies throughout the book are all based on direct interviews with those whose lives and work we explore. Many were clients, coachees, or simply people we identified and sought out because of the work they undertook. Our interviews with our subjects were both informative and inspiring. And in most cases, it provoked us to rethink what we wanted to write. We supplemented our interviews with additional material from public interviews, speeches, and academic research.

We acknowledge Charlie Massy and Colin Seis, two humble, genius Australian farmers; our friends from kibbutz Yizrael (and originally from Michael's homeland, New Zealand), Peter Pezaro and Shimon Zelas; Dr. Chris Sarra from Queensland; David Kalisch and Dr. David Gruen from the Australian Bureau of Statistics; René Jones and Kevin Pearson from M&T Bank (Buffalo, NY) and Jeff Lawrence who coached them; Dr. Martin Parkinson, David Tune, and Dr. Ken Henry previously Departmental Secretaries in the Australian Public Service; David Parker who we knew from the Australian Department of Treasury; Nyadol Nyuon who we were introduced to and came to admire; Sarah Mali and Diana Renner who were participants at the Harvard program and who became, and still are, colleagues and friends. We can't thank you all enough.

There are many others who gave their time, who we reference using pseudonyms and some, like our ex-Google colleague Geoff Mendal, who have so much to share as a result of their deep experience. Many others influenced our thinking and challenged us on the way, including our colleagues at the Kansas Leadership Centre and at Cambridge Leadership Associates (New York).

Several people read draft chapters and provided valuable comments and critique—Diana Renner, Marty Linsky, Anton Zelcer, Shawn Callahan, and Maya Bernstein. Thank you. A special thanks to Diana Renner who constantly nudged us to write and believe in this topic; and ultimately to Marty Linsky—our mentor and guide—he helped us stay the course and continues to keep us on our edge.

To our editor, Richard Martin, who not only reviewed and shaped our early drafts but became a thought partner. Thank you.

All of you have been generous and steadfast to us and to our endeavor, and generous with what you shared. Even without what we have written in this book, you have each enriched our lives. We hope we have interpreted what you told us fairly and accurately, and our interpretations have done justice to each of you and your achievements. Any errors are ours.

We recognize our three children (Danielle, Guy, and Summer) who continue to offer us unique opportunities to learn and grow. Experts in provocation, they still teach us to rethink who we are and what our job as parents and people is as it changes. And finally, to our eight grandchildren (Lillian, Madeleine, Samuel, Gabriel, Violet, Adelaide, Paloma, and Leo) who, as they grow and move toward adulthood, also take their part in helping us see the world anew. You each remind us that challenge and love are part of the same package and can come from unexpected sources.

INTRODUCTION

> *I provoke thought because that is what needs provoking. Humanity seems to hate thinking more than any other activity, and yet that is the activity most needed. I do what I can to force thought along, and I am hated and worse—ignored—for it. That's ultimately acceptable to me because the work needs to be performed.*
>
> Robert Peate, On Writing

This is a book about rehabilitation, opportunity, and growth.

The rehabilitation is of the word *provocation* itself and our understanding of what it means to provoke. The opportunity is to repurpose and make use of provocation as a powerful tool. The growth relates to how we want to help individuals, groups, and organizations learn and flourish. We want you to be much more capable than before, to successfully navigate the swirling waters and crashing waves of our globally connected times.

Many of us, from diverse backgrounds and fields, seek to bring about change, to exercise leadership but find that the status quo, existing attitudes, and patterns of behavior resist our efforts, especially from within our own organization or community. Because we take the view that leadership involves people and organizations facing the adaptations they must make to survive and thrive, we know that leadership is challenging. To foster change and adaptation, we have to deliver difficult news or help others adjust to a new reality. We understand viscerally that change requires a critical examination and disturbance of the status quo, the attitudes and behaviors of our everyday practice and routines. But most of us do not take kindly to being disturbed, particularly if our habits, traditions, and loyalties are involved.

Our history as community workers, systems family therapists, our training in and teaching of Adaptive Leadership, and our exposure to Robert Kegan and his Adult Development theory, all have influenced our thinking. They have helped us understand why change is so hard and how essential it is to create productive disturbance.

We would hazard a guess that more than one reader of this book will have had the experience of trying to bring a critical issue to the attention of other people. You may have found that those you engage with act as if they are not interested, even though it seems self-evident that change is needed and in everyone's interest. You may have wondered what other strategies and moves you could make to shake people out of their apparent complacency, out of their addiction to "how we do things around here."

DOI: 10.4324/9781003321200-1

You would not be alone. We have noticed this too, detecting three notable trends. First, despite good intentions, most people need a good reason, a nudge, to shift their way of thinking, learning, and behaving. Second, people learn best, and are more willing to make changes, when they experience what Jack Mezirow calls "a disorienting dilemma"—that is, a troubling situation or disruptive event. Third, to navigate through such events, people require a combination of support and challenge.

We have experienced firsthand what it means to be disturbed, as our clients, participants, colleagues, mentors, and family have challenged us. This has been both uncomfortable and energizing because we have learned a great deal about what does and does not work and why. In the process, we have also learned a lot about each other and ourselves. Through our working and life partnership, we have been drawn, sometimes to our peril, to the problematic, rocky work at the heart of the disturbance created during adaptation and change. Despite the occasional discomfort, we have thrived on being disturbed and on disturbing others, including each other—to provoke from a place of love and care which is at the heart of who we are. We do not always succeed, sometimes provoking each other unskillfully and, at other times, forgetting the love. But these lessons have given us a clear philosophy in our teaching and consulting work. Learning, growth, and change are possible but require skill, will, and deep commitment and love for individuals and their welfare.

This book is about leadership and change and the necessity of facing or creating disturbance in order to get there. This is not a self-help book, but it is intended to prompt both thought and action by those who have, or should have, authority and influence. It is an essential guide for anyone leading deep change, laying out a blueprint for when and how to provoke in the service of your mission.

Consider the following scenarios, which describe typical challenges we have seen and where some kind of different response is required to break an unproductive pattern or help an organization realize its potential.

1 Jade, a senior executive in a global tech company, was at her wit's end because there were frequent arguments in her team, members criticized and undermined each other, and some stakeholders were becoming concerned. She felt stuck because everything she tried was not helping and the group was caught in a cycle of blame and recrimination.
2 After decades of neglect, a small First Nations school in outback Australia appoints a new principal who discovers rampant absenteeism, dilapidated buildings, and children running wild. The teachers are despondent and believe this is the way it is and that "these children can't learn. It's who they are."
3 After the death of a well-regarded CEO, a growing regional bank in the USA realizes that its old and proven ways of operating are not sufficient to compete in the digitized marketplace. The new CEO and his colleagues face the unpalatable idea that they are wedded to ideas that serve them but not their clients. Adaptation is not a word anyone uses.

4 A new female team leader notices that her male colleagues rarely answer her questions or even look at her in meetings. Indeed, some don't follow her directions. She concludes that they are having trouble with her as the new group head, and would prefer not to have this particular fight.
5 Following a debilitating strike, the new site lead at a large industrial plant facing a dispirited workforce observes the hierarchical nature of the business and the way well-established but antiquated management and working practices get in the way of operational effectiveness.

Each of these situations offered a choice for those involved—continue with tried-and-true methods, with more of the same, or do something different. As we show throughout this book, the leaders and change agents we discuss here all did something unexpected, and more functional responses emerged. They all risked challenging the status quo, held steady during the ensuing disturbance, and broke through.

This book emphasizes the skill, will, and heart required to challenge that which people hold dear and is concerned with creating the conditions in which the beliefs and micro decisions we make unconsciously can be examined. We can then ask how current beliefs, values, or behaviors help or hinder progress in relation to any specific purpose.

In this context, provocation comes into its own by introducing productive disturbance. It questions the otherwise useful, daily rituals of politeness and avoidance of discomfort. Our work has taught us how to overcome people's natural tendencies to be polite, and careful, and to protect others from the consequences of their beliefs, and behaviors. It has shown us that the comfortable path is most often taken, even at the expense of what we say we care about.

We believe that it is possible for most individuals and groups to learn to be more purposefully provocative. We also believe that it is possible to create more productive disturbance than may previously have been considered reasonable. Provocation is a skill set, a mindset, an analytic process, and an emotional experience that needs to be crafted, practiced, and refined over time. Learning to be skillfully provocative to help others reshape their lives and their collective futures is an adaptation in itself. You will need to examine your own beliefs to say or share what, on the surface, might seem outrageous or even hurtful. You, like the leaders we coach and teach, can decide how much to experiment, and practice this new skill set, knowing that there is always the risk of getting it wrong. Yet, most learning and change comes from experiment, trial, and error.

If you are interested in change and human adaptation, you already know that there are situations when it is difficult for people to understand how to attend to an issue even when change is required. By the end of this book, we hope you will have a more sure-footed clarity about planned, purposeful provocation, and disturbance.

Each of the aforementioned vignettes illustrates the strength of the status quo. They demonstrate that a core task of leadership—at the micro family level, macro community level, or national level—is to gain people's attention and hold them to the critical issue, even when fully aware that this will create a disturbance. Without people's attention and their agreement that there is a problem to be faced, all efforts by those wanting to facilitate change and adaptation are futile.

As such, we want to make the tensions more visible. On the one hand, there are the usual, often useful, dare we say, comfortable, certainly acceptable ways of interacting, and behaving. These often serve us well. However, on the other hand, there are those occasions when to proceed in known and practiced ways would not only be insufficient but would amount to an abdication of responsibility.

Today, we face global disagreement on how to respond to issues that threaten to engulf us. These include the climate crisis, growing inequality and inequity, military conflicts, mass migration, the relentless pressure on business to adapt and innovate, and most recently, how to live in a Covid-19 world. There appears to be perpetual realignment on social issues and across the political spectrum.

In the face of so much disturbance, it is hard to imagine people tolerating any more pressure. Yet, across all walks of life, people are saying something has to change, that things can no longer continue as they are. People ask how can we best use this moment in time This is a question about change and adaptation, and, implicitly, is about how to hold people's attention to the issues they are swimming in.

This book attempts to address this question. How do any of us attract and hold people's attention in a world where there is so much noise and so many competing issues? What tools and strategies can we use to move things forward? How can people, with or without formal power and authority, effectively challenge the status quo?

In *Provocation as Leadership,* we provide an expanded view of leadership and argue for reimagining provocation and disturbance as fundamental to continued human evolution and adaptation. People can learn from and harness what is already happening in nature, as well as from what takes place in scientific laboratories, and innovation hubs around the world. There is a continual cycle of testing and challenging established ways of doing things, letting go of those ways that are no longer productive or functional, and finding new ways to operate. In nature, we call this natural selection and adaptation. However, given the demands and pressures people face in today's world, adaptation cannot be left to chance. Purposeful action is required now.

We encourage an everyday mode of leadership that can be practiced by all of us—ordinary, diverse people, community workers and activists, family members, mid-level business managers, and chief executives. Anybody committed to seizing a moment in time can raise hard questions about how, why, and where things are not fit for purpose.

The unabated pace of change, together with the complexity of the challenges we face, calls for a grittier view of leadership based on three core ideas. First, provocation is essential for long-term, systemic change—a fundamental resource for any leader or change agent. It is required to help people understand how they are stuck, held back by, and often gain from, the status quo. Second, provocation is a means to elicit new information and bring out hidden resources necessary to navigate change. It facilitates insight, discovery, and breakthrough. Third, being provocative is usually unappreciated. It is often not welcomed because it is challenging, uncomfortable, and considered anti-social. It can be overused, and it puts the provocateur at risk unless used with skill and awareness of the dangers.

In this way, provocation becomes a valuable and necessary tool for leadership work, but one that is potentially dangerous. Provocation can evoke strong reactions from others, responses that have the potential to undermine the leadership work and those enacting it. So, provocation as a leadership and change tool must be undertaken with a mind to understand how it works and how to use it wisely.

As we will discuss throughout the book, unless people can be encouraged to examine the attitudes and patterns that hold them back, it is much less likely that real change will take place. But without disturbance, or some clear motivation or shock, people will continue with what they have, even if it is unproductive or even maladaptive. We need to perturb just enough for people to start to pay attention to what is troubling them, but not so much that they cannot function.

Provocation as Leadership provides insight into the power of provocation by exploring theory, practice, and risks, brought to life, and exemplified by stories, conversations with many people, case studies, and our observations. We argue that new ideas and perspectives are vital in overcoming resistance to change, and provocation is the means to elicit missing information that makes change possible. As Gregory Bateson[1] shows us, information is life. Whenever people or systems are stuck, leadership is required to move forward, to identify innovative and potentially challenging knowledge and practices.

You will learn methods to provoke individuals, groups, and organizations skillfully. A range of unique forms of provocation are examined, illustrating how provocation is an essential tool for progress, adaptation, and change across a wide range of sectors and current problems. You will also understand the risks of provocation and of going too far.

We serve as guides throughout the book. We recognize the need for both optimism and care. Drawing on what we have learned, we explain how to succeed, as well as how to recover when you have overstepped. We aim to help you understand the importance and necessity of provocation, as well as the need to employ it with skill and forethought.

This book has five parts.

~~~

1.1 Part One: What is provocation and why is it necessary?

This part centres on Chapter 1. in which we want to help you rethink the role of provocation in your life and work. To that end, we provide an expanded view of provocation, attempt to demystify the term, and provide a framework that shows the full range of forms of provocation that can be used.

1.2 Part Two: Provocative capabilities and skills

In Part Two, we consider how to use yourself as an instrument for provocative purposes. Chapter 2 details the foundations of provocative action and the importance of
~~~

diagnosis, showing how the ability to make skilled observations and interpretations is essential, and provocative in itself. These skills sets are essential for all types of provocation expanded in the next Part.

Chapter 3 provides a practical focus outlining five core diagnostic skills required for effective provocation. The skills are based on five simple questions: why, where, when, what, and who? We demonstrate that provocation is both an analytical practice, as well as an action method.

Based on the lessons we learned from consulting and from teaching change agents, Chapter 4 examines five perspectives or attitudes necessary for effective provocation. These skills sets are essential for all types of provocation expanded in the next part.

1.3 Part Three: Types of provocation

Building on the foundations outlined earlier, in Chapters 5–7 we examine different forms of provocative action, including Paradox, Stories, Humor, and Counterfactuals. We illustrate with examples and anecdotes, including comments from the leaders and change agents we have interviewed, and show how different styles of provocation can have varied impact. Woven throughout Parts Two and Three are examples and case studies from politics, sport, education, and business.

1.4 Part Four: Application—practicing provocation

Our case studies describe how provocation was used by someone who faced their fears and their opportunities, and overcame the constraints of the status quo. Each chapter is based on conversations we have had with a client, a community activist, a friend, or someone we discovered through our research. The examples highlight one or two of the provocative schemas we have identified (Chapter 1) and show the advantages and risks of the approach chosen.

We have used several Australian examples because this is home ground for us but also because Australia is one of the most connected and interdependent societies in the world. It is a simpler microcosm of the developed world. What happens in Australia is noticed elsewhere and vice versa. For this reason, the case studies used in the book reflect much of what is occurring elsewhere—be it environmental change, food security, offshoring of manufacturing, changes in family life and social norms, transforming a business in response to changing customer needs, or the challenges of absorbing immigrants and refugees.

There are four types of case studies—individual and personal, very local, for example, within a small school, within a whole community or business, and across a large, complex, national system, such as water usage.

It is a challenge to identify a causal link between individual provocation and organizational or complex whole system change; the inevitable complexity muddies distinctions between instigation and results. However, looking at cases that shifted a national status quo across Australia may come close. Australia's relative geographical isolation and progressive nature provides a petri dish where we can weigh the impact of individual provocateurs. The level of provocation illustrated in Chapter 13 for example created profound shifts in sedimented beliefs, values, and behavior. New patterns were enabled with national effect. This level of change can rarely occur without the involvement of government, and so we show how several policy designers and politicians risked provoking noticeable change.

We offer two chapters with more individual and personal focus. First, we offer examples of several prominent people who put their heads above the parapet to speak out on important issues, the tools they used, the risks involved, and the results. And then explore the way personal life transitions are provocative for all of us because they require profound reevaluation of our values, of who we are.

1.5 Part Five: Risks and lessons of provocation

Following the examples of provocation in action, Part Five focuses on the impact and risks of provocation. Provocation can sometimes take people to places they do not want or have not agreed to go. In Chapter 16, we discuss seven key risks and what can be done to mitigate them.

Chapter 17 provides insights into how to help people, including yourself, as you live with and harness provocation and disturbance, whereas Chapter 18 discusses five key lessons about using provocation and concludes with some practical guidelines.

~~~

In summary, our central proposition is that to exercise leadership and create change, you must disturb people. But provoking without alienating people already under pressure, or shutting them down, can be a complex task. This book is designed to give those of you who are hesitant and those of you who are brave, the tools and encouragement to provoke more than you currently do. If your hesitancy to provoke is a barrier to you stepping out and getting closer to your purpose, then this book is for you. If you are ready, we provide a clear categorization of the tools required and a schema of provocative approaches.

In the words that follow, we hope to guide you on a path that helps you embrace your inner provocateur. We want to enlist you as a member of the growing wave of people prepared to risk, at least temporarily, their reputations as smooth operators who always get it right and always look good. We want you to be the ones who engage and enable others to use their hearts and brains when addressing the big challenges that confront us all. We hope the lessons will help you ignite change and break through on those challenges that matter most to you.

Note

1 Gregory Bateson was an English anthropologist, and systems thinker whose work influenced practitioners across a variety of fields including family therapy, cybernetics, mental health, and evolution. See *Steps to an Ecology of Mind* (1972).
~~~

References

Kegan, R. (1994). *In Over Our Heads: The Mental Demands of Modern Life*. Harvard University Press, Boston, MA.

Mezirow, J. (1991). *Transformative Dimensions of Adult Learning*. John Wiley & Sons, New York.

Peate, R. (2015). *On Writing*. Self-Published. https://rpeate.wordpress.com/on-writing/. Retrieved 1 July 2019.

PART 1

WHAT IS PROVOCATION AND WHY IS IT NECESSARY?

Provocation is a skill set, a mindset, an analytic process, and an emotional experience that needs to be crafted, practiced, and refined over time. Learning to be skillfully provocative to help others reshape their lives and their collective futures is an adaptation in itself. You will need to re-examine your own beliefs to say or share what, on the surface, might seem bad mannered, outrageous, or even hurtful. You, like the leaders we coach and teach, can decide how much to experiment, and practice this new skill set, knowing that there is always the risk of getting it wrong. Yet, most learning and change comes from experiment, trial, and error—exactly what you are asking your participants to do.

In Chapter 1 we outline what provocation is and how it can be used.

DOI: 10.4324/9781003321200-2

1 WHAT IS PROVOCATION?

I am deeply committed to challenging ways of thinking and behaving that I consider unhelpful and contrary to the conduct of a high expectations relationship. It does not serve any of us to leave such ways of thinking and behaving unchallenged.

Chris Sarra, Beyond Victims: The Challenge of Leadership

1.1 Introduction

In 1729, Jonathan Swift published *A Modest Proposal*, which he subtitled "For preventing the children of poor people of Ireland from being a burden on their parents or country, and for making them beneficial to the publick." He outlined the social and economic advantages of poor Irish people selling their children as food to the rich. He recommended, "buying the children alive, and dressing them hot from the knife, as we do roasting pigs." Many citizens were outraged, and it took time for them to realize that Swift had been purposefully provocative, shining a light on the plight of the socially and economically disadvantaged. He challenged the indifference of his countrymen, focusing attention and shocking his peers to reconsider their own values and behavior, as well as government policy.

Swift's work demonstrates that provocation is not a new phenomenon and how it might force the reassessment of values. Swift's satire also illustrates three essential leadership tasks when change is needed, requiring us to give up a belief or behavior that previously underpinned our existence. The first task is to help people identify their critical challenges. The second is to ensure the visibility of the challenges and amplify them if they are not given sufficient attention. The third is to jolt people into action while ascertaining that the adaptive issue remains front of mind. These tasks are as relevant for executives and team leaders as they are for change agents and leadership consultants.

As the world faces more problems that have no easy solutions, purposeful provocation becomes increasingly necessary. This is not something that we can leave to the brave few. We can all use provocation to navigate the situations and crises we find ourselves in, enhancing our lives and moving forward. For us, provocation should be viewed as constructive troublemaking rather than something negative. Indeed, we want to avoid any stigma associated with it.

Provocation encompasses a broad range of actions, from shocks to gentle prods. It includes the outrageous and the kind, the disturbing, and the calming. At times, we

DOI: 10.4324/9781003321200-3

have found, to our surprise, that it can even be provocative not to provoke, confounding others' expectations. Provocation is essential for leadership. You can act provocatively, you can respond to the provocation inherent in a situation, and you can be swept along by provocative moments that extend over time.

This chapter will outline how we see "provocation" and how we use the term throughout the book. We provide you with a framework to increase your ability to respond more surely to changed circumstances. Equally, we provide a set of essential tools and a schema of provocative approaches.

We will draw on three linked disciplinary traditions as we develop our ideas: systems family therapy, adaptive leadership, and adult development. These traditions shape our understanding of how change happens and are the basis of how we think about leadership, which makes provocation necessary. We will use politics, history, philosophy, comedy, and the arts to see how this works in practice.

1.2 Perspectives on provocation

We are admirers of Hannah Gadsby, an Australian comedian who has gained global prominence by challenging her audiences with her breakthrough show *Nanette*, which is available on Netflix. Gadsby confounded people's comedic expectations by raising highly evocative issues, such as misogyny and homophobia, requiring the audience to engage directly with our culpability. She created a temporary space so that we could see a different description of some of the less visible, more brutal ways we are with each other. We were tested, and some of our habitual responses began to melt in the heat she created as she morphed her role from comedian to catalyst and provocateur.

While speaking about her success, Gadsby offered a pithy definition of provocation when she said, "I broke the contract." Thus, Gadsby helps us understand what provocation is and how you, too, might draw on it. Her work can help you orient to the tricky world of provocation with a purpose, the goal of this book.

The verb *provoke* is defined in the *Merriam-Webster Dictionary* as "something that irritates, arouses, elicits or stimulates." It is derived from the Latin *provocare* meaning "to call forth." *The Cambridge Dictionary* defines the verb as "to cause a reaction, especially a negative one," as in, for example, "I was provoked into an argument." These definitions show that provocation has two parts. First, there is an action or stimulus; then, there is a reaction. Gadsby speaks and makes jokes, poking at our protective sensibilities, taking us to the very edge of what we can manage. We, the audience, react, disturbed, and squirming. We may reject the disturbance by hiding behind our comfortable assumptions or defensive routines, such as labeling the provocateur as rude, unskilled, or inappropriate. Our reaction to her provocation deliciously makes the case she prosecutes.

Provocation is not just something annoying or off-putting but also can be a productive and creative activity that can also bring something into being. Therefore, the third component of provocation arises from in between and surrounding the initial stimulus and response. Gadsby builds a relationship with her audience, steadily increasing the pressure. In turn, we develop greater awareness of the boundaries of our worldview and our own commitment and collusion in the world she describes. She cannot do the work alone and pushes us to carry some of the load. As a result, we find ourselves stimulated, thinking, and acting differently. Gadsby achieves this effect by speaking of her trauma and isolation as a gay woman, raising issues that the public generally doesn't discuss. Her story and the audience's reaction construct a provocative bubble, a moment in time when "business as usual" stops and deeper reflection can occur.

Like many systemic phenomena, the interaction between the comedian and her audience, between a change agent and an organization, produces something intangible. Skilled provocation creates emergent qualities that enable breakthroughs in our thinking and behaviors, which leap forward beyond the old routines. Its effect permeates our thought and action long after the original act. In the disturbance that emerges, time and space create a learning opportunity, a liminal zone where—as a parent, friend, team leader, facilitator, advocate, change agent—you can create new awareness and energy, helping others experience, even momentarily, the consequences of their beliefs and behaviors.

These provocative moments, generated by the shock of the unexpected, are what political scientists Giovanni Capoccia and Daniel R. Keleman call "critical junctures." These are intervals in time (or history) when there is a heightened probability that someone will act to affect change. They render the unyielding elements of the status quo more plastic and amenable to different outcomes, and suddenly things open up. What was rigid, becomes malleable; what was inaccessible can now be examined. During provocative moments, the rules, and assumptions of operation, in all units of analysis (whether in a family, school, institution, or whole society) are loosened, resulting in first, more engaged people who are ready for something different; second, a more comprehensive range of choices; and third, decisions and actions having more significant impact. Finally, during the opening up forged by provocation, critical actors can shape outcomes more deliberately in partnership with those affected. Provocative junctures, once started, are harder to stop, momentum is created, and it becomes possible for leaders and change agents to ride the wave together with their constituents.

Although provocative actions may appear to be timebound, they have the potential to shake people long after the initial event. They become what Karl Polanyi called in his epic 1944 book, *The Great Transformation*, "connecting stretches of time." As you will see in later chapters, the most effective provocations will stop time, so people can see and feel things relevant to them, and cross or extend time as people begin to learn and adapt while in a zone of productive disturbance. Gadsby's audiences similarly describe their experiences.

1.3 Four lessons

We have learned four fundamental lessons that show us that provocation is essential to generating the learning necessary for adaptation. First, despite best intentions, aspirations, and heroic self-descriptions, most people prefer their current situation to unknown ones. They will not easily let it go, and left to their own devices, most will choose to hang on to the status quo at almost any cost. People and systems thereby have stable patterns that are hard to move.

But, if significant, systemic change is required, advice, explanation, and logic are not enough because such strategies are more likely to engender deeper devotion to our existing ideas and greater resistance to change. Our advice and explanations only serve to activate the organizational antibodies.

Second, to create a new, more productive pattern that will help people move toward their stated purpose, an intervention is needed that can leap over the threshold of current commitment to what you see, do, and believe. For stable patterns to shift, we all need to be disturbed by an unexpected and often unwelcomed event or action.

Third, change requires taking people beyond their comfort threshold into what Ronald Heifetz, Alexander Grashow, and Marty Linsky refer to in *The Practice of Adaptive Leadership* as the "zone of productive learning." Adaptations will significantly "displace, reregulate, and rearrange some old 'DNA' aspects of an organization's way of doing things. People must be helped to navigate through a period of disturbance for which they may not be prepared and, inevitably, are reluctant to embrace." This displacement and rearrangement is part of adaptation and at the heart of leadership work. But as any systems or complexity thinker will tell you, change will be disorderly, unpredictable, emergent, and context dependent.

Fourth, while recognizing the need for provocation, we also understand that despite its potential benefits, we may inadvertently upset people and cause offence, sometimes unnecessarily and without apparent gain. If it were straightforward for people and systems to adapt and change, we probably would not need to provoke them. But it is neither easy nor predictable.

Before you can address the reasons for provocation, you must recognize the signs that people are stuck, and that the required change lives outside the realm of business-as-usual. Therefore, we invite you to be discerning about when only provocation will do.

1.4 Working hard at failure

When our clients come to us with a "big problem," such as team dysfunction or with strategy alignment, what we often find is that, despite their protests to the contrary, the way they interact and problem-solve is stable and perfectly designed to keep them comfortable and exactly where they are. Like the seabed, there are multiple layers of sediment built on the debris of repeated efforts to solve the problems they face. As a result, people become stuck in the mud, unable to move. The leadership task, then, is to help them become less stuck—individually and collectively—identifying and exploring other options that will lead to adaptation.

We think of groups of people, of any kind, as systems within which behavior and relationships show consistent patterns over time. People reinforce the patterns that they believe will serve their purpose, even though this reinforcement can lead to suboptimal outcomes that keep them repeating maladaptive ways. In human systems, responses to problems become indicators of the ways groups will succeed or fail in overcoming the barriers and contradictions they face. A repeated pattern of failure to address an obstacle leads to an escalating problem—in scale, impact, and urgency. Organizations and communities adapt, thrive, and grow when they learn how to confront issues. They become maladaptive when they do not. A problem only becomes salient when patterns of unproductive behaviors start to impede life and progress. The homeostasis is disturbed, and the disequilibrium becomes too much to live with.

Therefore, problems in groups and organizations develop over time as the inevitable outcome of vicious cycles and the cultural and behavioral restraints embedded within them. It is hard to persuade people away from known routines, even when they see that their habits create problems. Groups are accustomed to the status quo. While this may be recognized as problematic, it can also serve a purpose for the team, community, organization, or individual.

How can you help both individuals and groups see and feel things that the status quo keeps hidden? How can you help them reveal the "service" provided by the maladaptive grip of existing patterns?

When straightforward advice, suggestions, compelling data, and argument are not enough to alter behavior, it is necessary to provoke people to see beyond their current visibility threshold. As they do so, they can begin to learn more enabling patterns of discovery, knowing, and doing. Provocation instigates a battle between the wisdom people have in protecting themselves and what they are currently invested in and the wisdom of a larger, change-oriented perspective.

1.5 An affair with the status quo

For some years, we consulted to a college, helping to improve collaboration between the different educational departments, and foster an environment of trust and open exchange. In conversation, we discovered what was holding them back—they interpreted their strong commitment to their goals as "follow the rules and don't rock the boat." Consequently, alternative viewpoints and any dissent disappeared, and there was little or no robust discussion. While this was not what they wanted, it was the prevailing mode of operation, making change difficult to accomplish.

It can be so hard to let go of something you know—such as a relationship, belief, or practice—even when it is increasingly apparent that clinging on to it is misguided and may even perpetuate or exacerbate a problem. When current practice no longer serves your needs, it may be necessary to provoke and challenge to ignite change. When you realize that the accumulated debris of past problem-solving efforts themselves have become part of the problem, provocation can help shift us from the familiar, challenging the usual explanations and resistance to change.

In this sense, when groups of people are stuck, they need a push, a critique, or a shock, prompting them to assess the reality they face more consciously. Yet so much of the usual advice, exhortations, or data they receive goes unheard. As Gregory

Bateson observed in *Steps to an Ecology of the Mind*, information does not "pass the collective threshold of restraint."

Helping people see that they are not the sediment they are stuck in is at the heart of helping people change. People can see how their learned routines, recurring patterns—a response to initial symptoms—effectively hold them back. Members of a family or an organization can reflect on whether the rules and assumptions that guide them should be changed and how their problem-solving efforts undermine their goals.

As we found in the college, the people involved prevented the "real" problem from being seen. They were restrained by their habits and beliefs, which served as information barriers. Since change would require them to take a fresh look at where they were and where they wanted to be, we needed to curate information in such a way that it overcame their established habits and beliefs. For example, when we asked the teachers whether it was more important to be clear and consistent in their direction or to have an open and vibrant culture, they initially opted for the former. This question helped them see how they were stuck.

When someone did speak out at the college , they were often privately chastised for rocking the boat or being difficult. It was as if the school police were watching, and as soon as someone spoke up, the police could say, "Now we've got you." The braver teachers continued to speak out but, over time, were worn down by this recurring pattern—what we refer to as a *racket.* Drawing on Eric Berne's pioneering model of *Transactional Analysis*, rackets are unhelpful patterns of feelings, thoughts, and behaviors that undermine efforts to change. They cement psychological responses, preventing evolution. We discuss one typical pattern—"Yes, but"—in Chapter 5.

In this way, each action or intervention that makes new information available will elicit a reaction, enabling people to pay attention differently, seeing things from an alternative viewpoint. Provocation and the ensuing disturbance help make ideas newsworthy and increase the chances that new information will be received. In Bateson's words, it may become "the difference that makes a difference." The initial difference may be a random event, crisis, a variation or shift in social or political alliances, or as we explore in depth in this book, a deliberate action by one person. A different perspective on how people approach their problems can reveal the original symptoms, the responses, and whether a holding pattern or growth pattern is being created.

In summary, the main reason you provoke is to challenge an unproductive status quo. But it is hard to wrench people away from familiar routines, even when they can glimpse that their habits create the problems. And in the moment, don't expect them to thank you for it.

1.6 Signals that provocation is needed

The patterns we saw among the teachers were a clear sign that they were stuck and needed help to loosen the status quo's grip. As we do in all our consulting assignments, we used the following rubric to identify the key signals. You will also see how these signals appear in the case studies we describe in Part Four and how each one impacts the problem-solving ability of those involved (Table 1.1).

Key Signals
A repeated pattern of unsuccessful attempts to solve the problem—efforts to resolve the situation make it worse.
There are few attempts to broaden the information and perspectives available (i.e., reduced variation).
Failure to identify and plan for predictable changes in the environment.[1]
Success breeds complacency, pride, and arrogance.
People overestimate their capability and underestimate the challenge.
Overreliance on expertise and authority—an increase in the God complex.
Insularity and a lack of strong connections and interdependencies (both internal and external).
An increase in complaint, blame, and unproductive conflict.

Table 1.1 Signals that provocation is needed

1.7 An overview of provocative action

Not all change interventions are provocative. Some are necessarily designed to do the opposite—to calm things down, reassure people, or orient them. Others help you refine what you have, even though the underlying rules that govern the system do not change. But when you need to put pressure on a system, provocative moves are critical.

Provocative interventions come in different forms and sizes—from a challenging question posed or observation offered by a therapist, facilitator, friend, or family member, to a significant event or environmental shift that heralds something new. In each case, the provocation is a disturbance to a prevailing pattern, be it to a business culture, our family routines, social norms, or behaviors or even to supply and demand curves that govern commerce. The shock enables us to see the need for change in a different light. Connie Gersick's 1991 article on "Revolutionary Change Theory" describes these moments as punctuating the stability of a longstanding status quo. In this way, interventions and events trigger a shift. They open and fracture existing patterns of thought and action. In this sense, punctuation and provocation are the same. They both bring the problem into sharper relief, creating conflict over ends and means, and stimulating a period of productive disturbance, which leads to exploration, discovery, and change.

1.7.1 A spectrum

A range of methods from softer to more confrontational interventions can be used to provoke a system productively whatever the unit of attention. Individual actions, including questions, critique, observations, interpretations, stories, counterfactual scenarios, experiments, or decisions, are designed to bring forth a new response, to reactivate a group's capacity to learn beyond the current and exhibited range of thinking and action. Hannah Gadsby exemplifies this spectrum by using gentle jokes and prodding, followed by her deeply personal revelations, which directly challenge her audience.

	Conventional methods	Unconventional methods
Soft	Tell a story	Ask systemic questions
	Ask questions	Use an unusual metaphor or image
	Ask a person to reflect	Use psychodrama to illustrate
	Encourage interpretation	Use analogy (e.g., medical trials)
	Seek more specifics	Act as a nonverbal mirror
	Encourage deeper diagnosis	Restrain change
	Ask how ripe the issue is	Direct people to go slow
	Make assumptions explicit	Prescribe symptoms
Challenging	Name default roles	Use paradox
	Remove clarity and structure	Make a purposeful mistake
	Reorder agreed priorities	Be inattentive
	Make a strong interpretation	Refuse to answer a question
	Identify gaps in values and behavior	Utilize resistance
	Deliver hard news	Call out irresponsible behavior
	Don't protect people	Use powerful images to shock
	Describe the elephant in the room	Develop a counterfactual view
	Point to actions as evidence of intention	Emphasize immanent critique
	Relay an emotional scene	Use subversive narratives (a song or poem)
	Use an unpredictable role	Use anger to raise heat

Table 1.2 A spectrum of provocative action for a change agent or facilitator

There are also methods to stimulate behavior change across a large system, such as the water policy action described in Chapter 13 and those discussed in Chapter 12, for example, where the Covid-19 pandemic created an environment in which the Australian Statistician, Dr. David Gruen, challenged his organization to break the shackles of the past and emerge as an exemplar of public sector innovation.

Provocation occurs along a spectrum ranging from soft and playful to strong and aggressive. Your intervention may be experienced as a shock, threat, violation, stimulant, nudge, or an invitation to action. Whatever the form it is often the way you provoke rather than the content of the provocation that will create the biggest impact. Your approach may even use subversive humor or a more forceful stance. Again, flexibility and variation are key (Table 1.2).

Furthermore, successful provocation is not always respectful or compliant with social norms. Anthropologists have shown that it is possible to be aggressive with others and still be accepted and useful. We all are familiar with the friendly physical games that fathers, in particular, play with children, leading the youngsters to squeal with both fear and delight. We see, too, how adults enjoy the rough and tumble of teasing and friendly insults. Forceful provocation can be part of your toolkit, providing the recipients believe that you care and have their best interests at heart.

Conversely, provocation may be gentle and kind even though the recipients feel challenged and threatened. The late Lotte Weiss, a family friend of ours, was a Holocaust survivor. Her gentle approach to retelling the stories of the realities of Auschwitz was deeply confronting but arose from her kindness and hope. She would say, "I am part of an endangered species, trying to warn the next generation of what humans are capable of." Provocation is always designed to revitalize people and the systems they live and work in, unsettling their current thinking. It can be shocking—although that is not a prerequisite for its effectiveness.

1.7.2 Confounding expectations

Frank Farrelly, the founder of Provocative Therapy, taught us to confound expectations, one of the many forms of provocation. We have seen how people, individually or in groups, are more robust than most of us think and do not need coddling. Provocateurs can humorously take on the role of devil's advocate, playing on the client's ambivalence toward themselves and change, giving voice to the negative, and holding up a mirror to reflect their constraints. The change agent highlights how the person or group is holding themselves back, developing their self-knowledge and capacity to utilize disturbance for growth and change.

In his book *Provocative Therapy*, co-authored with Jeff Brandsma, Farrelly explains:

> I take the illusions, the belief systems, the assumptions of clients, and I say in effect to them: "Which one do you want to be real?" And if you maintain this view of yourself, of other people, of the structures within which you live, I know what you will get—more of the same!

He reminds us that targeted, loving disturbance of a system's infrastructure, its fundamental DNA, can be transformative.

1.7.3 Productive disturbance: Stimulus and reaction

Our starting point is that change can only occur if an individual, a group, or a more extensive system confronts and tolerates a disorientating experience. The observations we offered to the teachers mentioned earlier were the first steps in their growing encounter with the patterns of behavior and thinking that kept them stuck. Provocation is understood here as the disturbance of the school's homeostatic routines, affecting its communication and interaction. Overall, our critique tested and perturbed some of what our clients knew and believed about themselves and the actions that held their beliefs in place. Provocation disturbs established ways of thinking and peoples' narrative about themselves. It unsettles the historical sediment and attempts to render it less relevant, exposing the instructions, coding, and algorithms on which their current life stories depend.

As such, these interventions are not an end but a method with a range of specific tools designed to create moments that are sufficiently newsworthy to draw people's attention. Any intervention begins a process of discovery and experimentation, leading to problem resolution and innovation. Just as evolution teaches us how changes to DNA affect biological adaptation, provocation in human endeavors creates pathways to new possibilities and new narratives.

We liken these perturbing activities to medical drug trials that test the sensitivity of new drugs and antibodies by observing where and how a new medicine will elicit a reaction in the body. Regulating a new product's provocative properties is a critical part of determining drug strength and dosage size. As with drug trials, we learned through trial and error and the honing of our diagnostic skills how far we could go with the teachers, what was most helpful and what was not.

1.7.4 Getting over the threshold

Mary was the senior human resources advisor for a global resources company who wanted her colleagues to demonstrate more collective leadership at their monthly meetings. The team had committed to work across functions and tackle business-wide challenges, but they mainly discussed tactical issues when they gathered. They aspired to have more "real and authentic conversations," to debate issues and challenge each other. Mary lamented, "They know what is required, but just don't do it! Why is that?"

Mary wanted to help her team see and feel things that the status quo kept hidden, revealing the rackets and adverse effects of existing unproductive patterns. She tried different ways to discuss what she could see but to no avail. Her advice and exhortations failed to pass over the threshold for change because the group could (or would) not see their situation outside of their current view. Eventually, Mary realized that her leadership task was to provide information in a sufficiently different form to overcome the threshold of restraint. She needed to provoke her team to be open to new information.

When usual methods are insufficient, it is necessary to act differently so that the group responds differently, grasping their dilemma anew. As they do, they can begin to explore and experiment with alternative operating methods instead of a familiar defensive routine.

The more stuck or restrained a group or system is, the higher the threshold over which information[2] must jump to be seen and heard. In this sense, Mary's group needed a nudge to experience the reality they were avoiding, and to understand how their longstanding way of problem-solving was not helping them meet their stated goals. Mary decided, therefore, to use her frustrations as a tool.

Her ideas needed to be more newsworthy or "sticky" than before to increase the chances that a new perspective could be genuinely considered. This prompted her to speak uncharacteristically passionately, and forcefully. She highlighted the discrepancy between her colleagues' claims that they wanted to act more courageously with each other, and the timidity and politeness evident in their meetings. Mary used a critique pointing to the contradiction between the team's espoused values and what they did. In so doing, she encouraged a more overt focus on their current patterns of behavior.

The unpredictability, energy, and focus of her provocation led to a deep conversation in which all team members spoke directly, identifying their frustrations, including with each other. They became alert, energetic with an urgency that allowed them to redefine their reality, establish new learning conditions, and identify alternative ways to move forward.

As Mary's experience demonstrates, actions or interventions that get over the threshold will elicit a reaction, and result in people paying attention differently.

1.7.5 Create an opening

Provocative moves increase the chances that your ideas will jump over the resistance threshold, a principle that was reinforced during a strategic thinking exercise we facilitated for a senior team. In these activities, we usually see ourselves as having at least two roles. First, as facilitators who assist a group discuss their challenges but who are neutral to the outcome. Second, as pattern interrupters, whose job is to help people see how their behavior either enhances or constrains exploration and deep discussion.

In the early conversation, the executives did two things. First, they blamed resource cutbacks for their current problems and then focused most of their attention on what was working and why it should continue. The resource issue might have contributed to the slow pace of change, but it was an insufficient explanation for the problems the group listed. We deviated from our original plan offering a simple framework, a different lens, to invite another view.

We asked the group to determine what activities they should keep, those which were core to the business and what could be modified or discarded. The framework, taken from Adaptive Leadership, is inherently provocative because it requires people to consider threshold issues, such as what is a priority and what is not. The Trojan Horse in this simple design is that change requires something to be discarded or lost in order to move forward.

As the conversation became focused and productive, it became clear that the group had been avoiding their disagreements. But now people spoke honestly and contested ideas vigorously. The exercise breached the threshold of the existing narrative to highlight what was being kept invisible by the exclusive focus on day-to-day activity. No one wanted to give anything up, but everyone agreed that something needed to shift. The group began to name the potential losses required for their survival and acknowledge their uneven impact. That is, they named the inevitable and uncomfortable truth that not everyone would be affected evenly.

Our intervention nudged existing ways of doing business toward an alternative means of operating, allowing activation of new and underutilized behaviors. A unique quality of interaction emerged in response to our challenge, helping the group overcome its threshold for change.

Overall, you can choose from a wide range of provocative responses to target thought patterns and behaviors that help maintain the status quo. Each type of move has its own impact depending on form, timing, and intensity.

1.7.6 Intention and impact

Leadership is specifically about change that builds the capacity to learn and thrive in new and challenging environments. Collective or individual disturbance, the by-product of any provocation used, can be very confronting. The intention when challenging people is to keep the temperature within a productive zone of disequilibrium or discomfort. In this space, you have people's attention—they are engaged, and learning takes place. Like a thermostat controlling room temperature, your job when provoking others is to regulate the heat, ensuring they remain in a productive spot.

But a word of caution at this point as we remind you of the difference between your good intentions and the potential reality of your impact. Provocation always should be purposeful and target some unhelpful aspect of a group or organization's functioning. But you can never know precisely how it will land or what the impact will be. You can generate unpredictable and intense reactions even while believing that you have been respectful and moderate. Others may have a different view.

The range of people's responses was bought home to us during an executive development program we helped deliver at Harvard University's Kennedy School. The group had been disparaging an outspoken, theatrical woman who was involved in many exchanges. Michael described her contributions as "a virus the group needed to adapt, as she embodied some of the qualities, they needed to become more productive and innovative," suggesting that as with all humans, this group was using its "antibodies" to defend itself against the threat posed by the "virus."

This colorful metaphor and the interpretation inherent in it elicited strong reactions and a heated session. Michael got more than he had bargained for as many people objected to his terminology, informing him that the woman's partner had recently been ill because of an unknown virus. Michael had not predicted this possibility or anticipated the strength of reaction and, with the benefit of hindsight, might have used a more enabling metaphor. Nevertheless, it was a challenging and electric experience, with everyone engaged in the work before us. Although disturbing, the provocation ultimately focused people on the ways they were unintentionally silencing and marginalizing their colleague. A new interpretation and insight allowed them to consider the value of hearing different perspectives. They were generous in forgiving Michael for his clumsy feet.

It is never easy to point out problematic behavior, nor is there ever a perfect time to do so. The intervention, however, helped the group learn two things. First, to recognize an unproductive routine and adjust their behavior. Second, to link the dynamics of adaptation and leadership to the group's goals. The session served as a just-in-time case study of the very issue affecting them at that moment, and they could see and feel their sticky status quo in action.

1.7.7 Different strokes

To consider purposeful provocation, which we discuss in more detail in Chapters 2 and 3, you need to clarify why you would use a challenging comment, question, interpretation, or action. There is a big difference between asking a relatively soft, though testing question and drawing on a vivid metaphor. For example, we recently asked an executive team, "In the last two hours of our work together, which forms of interaction have been least productive for you?" The question was revealing because it invited a diagnosis of the practices used by team members even though it appeared to have a narrower, more behavioral focus. On the other hand, the "virus" example was more provocative because it bypassed standard rules of etiquette by unexpectedly labeling an individual's behavior and interpreting the group's responses (conscious or otherwise). As a result, those present came to see their contribution to the safe yet dishonest exchanges that were impeding their learning and progress.

Ideally, provocation should be purposeful and intentional, although there are times when spontaneity and improvisation will lead to better outcomes. While the two are not always mutually exclusive, it is harder to plan or be intentional in the moment. In our experience, the more contentious the intervention, the more unpredictable the reactions. We have also found that the more unpredictable the intervention, the more unsettling it will be. Therefore, it is crucial to know how much risk and pushback you can tolerate, given the benefits you might achieve. The nature of the storm or mess you have to clean up may also be a deciding factor, as well as how much credibility you have. Thus, if you are a senior manager trying to solve a problem in your business, you may be able to afford less disturbance than a Harvard faculty member provoking an executive leadership program.

1.8 Practicing provocation

Provocation is a skill and an art form. It takes time to develop this capacity, and, therefore, we recommend as much practice as possible. However, some of you understand intuitively what family therapists, philosophers, politicians, and satirists have learned about provocation—inducing a crisis will disturb the status quo, and disturbance contains the possibility of something new. It will force people to consider new options, inviting them to tolerate the discomfort essential for creating a new equilibrium that is preferable to the previous one. The practical examples that follow will illustrate these principles.

1.8.1 Kick out the ladder

In *Honda: The Man and His Machines*, Sol Sanders explains how Soichiro Honda discovered that an uninvited external perturbation focuses attention, and can be used to improve outcomes through forcing creativity and improvisation. It took a crisis, a steel shortage in his company's early years, for Honda and his engineers to discover that aluminum not only made lighter engine blocks but dissipated heat more effectively. Honda began a new production method using aluminum, and subsequently introduced short, sharp disruptions at critical points in the manufacturing process to force teams to stop relying on previous practices. They would provoke by "kicking out the ladder."

1.8.2 Create a crisis

Systems-oriented family therapists, such as Jay Haley, Lynn Hoffman, and Maurizio Andolfi, have observed how client families unconsciously ask their therapist to "fix us but don't change us." However, the therapist's task, particularly with families caught in rigid exchanges, is to induce a crisis because, despite overt statements to the contrary, the family wants to keep the stability created by their rigid patterns. Therefore, rather than restoring order, they push the families beyond their usual coping mechanisms by introducing a higher degree of complexity and disequilibrium. Thus, Andolfi declares, "for there to be a real improvement, the family's functioning must enter a crisis." In this way, to be provocative requires the initial identification of a system's status quo, including their entrenched ways of seeing and experiencing things and the beliefs that underpin the family's identity, followed by a "crisis inducing" provocation.

We learned from family therapy that provocation is the nudging, critiquing, and perturbing of the unhelpful behavioral rules in a family, group, or organization. Doing so creates a significant disturbance, and as provocateurs, we pose a counterfactual to our clients, asking them, "What if you could cope, even make a change, with more disturbance, rather than less?"

From a leadership and learning perspective, this induced crisis strategy illustrates how provocation is a means to jump over the current system's restraints to consider new options and keep people, regularly but unpredictably, in productive disturbance and learning. Provocation generates difference or what evolutionary biologists call "variation."

Honda learned by trial and error what strategies helped his company innovate and become a market leader. Kicking out the ladder is an apt metaphor for temporarily destabilizing a system, for finding a provocative means to help people take stock and learn. Honda also understood that indiscriminate ladder-kicking was unproductive because his workers also needed support and some degree of predictability.

1.8.3 The provocative sweet spot

Consider the following example. An elderly woman entered Frank Farrelly's room. She was stooped and shuffled her feet. With difficulty, she maneuvered herself to a seat. But a split second before her backside touched the fabric, Frank said, "No, not that one!" The woman rose and shuffled to the next chair. The therapist intervened again, and once again at a third chair. At this point, this frail woman took a deep breath, rose to her full height, and roared, "Well, make up your fucking mind!" What initially appeared rude, even cruel, elicited a moment of strength and capacity, inducing a crisis that led the patient to draw on her most capable and powerful self. Farrelly had created a platform from which to begin therapy. But the platform emphasized the woman's ability rather than her symptoms and disability. In provoking her to activate herself, he found the optimal place for new steps.

Provocation is designed to create sufficiently newsworthy moments for people to pay attention and give at least "a half-life" to a new possibility, a new narrative. But Frank Farrelly is subversive in turning the standard rules of engagement on their head and his use of plain, truthful language. He uses the truth of the everyday to push boundaries and find the Goldilocks moment.

There is a sweet spot of creative dynamism between nudging, cajoling, challenging, provoking, and offering enough support for people to stay in the game. Public health campaigns try to find the perfect means to pitch their message and target the regulatory response. As David Studdert and his colleagues at Stanford University Medical faculty found in their study of sugar intake, "there is a danger in treading too lightly." They concluded that increasing pressure up to a certain point leads to better outcomes. Thus, public health campaigns needed to push people to adjust their behavior.

Whether in the therapy room, on the factory floor, or in the boardroom, most types of profound change involve a crisis or disturbance, a disjuncture in the normal routine. This is a moment when you accept responsibility for the problems you face and the impotence that comes from feeling stuck. Without some pressure, it is unlikely that you can prompt a commitment to change. A genuine shift from the status quo only occurs when all the simpler options have been exhausted.

As we write, there is continuous debate around the globe about how strong the message should be regarding Covid-19 vaccinations and ongoing protective measures. Officials are wary of alienating the public but want to hold their attention. Their campaigns have urged us to maintain social distance, wash our hands, wear masks, and get vaccinated. Those who were persuaded by the scientific argument quickly changed their behavior, whereas some continued to dig their heels in despite persistent badgering.

People don't like disruption, even when advantageous, as evidenced by anti-vaccination protests, and the backlash against mask-wearing. Provocative moves can be helpful in these situations because they recognize that people are wary of or resistant to being told what to do. A balance between provocation and support is required—the sweet spot.

What each of these examples have in common is that they start with a temporary crisis or disturbance designed to prompt people to overcome their reluctance to change. You can never know for sure whether the initial kick will be too hard, too soft, or will hit the target. So, you need to stand by, respond to what emerges, and determine whether to hold steady or back off a little by offering support, understanding, or acknowledgment.

1.9 An architecture for provocation

In this chapter, we have explored the nature of provocation and its core features, looking at how it brings attention to what is hidden or ignored. Provocation restarts the process of adaptation, energizes engagement, and builds capacity. Provocation is, however, more than the simple act of saying or doing something that disturbs people. It is an interaction between people, events, and systems that creates momentum. Provocative learning is forged in the heat of a relationship between a group, a problem, and an unsettling stimulus. It is both orchestrated and emergent—a dance between the conductor, the orchestra, the listener, and the music.

We borrow from the principles of physics to understand the dynamics of creating a provocative moment. The Architectonics Course notes at MIT state:

> A "moment" is a measure of the tendency to cause a body to rotate about a specific set point or axis. A moment is due to a force not having an equal and opposite force directly along its line of action.

In human systems, a moment develops when there is some pressure or demand, a provocative action or force that requires you to adapt or consider doing so, throwing you off balance. When something you believe in is tested, you have the opportunity to reprioritize what is important. While there is also equal pressure to stay the same, the act of reconsidering what you hold dear unsettles established ways, and has repercussions for others involved.

Imagine the disturbance caused by devastating floods as peoples' lives and livelihoods are overturned. There is anger and disbelief that the authorities did not anticipate and plan for such disaster. Pressure mounts on government. For so long, policies have been in place which are seen as adequate to the task—the system was in equilibrium. But record flood levels suggest that the Bureau of Meteorology's forecasting systems are not fit for purpose, raising hard questions about the assumptions that underpin the modeling. All of a sudden, the balance is disturbed, and the public and experts reassess. Policy makers throw out old emergency protocols and experiment with new approaches. The emergency forecasting and response no longer "rotates around a set point," it is provoked to do adaptive work.

This temporary disturbance is what physicists call a moment. The change in dynamics causes the interactional system to oscillate, to act differently, creating the potential (and need) for some growth and progress. These interactions became vital moments that disturb the equilibrium of a group or whole business over time, and the values and beliefs of those involved are thrown up in the air.

If we simplify, provocative moments, therefore, occur through three interconnected elements:

1 an *action*, a behavior that challenges the status quo and helps to further shared goals, or an external force that impacts a system and requires a response;
2 *a reaction* from a person or system to point 1; and
3 an *experience* that contains each of these, creating a zone within which transformation is possible.

Together these elements help us construct an architecture of provocation and indicate our role in creating it. They show the choices available within even the simplest moment, and therefore the opportunities to help shift a person or system towards learning (Table 1.3).

Element	Description
Action or external stimulus (1)	An action is undertaken to help make progress on shared goals or an external force or change can impact a system. Either may be a stimulus, eliciting discomfort, disturbance, or threat. The force has knocked the group off its normal axis.
Reaction (2)	The reaction will be a psychological state in response to a provocative stimulation and may lead to openness to the provocation or, conversely, rejection. An individual's or a group's reaction may have ripples extending over time and thereby creating a provocative process.
An experience (3)	A process of creating a provocative moment: The interaction between stimulus and response creates a provocation bubble within which usual ways of thinking and behaving are suspended because belief, values, and behaviors are unsettled or challenged, thereby puncturing the status quo, and allowing new ideas to be considered.

Table 1.3 Architecture of provocation

1.9.1 Provocative schema: A guide for action

Several broad blueprints for provocation emerge from these three elements, exemplifying ways to address the challenge at hand. As provocative actors, we use a range of specific tools, capabilities, and mindsets within each blueprint, flexibly intervening moment by moment, as well as, with a strategic longer-term view (Table 1.4).

We will use the schema to understand the approach used in our case studies later in the book. They also can be used to guide facilitation of learning and change work. The skills and capabilities that underpin these are discussed in the following chapters, where we also extend the discussion of different types of provocation.

Blueprint	Description
Advocate a paradigm change	Advocate a compelling view of what can or should be.
Confront vulnerabilities	Identify critical pressure points to ensure survival.
Radical scrutiny	Open yourself and the organization to scrutiny and accountability for mistakes.
Orchestrate conflict	Bring different, often competing, groups together.
Distribute loss and responsibility	Mitigate risk and disadvantage, and give the problem-solving back to the group.
Create or harness a crisis	Shock the system.
Introduce variation	Test the community's values and experiment widely and wildly.
Confound expectations	Confound expectations and use the unexpected. Value unpredictability and break the rules.
Put yourself at risk	Become a catalyst and figurehead by sticking your head above the parapet.

Table 1.4 Provocative blueprints

Notes

1 We are grateful to our colleague, Natalia Weisz, for bringing this pattern to our attention. Together with Roberto Vassolo, she examines this idea in their book *Strategy as Leadership* (Stanford University Press, 2022).

2 We use the term "information" to refer to all forms of communication: data, ideas, comments, questions, observations, interpretations, and stories.

References

Andolfi, M., Angelo, C., Menghi, P., & Nicola-Corigliano, A.M. (1983). *Behind the Family Mask: Therapeutic Change in Rigid Family Systems.* Brunner-Mazel, New York.

Architectonics (no date). *What Is a Moment?* Online lectures notes, MIT Architectonics: The Science of Architecture. http://web.mit.edu/4.441/1_lectures/1_lecture5/1_lecture5.html. Retrieved 16 October 2020.

Bateson, G. (1972). *Steps to an Ecology of Mind: Collected Essays in Anthropology, Psychiatry, Evolution, and Epistemology.* Part V, Chapter Four, Substance and Difference. The University of Chicago Press, Chicago.

Berne, E. (1964). *Games People Play.* Ballantine Press, New York.

Cambridge Dictionary (2020). Online Dictionary. https://dictionary.cambridge.org/dictionary/english/provoke. Retrieved 10 August 2019.

Capoccia, G., & Kelemen, R.D. (2007). The study of critical junctures. *World Politics, 59* (April), pp. 341–369.

Farrelly, F., & Brandsma, J.M. (1981). *Provocative Therapy.* Meta Publications, California, USA.

Gadsby, H. (2018). *Nanette.* Netflix Special. Recorded at Sydney Opera House. https://www.netflix.com/watch/80233611?trackId=14277281&tctx=-97%2C-97%2C%2C%2C%2C. Retrieved 1 June 2021.

Gersick, C.J.G. (1991). Revolutionary change theories: A multilevel exploration of the punctuated equilibrium paradigm. *The Academy of Management Review, 16*(1), pp. 10–36.

Haley, J. (1973). *Uncommon Therapy.* W.W. Norton, New York.

Heifetz, R. (1994). *Leadership Without Easy Answers.* Harvard University Press, Cambridge, MA.

Heifetz, R., Grashow, A., & Linsky, M. (2009). *The Practice of Adaptive Leadership: Tools and Tactics for Changing your Organization and the World.* Harvard Business Press, Cambridge, MA.

Hoffman, L. (1981). *Foundations Of Family Therapy: A Conceptual Framework For Systems Change.* Basic Books, New York.

Merriam-Webster (2020). Online Dictionary. https://www.merriam-webster.com/dictionary/provocateur. Retrieved 16 August 2020.

Polanyi, K. (1944). *The Great Transformation: The Political and Economic Origins of Our Time.* Beacon Press, Boston, MA.

Sanders, S. (1975). *Honda: The Man and His Machine.* Little Brown, Boston, MA.

Sarra, C. (2014). *Beyond Victims: Dr Chris Sarra on the Challenge of Indigenous Leadership.* Speech on ABC Big Ideas with Paul Barclay, 8 September 2014. https://www.abc.net.au/radionational/programs/bigideas/beyond-victims:-the-challenge-of-indigenous-leadership/5727864. Retrieved 12 February 2021.

Studdert, D.M., Flanders J., & Mello, M.M. (2015). Searching for public health law's sweet spot: The regulation of sugar-sweetened beverages. *PLoS Med, 12*(7), p. e1001848. 10.1371/journal.pmed.1001848. Retrieved 29 October 2021.

Swift, J. (2008). *A Modest Proposal.* A Project Gutenberg ebook. Originally published in 1729. https://www.gutenberg.org/files/1080/1080-h/1080-h.htm. Retrieved 2 October 2017.

Vassolo, R., & Weisz, N. (2022). *Strategy as Leadership.* Stanford University Press, Stanford, CA.

PART 2

PROVOCATIVE CAPABILITIES AND SKILLS

There is a range of methods and tools that help provoke a system and cause sufficient disturbance of well-practiced routines. All forms of provocative intervention are designed to elicit and bring forth a new response, to reactivate a group's capacity to learn beyond the current and exhibited range of thinking and action. They offer news of difference, which is created through a variety of viewpoints, interpretations, and approaches. We adopt Ross Ashby's notion of the Law of Requisite Variety, outlined in his 1956 book *An Introduction to Cybernetics*, which states that the person or system with the most variation and flexibility is more able to respond to the complex situations they face. Therefore, using a multifaceted toolbox allows you to respond more flexibly and effectively. The forms of provocation range from softer to more confrontational means of intervention.

When you watch a seasoned provocateur delicately nudging and pushing a group of people to the edge of their understanding and competence, what do you see? First, you will see someone just like you and us. Yes, there may seem to be some magic in what they do but it is a magic that is well rehearsed, based on solid foundations. Second, you will see a practitioner working in real time, spontaneously responding to what is in front of them, drawing on their experience and driven by endless curiosity, and a willingness to get it wrong.

The following three chapters examine the foundations of provocative action and provide examples of how they can be used. We start with the basics of observation, interpretation, and questioning, which are the foundations for effective provocation. Diagnosis is at the heart of provocative work. But this is diagnosis with a twist because every diagnostic move, be it asking a question or sharing an observation, also has the potential to provoke, as well as provide data. Provocation begins with diagnosis and situational awareness, and requires a fine ear for listening as well as skillful questioning, especially those that help open a system up.

In addition to five basic skills sets outlined in Chapter 3, it is necessary to develop a supportive mindset (Chapter 4). The five elements of a provocative mindset include an appetite for risk, being nimble, a willingness to be scrutinized, unpredictability, and an appreciation of diverse inputs.

Reference

Ashby, R.M. (1956). *An Introduction to Cybernetics*. Methuen, London.

DOI: 10.4324/9781003321200-4

2 OBSERVATION, INTERPRETATION, AND QUESTIONING—FOUNDATION SKILLS FOR PROVOCATION

Everyone in a complex system pays attention to and emphasizes different things, and each has a slightly different interpretation of events. The more interpretations we gather, the easier it becomes to gain a sense of the whole.

Wheatley, M. (2002) *It's an Interconnected World*

Our clients typically come to us because they want to solve a problem or improve something. They initially are apprehensive about our advances and eventually push back, argue, and storm against us. And yes, they argue amongst themselves. The differences, tensions, and fissures escape the confines of what our clients call "the real world" and infuse the so-called unreal discussions we have with them in the training venue, retreat, or boardroom. They will show us what they won't consider or discuss, and which ideas are taboo—the early signs of problems.

For example, a professional services firm (we'll call them NextXa) was trying to rebalance their relationship with a major client. There was growing frustration on both sides, because NextXa was one of three vendors to the client, and from time to time, all three had to work together. Each player thought the others were not sharing information and undermining each other. But the contractual arrangements made it difficult to collaborate and they were at an impasse. NextXa asked us to facilitate a problem-solving session which, in brief, went something like this:

- *We asked, "Who or what is benefitting from the impasse?" After a little exploration, the answer was revealing. "Well, it stops us from having to confront the client, and we keep things calm."*
- *"Who among you does this most suit?" "Well, none of us. But it suits Harvey the project leader most because he can avoid the hard discussion."*
- *"And how does that benefit the rest of you?" we followed. "Well, we can watch from the sidelines and not get our hands dirty," Megan called out.*
- *"So, you are all in agreement that Harvey needs to talk to the client while the rest of you wait?"*
- *"Well," Megan answered, "as a matter of fact, I have contacted the other providers."*
- *"You have done what?" her colleague Anthea yelled, "Who authorized you to do that?"*

And so, the discussion continued, with increasing heat, as the once aligned colleagues turned on each other. The fracture lines were on show, and issues of autonomy,

DOI: 10.4324/9781003321200-5

boundaries, and team cohesion became apparent. They were blind to the impact of their current approach, preferring to see themselves as the "good guys," and some members had very different views of how to respond under pressure. But, when they stepped back and looked at themselves, they could see the patterns of avoidance and self-protection more clearly.

Our goal is to help our clients understand how their system (team, organization) operates, what the rules are (even if they are unstated), and which patterns of interaction and communication support learning and adaptation and which hinder it. We do this by using three core skills—observation, interpretation, and questions. These are the three foundations of provocation and simultaneously are diagnostic activities and provocative actions which allow you to assess a situation, expand the context and frame the challenge faced.

Observation, interpretation, and questions are "strong forces,"[1] which shift the patterns holding people in place or restrain change. As a physicist might say, "The status quo tends to stay at rest unless motivated to move by a strong force." They are confronting, a "strong force," precisely because they offer a twofold and iterative energy—they diagnose, making more information available while also challenging the system. In addition, they are provocative because they help people see and feel their challenge from a new perspective, thus overcoming inertia and creating momentum. Had the NextXa consultant moved her team to take more active responsibility for the problems with their client, their interactions may have been more productive. As consultants and change agents, it is your job to help clients do this when they are unable or unwilling to do so themselves—always a challenging task.

2.1 Observation

Lien was the manager of a new IT division and became concerned that her colleagues had an issue with her appointment as the only woman on the team. She noticed that they rarely responded directly to her comments and directions and instead waited for Tommie, a senior engineer, to reply. Lien was puzzled but decided to watch and wait. In most meetings, it was Tommie who led the discussion. Her colleagues frequently didn't reply to her. The pattern continued, and she slowly concluded that there was an issue with her authority. Finally, she plucked up the courage and shared her observation with the team.

She said,

> I know that my appointment as team leader was a surprise to many of you. But let me remind you that I have been an engineer for over ten years. I have seen how Tommie is the only one who regularly responds to my input. The rest of you remain silent. This leads me to think that you might have concerns about my expertise and position. I think we need to be open and discuss these.

Lien's intervention was the first step in a provocative process. She used her observations to describe what she had seen and new interpretative skills to unlock an unproductive pattern. By making a tentative interpretation, she invited her team into a more open conversation. While this was a relatively mild challenge, it was a big move for Lien and pushed her team to be honest about their attitudes to her and their collusion with the growing dysfunction of the group.

Lien had first collected relevant data from a detached perspective: noticing, listening, and feeling. She then crafted these observations into a straightforward interpretation designed to affect her team's dynamics. Her comment enabled her team to see and describe less evident and hidden facts when caught up in immediate activity. Of course, like all observations, her comments were not neutral because she, as the observer, was part of the situation being observed.

Effective disturbance requires you to see yourself and others in action before considering solutions. Lien learned this, and instead of relying on instinct and just reacting, she gathered "data" to use when she intervened. Her provocation created energy in her team, part of her initial efforts to crack a problem open and her ongoing efforts to keep it open. Understandably, Lien was apprehensive when sharing her observation with her team because she did not know how her staff would respond. But she felt compelled to do so because she was stuck and wanted to solve a problem.

2.1.1 Generate data while gaining perspective

Observation is sometimes described as "being mindful" or "being socially and contextually aware." When you pay attention, patterns stand out and the impact of actions on people is more evident. In this way, observation helps resist the temptation, the universal default, to jump quickly into action. Even the simple act of saying to yourself "what is going on here" will slow you down and give you time to read and absorb the situation.

Of course, you can make observations at many levels of analysis, from an individual to a whole society and beyond. We have emphasized a mid-level perspective with groups and in smaller systems such as communities and organizations. However, diagnosis and analysis of social and economic trends provide a form of meta-observation on a wider scale. For example, Nesta, the UK-based innovation agency, used a national network of volunteers to watch and report on changes in people's behaviors following the outbreak of Covid-19 in early 2020. Their report "The Moment We Noticed" made several startling observations that influenced subsequent social policy. For instance, they observed increased social bonding and caring for others despite physical and social isolation but also decreased mental health, This information would not have been used to make policy had it not been observed so rapidly.

Observation is thus a critical skill that can help you decide what is required at any moment. It enables you to determine:

- How much pressure a system is experiencing;
- Which relationships are most meaningful;
- What trends and patterns are most salient;
- What questions to ask;

- What role to play; and
- What the risks might be.

Observation also helps build momentum when you share what you see. And as the American baseball player Yogi Berra once said, "You can observe a lot just by watching." Recognizing some of the typical patterns found (See Application Box 2.1 for details) allows you to explore how your team or business keeps itself exactly where it currently is despite people's protestations to the contrary. This stuckness becomes the target for provocation.

What would you notice if you paid attention to how certain people and specific roles within a group communicate with others or how people coalesce or splinter when they face a contentious issue? A summary of typical patterns to observe is found in Application Box 2.1 at the end of the chapter.

2.1.2 Levels of attention

After the Global Financial Crisis in 2009, we worked with the executive team of a government agency, assisting them to interpret a culture survey, which suggested that the leaders were not paying enough attention to staff and had neglected internal communication. The six executives were perplexed because they prided themselves on how they "looked after their people" and how "they kept people informed." After listening to their definition of the problem they faced, we made several interventions, including the observations and questions described here.

> Observation: *"We noticed that you all express confusion over this feedback and are doing so by defending your past actions. We have also heard how much time you each have had to spend with the Prime Minister and Cabinet Ministers and how it has meant you have been absent from the organization, often for days at a time. Your absence seems to have created enormous pressure for you even though the circumstances would warrant you giving the government most of your attention."*
>
> Question: *"How long can you continue to deny that you all get so much satisfaction from being valuable for government and being in such demand? Is it any wonder you have been paying less attention to the internal functioning of your agency?"*

For a few minutes, the team sat in silence, absorbing our comments. They initially were shocked but gradually began to respond. The tone and focus of the discussion changed as they acknowledged that they had been neglecting their people despite their best intentions and that the feedback made perfect sense. The focus shifted from denying the reality they faced and their part in perpetuating it to exploring the conundrum before them and, ultimately, identifying responses to it. Observations and questions assisted this group of talented people to become unstuck.

In this case, as we usually try to do, we used a simple rubric (outlined in Application Box 2.2) to observe different levels of problem-solving behavior.

Here we saw a team using more benign individual explanations for their problems and not taking collective responsibility. Therefore, we intervened to push their thinking toward more contentious and systemic descriptions, recognizing the contextual pressures they faced.

The rubric notices individual actions, interactions between 2 or 3 people, patterns in the group as a whole, and how the external context affects a group's work together. Each level requires a degree of mental control by focusing attention on different parts of the social system in question. Observing at different levels helps you realize just how much the observed do not see about themselves and the patterns they are creating; and how critical aspects of their operating and communication style affect their desired goals.

Increasing people's awareness is, by its nature, provocative because previously invisible information, such as who or what is privileged and at what cost, is now available. Therefore, it becomes difficult for a group to ignore how they are contributing to holding on to how things are.

2.2 Interpretation

Interpretations, which often follow behavioral observation or emotional reflection, are hypotheses, speculations, or conjectures about the dynamics of a group or system. Lien interpreted when she shared her observation with her team. To recap, she said:

> I have seen how Tommie is the only one who regularly responds to my input. The rest of you stay silent most of the time. This leads me to think that there might be concerns with my expertise and position, and I think we need to be open and discuss these.

She clarified what she had seen and how she understood (interpreted) it and used it as a springboard into discussion and problem-solving.

Interpretation is a technique that combines selecting and naming facts with the power to highlight less visible meaning or assumptions or draw attention to an unnoticed or unexplored element. If you want to help others make progress, you need to know how to take their poorly constructed or narrow descriptions of what they face and apply their curiosity. Your task is to help others create more meaning from their complex situation and build a bigger picture that provides a broader field of understanding and action. Therefore, this way of working requires moving to the edge of what is apparent and then beyond.

Interpretations are provocative by nature because your unexpected perspectives will push others to reconsider their views, challenge prevailing beliefs, and, depending on your focus, will touch on unstated and sensitive truths. While we all know that a sign of a healthy organization is its ability to name the elephants in the room, initial responses may well be, "what elephants?." Lien discovered this as her colleagues initially denied there was any problem. In truth, no one likes or encourages someone else to interpret their behavior, and rarely will anyone invite you to do so. As such, interpretations should be treated as hypotheses to be explored and tested, stepping-stones to further inquiry and curiosity. After all, you can never have all the data or opinions available, and there can be many possible, occasionally conflicting, interpretations. An interpretative act requires cognitive skill and personal agility, and a stomach for ambiguity and pushback. In essence, an interpretation is an intervention that asks others to reflect on the different ways to consider the challenge at hand, be it immediate or more significant, and longer-term.

Your goal is to:

- Shine light on a disabling (or enabling) idea, belief, or pattern of behavior;
- Notice the group's defaults and reframe them; and
- Generate a range of different interpretations to maximize possibilities and help people to identify their boundary judgements.

2.2.1 Everyday interpretation

People from every sphere of life have used compelling but contentious interpretations effectively. For example, Shimon, a member of a kibbutz in Israel, identified the aging demographics of his community as a problem and challenged his colleagues with a provocative interpretation when he said, "We're on a path to dying out given that we're not taking in any young people." Although there was outrage, the members of the community could no longer look away from their challenge.

Similarly, Zoe, a not-for-profit board member, challenged her colleagues when she noted, "most of us seem comfortable with the slow pace of decision making. But it appears we do so because we are trying to avoid difficult conversations and having to disagree with each other openly."

Both examples are provocative because they increase the likelihood that those involved can no longer avoid an unaddressed issue. They make what we call an "interpretative shift" (see Figure 2.1), highlighting the need to take people away from the familiar, from their default ways of thinking and hold less usual, more unsettling ways of thinking and diagnosis. Shimon's views were controversial because of the colorful language used—it is hard to avoid a comment such as "we are at risk of

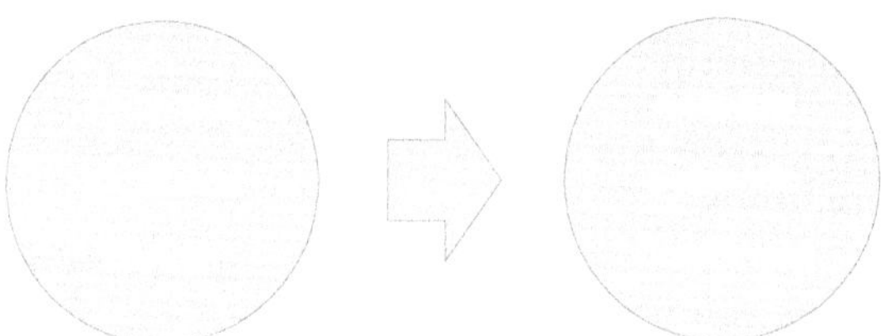

Figure 2.1 Interpretative Shift

Source: Adapted from Ronald Heifetz, Alexander Grashow, and Marty Linsky, The Practice of Adaptive Leadership (Harvard Business Press, 2009).

dying out!" Many of his colleagues hated the ideas, but it led to a productive discussion, and he was prepared to weather the storm.

A team we worked with would regularly defer to their bosses when they were unsure and unable to make decisions. "This is the way it is," they would say. "This problem is structural, and until the reporting arrangements are changed, we have to rely on this arrangement." Though this typical interpretation was factually accurate, it also removed responsibility from the team members. It reinforced their dependence and apparent powerlessness. And it was benign because it avoided the contentious aspects of the issue at hand. We responded with the following interpretation: "This arrangement works for you since whenever something goes wrong, you can defer to those above you, and your bosses can wonder where your leadership has gone." There was a long silence, and then one member declared, "that's unfair; we would lead more often if we were allowed!" There, in front of them, was the core of their dilemma and "stuckness."

Our intervention shifted their attention to the right-hand side of Figure 2.1 and created more energy in the team, even if they were initially defensive. They saw their ability to exercise any leadership as contingent on others and the problem as not of their making. As soon as they could glimpse their lack of agency and find the courage, they could consider and build other options.

2.3 Questions

Questions become provocative, not so much because of the answers provided but through examining what appears unknown, the space you open up, and the momentum generated. As Nobel Prize winner Arno Penzias said when asked by Polly La Barre in a 2001 interview, what accounted for his success, "I went for the jugular question." Questions are leverage, allowing you to prize open the locked box of prevailing thought and behavior, where you can dig deeper, revealing unexamined and divergent beliefs and stirring creative thinking and discovery.

Lien, like many, didn't like confrontation, but her initial intervention led to a series of increasingly provocative questions. She initially asked a simple question—"So, what do you think?" However, this seemingly benign question packed a punch because it required others to comment on her interpretation, and it led to a long conversation about the team's history and her outsider status. Lien now had fuller information to work with.

Geoff Mendal was a senior engineer at Pandora who facilitated strategy sessions with his team. Geoff had learned the power of sharing his observations and how he could provoke people even by asking simple questions. He usually left the discussions unstructured, providing time to get underneath the daily tactical work and focus on more complex issues, including how they worked as a team. At one of these sessions, as the group was debating competing technology options, Geoff observed the team overlook the contribution of one of the engineers ("Nivan")—someone whose ideas were somewhat different. After watching this pattern play out several times, Geoff called time out and invited his colleagues to reflect on what was happening. At first, they were somewhat confounded and couldn't remember the details. Geoff nudged them by asking fact questions such as "who spoke after Nivan" and "and then what happened." Gradually, the team built up a shared picture of how they interacted. His questions and prompts helped them step back and get perspective, which was challenging enough because it was unfamiliar. Finally, Billy exclaimed, "Now I get it. We have been ignoring what Nivan said." The group could see how they had unwittingly ignored and sidelined Nivan and his ideas—ideas that might have been useful had they been considered.

Geoff had shone a light on a hidden pattern of interaction and challenged his team to take ownership of how they overlooked quieter voices and less conventional opinions. On discovering their part in this behavior, many were quite shaken because they prided themselves on collegiality and cooperation. Geoff's observations and questions had gently provoked the team to have greater awareness. He reports that communication and productivity in his team improved as all members began to pay attention to their dynamics.

Questions are a necessary form of provocation because they help surface, expand, and critically examine the ways groups think about the problem they face, decide what is relevant (and therefore legitimate), and reveal hidden assumptions, values, and alliances. In his influential 1983 book, *Critical System Heuristics*, Werner Ulrich calls these elements "boundary judgments" because they help you determine what you include (and exclude) in your problem-solving, perhaps what you shouldn't address, and what your limits are. Critical questions increase your perspective and the "data" you have available by identifying what is considered discussable, accessible, by whom, and for what purpose. Ulrich identifies four categories of inquiry related to sources of motivation, power, knowledge, and legitimation. For example, we once asked a group "In what situations does (or should) your leader make key decisions or not?" This is a boundary question because it pushes people to make critical distinctions and identify the different views on such distinctions.

Overall, questions serve as a form of interpretative intervention because they draw on or highlight some value or way of seeing the world. Provocative questions, especially what family therapists call circular questions, can reveal alliances or splits in a group, surface themes about participation and inclusion, identify potential struggles, and help highlight barriers to move forward. In this way, the distinction between interpretations and questions is artificial because questions frequently arise from an (invisible) way of seeing things (an interpretation).

The method of questioning, making connections between actions, people, and critical issues, must involve all those in the group to see how they are affected by the demands of making progress and gives all group members a more comprehensive vocabulary for action.

Maxime recently challenged a group of executives who were all in "wild agreement" with each other. She asked, "Do you think you are more or less likely to generate new insights by continuing to agree with each other?" The group was silent for a minute, and then someone said, "Oh no, we are fine; it is a good thing that we agree and get along so well." There was a high threshold against thinking differently, a highly restrained system. So, she confronted them by replying, "Well, that sounds like tyranny. You are all stuck! Imagine the challenge for any person here who did have a different opinion if rule No. 1 is to "get along well and agree." The group reacted strongly, criticized her, and did not appear to understand her provocative stance. She left them to stew. It was only the following morning that someone said, "I think I understand you were suggesting that we were captured by groupthink, and this is unhealthy for our work." The question and interpretation ushered the group to deeper reflection overnight, which led to insight, revelation and the hidden dynamic that had governed their work.

2.3.1 Circular or systemic questions

A group asks themselves, "Why doesn't our boss provide better direction?" This focuses on an individual executive and relieves the team of any responsibility or ownership. Whereas "What pressures does the Division face and how might this explain how the boss is operating?" requires a different diagnostic focus.

Or in another example, we asked a team who did not complete agreed tasks, "What are the indicators that you are serious about change, and where are the signals that you are not committed?" This was a diagnostic question that pushed the team to understand more about their ambivalence. Without directly saying, so we had asked them to decide where they wanted to put their energy. It also addressed the tendency we see in people to want change but only if it doesn't inconvenience or cost them.

Systemic questions, by their nature, are provocative because they confound expectations of a more individual and benign discussion, and they have the potential to connect more parties in the group or system. They highlight the connection between individual and collective behavior, the behaviors under scrutiny, and the continued problem faced. They also explore underlying power dynamics, reveal contrasting views of those with most to gain and to lose including those who are left out of the conversation.

Application Box 2.3 at the end of the chapter includes a series of examples, each based on one core principle. Practice designing questions for yourself. Observation, interpretation, and questioning are diagnostic skills that provide a means to understand better the challenge you face. In addition, these three core skill sets provide a foundation for several more complex forms of provocation: paradox, stories, and humor, as well as some other distinctive forms.

Application box 2.1

Typical Patterns in Groups

Pattern	Description
Reliance on authority	People turn to the designated authority for answers, direction, and management of disturbance. When this is not provided, the group can become passive, aggressive, directly angry, or critical.
The usual suspects	Only a few people speak/contribute regularly, or only a limited number of perspectives are heard.
Heat avoidance	The group, or many people, works actively to avoid or reduce heat, disequilibrium, or conflict.
Flight to health	Instead of facing a challenge, a group displays sudden, either temporary or persistent constructive behaviors. This is often a response to anxiety. Something is being protected.
Focus outside the room	The group, or some parts of it, avoids talking about their functioning as a source of data for learning and focuses on outside issues.
"We're fine" (so it must be you)	The group uses benign interpretations of themselves or the challenge at hand.
Marginalization	The group allows dissenting (or minority) voices to be silenced. The group scapegoats a minority voice to distract from learning.
"I've got the answers"	Someone, or a faction, is elevated to the role of an expert in possession of the answers. The group offers a new authority to distract.
"That's not fair or justified"	Someone rescues a group member because they believe they shouldn't be treated that way, spoken to in that way, or put in the spotlight.
Role rigidity	Participants are stuck in a limited number of roles and insist that other learners stay in a familiar position.
Join the club	Learners only respond to "like type people" and encourage others to disagree with another faction.

Application box 2.2

Levels of Attention

Level	Description
Individual	Comments, questions, observations, and interpretations of an individual's contribution. The focus is on one particular person, their behavior, self-awareness (reflection), emotional expression and impact, and their ways of thinking (cognition), capacity, and skills.
Interpersonal	Comments, questions, observations, and interpretations about a relationship or pattern of interaction between two or three people. What does the shape of interaction between two or three people help us learn? What impact does this pattern have on how the group functions and what it considers? What interests or needs does a particular relationship bring to the work of a group? This level of intervention invites reflection on emergent patterns between specific people in a group.
Group or System	Comments, questions, observations, and interpretations about issues, themes, and patterns of exchange impact all members of a group and help describe the nature of the challenge they face. This level allows people to identify relevant systemic issues, relevant challenges, and the subgroups (factions) involved.
Context	Comments, questions, observations, and interpretations on issues that reflect participative, organizational, communal, national, ethnic, social, or political issues. It helps the team consider the broader context in which they operate and how environmental pressures may be affecting them.

Application box 2.3

Some Principles for Crafting Systemic Questions

Principle	Example
Focus on competing values and/or behaviors to identify any polarities.	"What difference does it make to your effectiveness that speed and politeness conflict here?"
Focus on responsibility and influence.	"How do you understand the impact that missing this deadline has had, given how you allocated the current tasks?"
Focus on constituencies and their differing ideas of success and loss.	"Which group here in this room do you think has the most to gain by agreeing with me"? "How would the men in the room benefit from listening more closely to the women?"
Identify cyclical sequences of interactions that may connect with beliefs or assumptions.	Under what conditions does your collective indecision most have you in its grasp?" "When it does, who is most likely to react?"
Ask for specific interactive behaviors that take us from the abstract to the particular.	"You say you have good reasons to withdraw from others. Can you name three of them?"
Ask about differences or changes.	"Who in this room will feel better about their skillset if you desist from testing your own ideas with me?"
Ask group members to explain the problematic behavior.	"Given your current explanation of this problem, how might you interpret it if you were at the receiving end of how you do business?"
Test the capacity of established routines for their flexibility or potential for change.	"How long do you think this way of operating can resist your efforts to disrupt it and keep it at bay?"
Ask questions that positively describe problem behavior, directing them at those who are most rebellious in the group.	"How have you learned to be so creative, and who in the team either encourages you the most or benefits the most from you being so?"
Build triadic questions that invite a third party to comment on or interpret the interaction between two other parties.	"How do you understand what's going on between Bill and Mary, and what values or positions do you think they each represent?"
Use colorful metaphors.	"Do you think your team needs to defend itself or, like you, continue to invite the world to use them as a doormat?"

Note

1 The concept of a "strong force" is borrowed from physics. See Rehm and Biggs (2021).

References

Heifetz, R., Grashow, A., & Linsky, M. (2009). *The Practice of Adaptive Leadership: Tools and Tactics for Changing your Organization and the World.* Harvard Business Press, Cambridge, MA.

La Barre, P., & Webber, A.M. (2001). Interview with Arno Penzias in *The Innovation Conversation.* Fast Company. 30 June 2001. https://www.fastcompany.com/43221/fast-talk-innovation-conversation. Retrieved 1 June 2020.

Nesta (2020). *The Moment We Noticed.* Report from The Relationship Project, Nesta.org. https://relationshipsproject.org/content/uploads/2020/07/The-Moment-We-Noticed_RelationshipsProject_202.pdf. Retrieved 1 May 2021.

Rehm, J., & Biggs, B. (2021). *The Four Fundamental Forces of Nature*. Space.com. 24 December 2021. https://www.space.com/four-fundamental-forces.html. Retrieved 17 May 2021.

Ulrich, W. (1983). *Critical Heuristics of Social Planning, A New Approach to Practical Philosophy*. Revised edition, J. Wiley & Sons, London.

Wheatley, M. (2002). *It's an Interconnected World*. Shambhala Sun, April 2002. https://margaretwheatley.com/wp-content/uploads/2014/12/Its-An-Interconnected-World.pdf. Retrieved 15 August 2021.

3 PROVOCATIVE CAPABILITIES

If the atmosphere in my team is getting too comfortable, now I will try to create some sort of surprise. Learning is about pushing the boundaries.

Comment from Joel,[1] a coaching client, following a series of behavioral experiments

Eddy Jones, the controversial Australian coach of the English national rugby team, describes in his autobiography, *My Life and Rugby*, that he used provocative methods to push his team beyond what is comfortable and familiar. For example, he gives his players unusual feedback and changes training techniques. "I am a fan of using surprise as a way of keeping people alert and on their game," he explains, clarifying that he is "impatient with tedium and will adapt training sessions so that players feel that things are different while developing the core skills required."

Jones understands the power of unpredictability to create productive disturbance and drive learning. "High-performance sport is about being on edge," he observes. "But I am constantly looking to challenge people." Like Jones, we believe that challenge helps people learn and grow. But provocation is also a diagnostic skill, as we explored in Chapter 2. You observe to understand and interpret before acting. Unfortunately, for all his success, Jones has a reputation for being impetuous. At times, therefore, he missed the mark.

In this chapter, we discuss five skill sets central to the use of provocation. They are based on a set of simple questions summarized in Table 3.1. Why? Where? When? What? And How (to begin)? These capacities help with diagnosis as well as being guide rails for action.

Question	Description
Why?	What is your purpose? Why are you intervening? What do you want to achieve?
Where?	In what situations are you acting? What is the context? Is the frame you are placing around the problem the most useful one?
When?	How do you know or decide when to intervene, provoke, or reduce the disturbance?
What?	What is the nature of the challenge you face? How do its qualities affect your action choices?
How (to begin)?	Who is in the room or organization or conversation now? Who will be affected by the intervention? What capacity do people have to engage in unsettling conversations? How are you preparing people for adaptive work?

Table 3.1 Five diagnostic questions for provocative action

DOI: 10.4324/9781003321200-6

3.1 Why provoke?—Purpose

Provocation must be a purposeful activity. It makes little sense to confront others if you don't understand either why you are doing so, or what short and longer-term goals you have. Why would you put yourself at risk for something you and others didn't care about?

It is also necessary to consider your purpose moment by moment. With each intervention, consider what you are trying to do. What are you bringing attention to? How is this relevant to the situation and the timing of the work? What are you testing? Why is that important now?

While it may seem obvious to remind you about your purpose, we see many leaders and change agents who challenge others out of a mistaken belief that "You have to shake them up when they get too comfortable or complacent." At times, Eddie Jones held this view. Yes, being too comfortable or complacent is a reason to be concerned if a change is on your mind, but sometimes there are good reasons to hold onto comfort. As Jones discovered, there must be some reason for your challenge, some gap that needs closing for which complacency is a clear impediment.

There are four broad reasons to provoke, which may overlap depending on their timing and intensity, and each has a diagnostic purpose and a temporal dimension:

- Help people learn more about the problem.
- Bring competing interests together.
- Identify an individual faction's part in the problem.
- Try new things out and experiment.

Provoking in the moment has a different purpose and impact than a longer-term effort. For example, notice the difference between the question "what did you see people doing in that last exchange that is indicative of the problem they face"? And "how could you learn more about this problem by using your team meetings as a case study"?

3.2 Where to intervene?—Reading the context

Many leaders have a bias toward action and need help to slow down, and consider the circumstances they face. Indeed, many think of themselves as firefighters rather than forecasters who read the signals that the situation generates. This is particularly true if there is volatility and anger such as that following a flood emergency or prolonged industrial action. A series of anecdotes will illustrate how using provocative capabilities have helped respond to demanding situations.

Noel[2] became the executive director of a large industrial facility (we'll call it Capato) just after the end of a damaging strike, which disrupted the local economy and created hardship for the workers. A new agreement was wrought from difficult negotiations, but Noel and his team faced a dispirited workforce, which led them to reflect on staff-management relationships, and a range of rigid work practices. Noel, who came to the job with experience in continuous improvement and a reputation for good people skills, was determined to use this volatile situation to begin a healing process, and make significant changes.

Noel and his team began by considering the broader context—taking time to discover how the workforce thought, and the effect of industrial action on their families. They also realized that no one on site could tolerate more disturbance, given the heated situation. Despite the cessation of the strike, pressure was mounting, and Noel was determined to reduce it. The context spoke to him strongly, and he heard it. In particular, he also saw that people didn't feel safe to speak up because they had lost hope, and didn't believe management would do anything. His observations reinforced the adage that it was all about culture. Innovation and change require new behaviors from leaders, as well as employees, and established ways will be unsettled.

Provocative action does not occur in a vacuum. Instead, it is connected to a group's work and its context. Noel's action was informed by what he observed and felt in that unique situation. You, too, also must consider the context of the job at hand, including what shapes it, and the people involved.

We define context as the dynamic environments within which leadership action occurs. These range from the micro to the macro level, from a specific moment in a group's life to an organization's, or the community's longer-term strategic pressures.

3.2.1 Context colors our view

Context is the invisible product of location, history, and prior decisions. A change agent or team leader must learn to see as much as possible and reveal existing pressures, to understand the "colors" or tone of the situation. While you can never totally comprehend your context because you are subject to it, you need to step back and investigate visible patterns, and what might be hidden but still inhibiting progress.

At the macro level, you need to be aware of how an institution's context affects people, and their thoughts, feelings, and actions. There is a big difference between challenging a group of consultants gathered at Harvard's Kennedy School for professional development, a cohort of indigenous children in a neglected school, or the exhausted workers on an industrial site. Each type of audience will have its own history and experience in dealing with crisis and disturbance, working collaboratively, and with forming trusting and transparent relationships. So, again, building contextual insight becomes critical.

Considering context is, therefore, essential, but remember, the moment you intervene in a system, you perturb it, even if only temporarily—the complex set of relationships and networks are disturbed. Problems are not the inevitable consequences of bad or incompetent individuals but can result from specific circumstances that can be changed. A community, for example, can reflect on its culture (its context), and change what is expected and essential. We demonstrate how this occurs in Chapters 9 and 10.

Therefore, you need to consider your interventions like an inoculation containing antibodies that the body may accept or reject. The context includes the rules of engagement, including the absorption codes, that is, the invisible habits and protocols that control what is acceptable or not. What can be learned from how the people take in or reject what they have just received? All elements of this code contain clues about that system's capacity to learn, and shape future and ongoing interventions. Thus, learning to examine and consider context is a core skill for leadership, and an essential part of the platform for provocation.

3.3 When to intervene?—Ripeness and readiness

When Noel started at Capato, he immediately faced escalating problems—although the strike was over, the workforce was agitated and untrusting. Workforce discontent is usually an indicator that some fundamental issues have not been addressed. Such situations are highly volatile and put pressure on all those involved, ripening the problem, particularly for management, who are used to being in control. But change does not happen by decree. People must be recruited to action, and momentum built.

Noel's team saw that the resumption of work was an opportune time to make a significant change. Although it was a demanding undertaking, the company had to reconfigure supervisory relationships, and workforce engagement. They had to reduce the power imbalance between management and workers, and provide greater autonomy in day-to-day problem-solving. The moment was ripe, and people were ready. Thus, Noel had a view of the ripeness—readiness equation at Capato. However, such a view is, at best, an interpretive act, and it is possible to generate more data by asking different people to make their own assessments.

The senior team became aware of many ingrained habits and restrictive work traditions on both sides of the operation. They determined to use the crisis to challenge the workers, and also their own ways of thinking and behaving. They started from some simple but powerful principles: reengage the workforce, fix broken relationships, and rebuild trust. As Noel said, "From a culture and production standpoint, it is important to have an engaged workforce."

Together with his team, Noel used action learning and Kaizen improvement principles, including quality circles, to involve operators in decision-making, devolving more responsibility to workers on the ground. They collaborated with their front-line supervisors to create new roles, pushing supervisors to spend most of their time on site with operators. They insisted that old command and control methods be put aside, and more collaborative problem-solving techniques be used. They turned the old equation on its head, telling workers:

> We are not only going to do something about this situation, but we are going to empower you. The problems we face are well within your power to solve. We will give you the tools and resources to tackle what we face here.

While most workers were hungry for more responsibility and welcomed the changes, some front-line supervisors were hesitant because they needed to make the most significant adjustments. Some felt confused, asking whether the company still valued their work. It took supervisors longer to "get on the bus," not because they were resisting but because they had to learn new, more cooperative ways of supervising. People prepare themselves for disruptive change in various ways, and need different kinds of support to become committed.

Though not a new idea elsewhere, the introduction of Kaizen methods and team-based problem-solving was a radical departure for this industrial plant, and proved to be a masterstroke. Noel introduced the new practices modestly, starting with just one action team, allowing more as opportunities arose. They framed the challenge simply, and had quick wins, building momentum and trust. Training and immediate application of new methods led to some remarkable safety and productivity gains, and started a process of operational adaptation and staff engagement. For example, in one case, a team solved the problem of worker safety around large mobile equipment by placing a flag on the machine's exterior to indicate it was occupied. A simple solution to an unresolved problem, which made an immediate difference. The flag's visibility fueled motivation for the new experiments.

Over time, the anger and distress that the strike had generated dissipated. A new balance was created, a new status quo emerged. However, it was clear that there would have been no progress without the strike—that initial stimulus. Without the turmoil, the management team may not have examined their own part, and intervened in such a constructive manner. Many companies find transformational efforts difficult when there is no burning platform or problem to solve.

Noel's team seized the moment in time, highlighting how provocative interventions need to be tailored to the situational conditions, which help determine both the timing and intensity of your actions (see Table 3.2). The prevailing mood was reconciliation—the issues of greater worker engagement, and autonomy had been simmering for some time. After the strike, managers and supervisors were more open to change.

3.3.1 Ripeness

Ira William Zartman, from Johns Hopkins University, has written extensively about ripeness in *International Conflict Resolution After the Cold War*. He shows how timing is all-important and that the pressure and urgency of a ripe situation increase people's commitment to change, increasing the chances for productive action despite the disequilibrium and the hard choices to be made.

Diagnosing ripeness will help you determine a good time to intervene, the intervention style to use and the best intensity for your action. A sudden shock or crisis rapidly communicates the urgency of the situation and the need for different behaviors, revealing how ripe the challenge is. But a disturbance doesn't necessarily mean you are ready and have the capacity to adapt. For example, witness the slow uptake of mask-wearing during the early stages of the Covid-19 pandemic in many countries. When an issue is ripe, the situation is charged anyway, and more

Condition	Description
The **mood or prevailing sentiment** of the group, including the current level of disequilibrium.	There is no point, for example, being provocative or raising a significant new idea if the relationships are strained, engagement is tense and hypervigilant, or energy/tone is overly enlivened. One way of lowering the "temperature" is to ask appreciative questions which remind others of the positives while still expanding what they can see.
The **ripeness of the issue**: the degree to which there is an existing or emerging consensus that something needs to be done about the problem; that the case warrants attention and is severe enough, even if there is a disagreement between interest groups about how to define, let alone resolve it.	There is no point in experimenting or trying something new if the issue isn't ripe or relevant parties are unwilling or unable to pay attention. Consider which parties find the topic "hot" and which find it "cold." How can you warm people up, and bring their attention into the room or conversation?
The various constituencies' **readiness** to engage (which relates to their willingness to contribute and be involved) and their capacity and skill to engage in adaptive work. Readiness is, in effect, an assessment of their skill and will.	Even if people agree that an issue is "ripe," do they have the time, energy, commitment, and skills to take any action? Which alliances need to be built, and for what purpose? Where does pressure need to be applied? Which interest groups need to learn what to progress and what to let go of? Here learning could refer to people understanding what is at stake for others or examining their own priorities to identify what could be given up.

Table 3.2 Situational conditions to determine provocative action

stimulation may be counterproductive. On the other hand, a challenging observation or question can help ripen an issue and make the group more likely to give it serious attention. Ultimately, you must determine just how sharp and hot an intervention needs to be, given the particular circumstances.

As you see with Capato, a crisis requires immediate and targeted action. But many adaptive problems, held in place by a history of habits and hidden practice, may lack urgency. Instead, they are creepers—critical issues that slowly become evident for a community. After arriving at the site, Noel discovered this and set about the essential task of knowing what kind of problem he faced.

3.4 What kind of challenge?

Helping to shift the anger and mistrust after a protracted industrial dispute, such as Noel faced, is confronting because it involves contested territory where not all players agree on what to accept and where to resist. In this sense, therefore, adaptation and disturbance go together. When environmental pressures (a strike) unsettle the status quo (labor conditions) and the established rules are punctuated, there will be less reason to provoke people. The system is already vibrating, and at least some are paying attention and hoping that movement is possible. As the new site director,

Noel believed only a radical shift in how the plant was managed would resolve the underlying issues. His proposals met workers' demands but also challenged long-standing work practices.

However, you shouldn't leave change to chance and goodwill. Leadership involves putting pressure on people at critical times and building their capacity to do the same with each other while keeping in mind the context and the type of challenges faced. You must tailor your interventions to each situation.

We use Dean Williams' framework found in *Real Leadership* to consider different types of challenges. Each has a different ripeness—readiness equation. Each requires different forms of action to move forward, and helps determine how much heat to apply in distinct circumstances, and whether your efforts will help ripen an issue or pay attention to an already ripe topic. For example, when facing what he calls an activist challenge, the barrier to progress is people's resistance or denial that something is happening, and therefore getting their attention to the situation is essential.

This was initially true in Noel's facility, where some managers did not see the underlying causes of discontent. But when a different approach, including the action teams, was used, the widespread behavior change indicated how ready the system was for something different. Noel's strategy was highly contentious because it pressured all workers' behavior, including the managers. He placed increased responsibility for the well-being of the operations on all staff's shoulders, which was a significant departure from previous practice. The strike was a form of activism because operators initially believed management was denying the problem. And Noel, in turn, provoked workers and managers alike by overturning years of hierarchical working practices which remained in plain sight but were accepted as "the way things were." He became an activist for change by insisting that all staff build new ways of working. After a year's trial, there were over 100 action teams on site making improvements in a range of operational procedures, but most importantly, workers were feeling more responsible and valued, and industrial relations were at an all-time high. Noel and his team focused on activating the workers' latent capability and developing their collective skill-set.

3.4.1 Mobilizing latent capabilities—An example

We worked with a pharmaceutical team where one member (Morgan) reported difficulties implementing his strategy, and noticed how they saw the problem as one of poor definition and poor communication. We suspected this definition served to protect the status quo, and so we attempted to ripen the issue further by introducing an alternative perspective:

> While better definition and communication may help you, your focus on these solutions blinds you to your part in keeping this problem alive. We notice you all cheering while Morgan goes out on the ice by himself, trying to implement a strategy that will benefit all of you. He can hear your encouragement, but today's discussion reminds him of just how alone he is. He is only just realizing that you are not there with him on the ice, sharing the risks. You're leaving it all to him.

The group was initially shocked, as they had not considered how they had "ignored" Morgan's efforts. But the conversation shifted to their joint responsibility for implementing the strategy rather than seeing it as his problem. The need for collective action and accountability was now at the center of their conversation. It was riper, and the team was willing to consider alternative responses.

Morgan's team faced what Dean Williams calls a developmental and transitional challenge. They had to build new competencies where the business's success depended on all team members taking responsibility for the whole company, not just their part. Unfortunately, the team been inadvertently protected from recognizing the changing nature of the world around them and remained committed to old skills, attitudes, and allegiances, reinforced by previous company structures and incentive schemes. Before the team intervention, the issue was simmering but not ripe.

Early interventions were simple, increased pressure on the team, and provided an opportunity to reflect on past success, identify what was precious and should be carried forward and which behaviors were no longer as important. We gently perturbed them and built awareness and momentum. As there was no emergency, we had to allow time to ripen the need for more collective work. We used problem-solving exercises to demonstrate what joint work looked like, providing a sense of accomplishment, and highlighted both outmoded and newly desirable behaviors.

Shining a light on what was growing and what was holding them back was disturbing in several ways. First, no one likes to be shown up or caught out, even though they have agreed to feedback. Second, cultivating new behaviors requires practice, which frequently involves failure. Senior executives do not like to appear incompetent. Third, you cannot guarantee your goal of a better outcome, it is just a dream or aspiration and therefore risky.

3.5 How to begin? Build a holding environment

Provocative work requires a "holding environment[3]"—at its simplest, a process that fosters difficult conversations and learning by creating a mixture of safety and discomfort. A holding environment can be a space, a set of relationships, or an agreement that creates sufficiently firm boundaries and a clear enough purpose to keep people together to work on difficult issues over a sustained period. There must be enough cohesion to offset the disequilibrium generated when you undertake adaptive work.

Think of the relationship between a father and child as she learns to ride a bicycle. The father runs alongside the child and catches her if she falls. He creates a sense of safety and encourages her risk-taking and experimentation. The child is uncomfortable as she wobbles from side to side and bumps into things, but she is doing new work and learning new skills. Only she can do this work. The father can't do it for her and must watch and hold, both psychologically and, at times, physically.

An essential task for sustained provocative work is creating and maintaining these holding environments. You become an orchestrator, a cultivator, a barista—that is, the regulator of heat, disturbance, and conflict. You must regularly play these critical roles to sustain a productive container allowing you to hold and direct the creative forces in a group and use them to face the conflicts, tensions, and emotions that could bubble over.

A holding environment will look and feel different in each setting though they will all share common ingredients:

- A dedicated space or moment for learning away from the routine;
- A set of guidelines and ground rules;
- Some shared experiences and values that bring people together;
- Known rituals that provide orientation and comfort;
- Commitment to a purpose; and
- A degree of psychological safety.[4]

Holding environments very in. We use the metaphor of the difference between a wok and a pressure cooker to explain. With the former, you require high heat, and everything cooks quickly but risks flying out of the pan. With the latter, you regulate the heat within firm boundaries, release the steam, and all the ingredients experience similar heat. Most productive provocation occurs within the more regulated environment of a pressure cooker. Capato's strike was a wok—highly volatile and difficult to control. But Noel's use of action teams is an example of a pressure cooker with a set of rules and protocols to solve previously unnamed or contentious problems. By putting workers in charge of problem-solving, Noel and his managers inverted the power dynamic, and by creating simple forms of collaboration between managers, supervisors, and workers, new rules of engagement grew—rules that gave the dispirited workforce new hope.

3.5.1 In the wok: Sexual assault in parliament

It is not surprising that there were widespread calls for formal inquiries into sexual assault in Australia's Federal Parliament in March 2021. The issues had been simmering for a long time, but the advocacy from two young women, Grace Tame and Brittany Higgins, ripened them, putting pressure on the government to act. Unfortunately, the government's slowness to respond meant there was no holding environment to deal with the issues, which compounded the problem. It now had multiple issues to deal with: specific cases of abuse, questions about systemic sexism, and poor behavior in parliament, as well as all the political pressures that ensued. This is another example of provocation occurring in a wok, with all the ingredients flying about uncontained rather than within a more productive container.

3.5.2 The CEO is not ready: Go slow

We have seen the risks of proceeding without a strong holding environment. For example, in an assignment with the top team in a global medical products business, we began our diagnostic work to understand the context and the organization's issues. As part of our first exchange with the Chief Executive Officer (CEO), we asked what he hoped for. A part of his answer led us to wonder just how committed to change he was. So, we told him:

> If you are successful together, it is likely that your executives will be asking more questions of you and your Board. They will test how you do things here, and temporarily it will feel more unsettled as you all find new ways of interacting.

His response was both surprising and illuminating. "Oh no," he replied, "I don't want that. This place can't afford to be unsettled right now."

It was clear to us that this organization's tolerance for disturbance was low and that the CEO, like many authority figures before him, wanted change just so long as it didn't upset anyone. So, we concluded that the holding environment was not robust. As a result, we went back to the drawing board and designed our interventions to emphasize incremental challenge and a focus on strengthening the trust between executives and their teams.

As Google learned through Project Aristotle,[5] the number one factor for team effectiveness is team members feeling safe to take risks and be vulnerable in front of each other. Our conversation with the CEO of the global medical business alerted us to the need to build a robust holding environment and do so slowly so that the team could eventually address more challenging, more controversial issues.

3.5.3 Warming up for provocative work

Like us, many of our consulting colleagues have found that inserting structured team-building activities into the beginnings of major projects promotes the kind of trust and openness that helps major works succeed. First used by British Petroleum, what is now called "project alliancing," encourages partners to focus on people and relationships and provides tools to foster better communication. Partners work as an integrated team where everyone's profit margins (or other preferred rewards) are put at risk by committing to a range of reciprocal trust-building practices. They share the commercial risk and reward. Therefore, it is in the interests of all participants to work cooperatively and openly. As a result, cooperation is enshrined in the formal contract, thereby becoming a tool and reference point for the holding environment.

Introducing collaborative practice into physical industries such as infrastructure or construction is inherently provocative because it departs from historical practice and is therefore challenging. Even when it becomes accepted practice, collaborative alliancing continues to be subversive. It is a means to hold people to the values and agreements made at the beginning of a project.

We use various methods to build a strong holding environment when starting our longer-term engagements. Typically, we begin by "warming-up"—a term borrowed from sport and theatre. Warm-ups can entail simple introductions outlining our purpose, physical activity, or a trust-building activity.

Overall, warm-ups are part of building a platform for a robust holding environment in which we build relationships, reduce anxiety, and foster creativity. Warm-ups help the group focus on its learning or problem-solving. As a facilitator or change agent, the responses to your preparatory activities provide you with valuable insights into how each group functions. You can learn about people's capacity for openness and creativity, their willingness to experiment and be challenged, and their ability to learn from each other, rather than relying on you as the designated authority. Your goal is to regularly stretch the boundaries of what is possible and what the group will tolerate.

Trust and a shared purpose are essential ingredients but not sufficient alone because attitudes, needs, and capacities are iterative, changing over time. You need to balance two opposite forces: on the one hand create enough cohesion to offset the centrifugal and disruptive forces that arise when a group confronts a problematic issue but on the other keep people in a productive zone of disturbance long enough to have the more demanding and unsettling conversation.

Provocation is part of the ongoing process of adaptation in which new practices create a foundation of continuing change. However, adaptation in human systems should not be left to chance and requires disciplined attention. The five capabilities mentioned in this chapter support this discipline, while the next chapter explores the mindset necessary to provoke.

Notes

1 Joel (a pseudonym) was Michael's coaching client for eighteen months. We discuss his experience in detail in Chapter 7.

2 This scenario is drawn from our client's experience, but names, places and details have changed to respect confidentiality. Noel is a fictitious name.

3 Holding environment is a term first coined by psychiatrist Donald Winnicott (1960) to describe the optimal environment for good enough parenting that facilitates the transition to autonomy.

4 For a discussion on psychological safety, please see Rozovsky, J. (2014) *The five keys to a successful Google team.* https://rework.withgoogle.com/blog/five-keys-to-a-successful-google-team/. And Edmondson, A. (1999) *Psychological Safety and Learning Behavior in Work Teams.*

5 Google's Project Aristotle researched the secrets of effective teams, re:Work with Google, https://rework.withgoogle.com/guides/understanding-team-effectiveness/steps/introduction/.

References

Edmondson, A. (1999). Psychological safety and learning behavior in work teams. *Administrative Science Quarterly, 44*(2) (June 1999), pp. 350–383.

Jones, E. (2020). *My Life and Rugby: The Autobiography.* Pan McMillan, United Kingdom.

re:Work with Google (2016). *Project Aristotle – Team Effectiveness.* https://rework.withgoogle.com/guides/understanding-team-effectiveness/steps/introduction/. Retrieved 29 March 2021.

Rozovsky, J. (2014). *The Five Keys to a Successful Google Team.* re:Work Google. https://rework.withgoogle.com/blog/five-keys-to-a-successful-google-team/. Retrieved 22 May 2021.

Williams, D. (2005). *Real Leadership: Helping People and Organizations Face Their Toughest Challenges.* Berrett-Koehler Publishing, San Francisco, CA.

Winnicott, D. (1960). The theory of the parent-child relationship. *International Journal of Psychoanalysis, 41*, pp. 585–595.

Zartman, W.I. (2000). *Ripeness: The hurting stalemate and beyond.* Chapter 6 in Stern, P., & Druckman, D. (ed) *International Conflict Resolution After the Cold War.* The National Academies Press, Washington DC. pp. 225–250. https://nap.nationalacademies.org/read/9897/chapter/7. Retrieved 29 August 2020.

4 DEVELOPING A PROVOCATIVE MINDSET

Provocation is not for the faint-hearted. Whether you are perturbing an individual, organization, or community, or at the receiving end of a disturbing event or intervention or experiencing push back when have tried to dislodge the status quo, provocation is challenging and risky. Therefore, it is crucial to have a solid foundation from which to provoke.

Comment made by authors during a workshop

4.1 Introduction: Building a provocative mindset

Provocation is not for the faint-hearted. Whether you are perturbing an individual, organization, or community, or at the receiving end of a disturbing event or intervention, provocation is challenging and risky. It is tough because you are unsettling an existing system with its established ways. You can never be sure how others will respond to your action; let alone what effect it will have, and people rarely thank you for suggesting they should question established practice. Even when people say they want to be challenged, being provocative is challenging. Therefore, it is crucial to have a solid foundation and a supportive mindset from which to provoke. It is a skill that takes time to develop. We both began learning some of these skills early in our careers, as the following stories illustrate.

4.1.1 Maxime's beginning: A big man and a big stick

Early in her career, Maxime worked as a community outreach officer in an area of disadvantaged families. Unfortunately, she had no formal qualifications for this role—only acquiring them later—and little training for the duties she was responsible for.

Coordination between agencies encouraged health staff and local police to visit crises together and there was enthusiasm for collaboration on both sides. Then, one day, a man went berserk in a nearby suburb and needed assistance. Maxime was asked to attend, but she discovered that neither the police nor other health workers were present when she arrived. As she waited near the house, she could hear banging and crashing sounds.

Too inexperienced to know better, Maxime approached the house. The front door was ajar, and, as she pushed gently against it, she saw a big man wielding a two-by-four

DOI: 10.4324/9781003321200-7

plank, shattering light fittings, glass, and timber, and putting holes in the walls. As she entered the house, Maxime called out to him, "Hello, I'm Maxime, I've come from the health center, and I'm scared." The man looked at her, dropped the plank, and asked, "What are you scared of? Are you scared of me?" The idea shocked him. Whatever he had been experiencing, he did not see himself as threatening. Maxime's words had jolted him, preventing him from doing further harm.

Maxime remembers this moment mainly because of the emotional depth of the experience. Despite her missteps, she began to learn the attitudes necessary for her to successfully undertake her job, primarily to manage uncertainty, make judgments about risk, and hold steady in the face of pressure. Her subsequent professional life as a therapist, leadership consultant, and coach has given her ample opportunity to develop this mindset. She also learned viscerally about the power of hidden description.

4.1.2 Michael's beginning: Dirty boots beget wisdom

As a graduate student Michael undertook research into illegal squatter settlements in Malaysia. He had lived in other countries before, but this was a significant foray into the unknown. Michael had few contacts, spoke limited Bahasa Malaysia, and had no idea how to choose, let alone live in a squatter settlement. For several months, he circled this dilemma, somehow hoping that a solution would magically present itself. Every day Michael drove past several shanties that hugged the highway between the city and his home. But the edge remained. Each time he got close to jumping off, fear got the better of him even though he had experienced real danger during his army service. He knew that he would have to jump sooner or later, but there was no map or established protocol to follow.

To prepare himself, he developed a sensitization program founded upon the notion that "dirty boots beget wisdom," which would enable him to overcome a fear of incompetence. First, he arranged to meet a *ketua kampong* (village head) willing to talk about his research. Next, he began regular visits to shanty villages talking to locals about their lives as squatters. After doing this for several weeks, Michael realized that he had stepped beyond the edge, becoming immersed in village life. He had transitioned from fear of the unknown, to letting his nerves guide him, to finding enjoyment in what he was doing.

Michael warmed up for the jump, practicing every day and building tolerance for feeling out of his depth. He also realized in talking to the squatters how unhelpful his earlier outlook had been. Initially, he had relied on his expertise, convinced that he should know what to do. Now, he realized that all the knowledge and expertise resided in the squatters. All he had to do was create space where he could inquire about their experience and let them talk about what mattered to them. They educated him.

The lessons we have learned about engaging with the world through our work and professional development inform the five core elements of a Provocative Mindset. All five aspects are linked, providing a way to act in organizations, communities, and groups.

4.2 Develop an appetite for risk

Provocation is a little like parachuting. You can't do it until you jump into the void. But talk to soldiers or skydivers, and they will tell you that leaping out of an airplane is a discipline built around repetitive training and practice, as well as making sound judgments about risk. Parachutists rely on their eye for detail, checking their equipment and that of their colleagues before a jump. They also become attuned to the context, monitoring weather conditions, who else is jumping, and the kind of aircraft used, not to mention the joy they experience in anticipation of and during the jump.

A risk appetite, therefore, involves holding several contradictory ideas simultaneously. The details matter as much as the context. It is necessary to accept the fear and the exhilaration. It is also essential to focus on preparation as well as fully experiencing the moment.

Dr. Richard Harris is an Australian doctor and cave diver who came to international prominence in 2018 because of his role in rescuing the trapped soccer players from the Tham Luang caves in Thailand. He and his colleague Dr. Craig Challen shared the 2019 Australian of the Year Award to recognize their rescue efforts.

Harris's *Real Risk Podcast*[1] reveals that risk-takers are very thoughtful, methodical, careful people—they just do things that frighten the rest of us. These people are not impulsive or reckless. Instead, they are highly disciplined and have in-depth knowledge of their environment. Harris's guests reveal that they don't consider their preferred activity risky because they are confident in controlling the variables. But ask a downhill speed skier to run the same course on a snowboard, now "that feels risky."

Even if you don't see yourself as a natural risk-taker, it is possible to develop a risk appetite through training and acclimatization. The social environment in which you practice also contributes. As teenagers at skateboard parks demonstrate, practicing among peers leads them to take on more graduated risks. Friends egg on fellow skaters to attempt riskier maneuvers, refining their practice after falling and trying again.

The renowned BASE jumper, Steph Davis, didn't start her career with a free climb of the sheer heights of El Capitan in Yosemite National Park. But, like other risk-takers, she circled her way into it. She trained, undertook drills, examined contingencies, built routines with her equipment, and practiced more. In her book *Learning to Fly*, Davis describes how she has become an orchestrator of her fear. Despite having lost her husband and other friends to this extreme sport, Davis learned to survive by being thoughtful and deliberate. Likewise, elite risk-takers of all persuasions draw on their training and recognize the repercussions of poorly considered risk.

Whether you are a change agent, community leader, or leadership consultant, you too can learn from pioneers like Davis. Just because you have seen a guru provoking people, doesn't mean you should start with an El Capitan moment. Instead, build your range and repertoire through drills and practice. Better to be driven by purpose than adrenalin.

We have noticed that some of the most effective provocations occur when we act without a plan or preconceived idea. This requires being "in the moment"—what psychologist Mihaly Csikszentmihalyi has termed "flow." Flow occurs when individuals forget about the outside world because they are thoroughly engaged in a process or activity without questioning what should be done and how.

Taking risks involves three aspects drawn from flow theory. First, the idea of committing to a deep engagement with people that is likely to be messy but stimulating. Second, the notion that provocation has a set of rules and guidelines that, once mastered, make it possible to act both purposefully and spontaneously. Third, the understanding that once initiated, a provocative moment creates a pocket of time and experience in which people feel "on the hook" and are ready to undertake deep work. Some people describe these experiential moments as "flying." Indeed, we often use the metaphor of a young albatross leaping off a cliff in its first flight to illustrate the idea of risk-taking as a leap of faith with a somewhat unknown outcome.

Fortunately, provocative acts do not involve physical risk, but there are other elements to developing a risk appetite. While jumping out with a constructive purpose in mind, you will need to learn to love the unknown—the complex, messy territory you enter when unpacking a well-practiced routine, racket, or mode of thinking. Not knowing is at the heart of provocative work. When your head is swirling with the imponderables of a situation, you will frequently misjudge the moment, the intensity of your intervention, and even your understanding of what you are stepping into, as Maxime found with her "wild man" and a stick. She felt like she had been pushed off a cliff. So, part of this way of operating requires that you recognize your own fallibility and remain open to scrutiny. This is what we mean when we advise people to "own your piece of the mess."

Learning to live in the heat and listen to people's frustrations, fears, and hurt is critical because it demonstrates that you are in the mess together with your clients, or community. You may become a lightning rod for how people feel, and you must withstand the wave of emotion that could come your way. This is equivalent to the rush, fear, and exhilaration experienced the moment before a parachute opens.

Fortunately, as a leader or change agent, it will usually only be your ego that is bruised, unlike the parachutist or downhill skier who can take a risk too far with catastrophic consequences. Sadly, there are also examples of political and community leaders provoking people[2] and being killed for doing so.

4.3 Be nimble

Cassius Clay was only twenty-two years old in 1964 when he unexpectedly beat Sonny Liston, the reigning world heavyweight boxing champion. Clay relentlessly taunted Liston before the fight,[3] promising to "Float like a butterfly, sting like a bee. The hands can't hit what the eyes can't see," and predicting a knockout. Soon after his victory, Clay changed his name to Muhammad Ali and became an iconic sportsman and fighter for social justice. Ali's nimble footwork was a hallmark of his prowess and the unpredictable strategies he used to confound, tire, and then beat his opponents.

Over the years, Ali not only won boxing matches but also captured the hearts and minds of many people. Ali was an expert provocateur, sharing his opinions on race, war, and other humanitarian issues. He also became a master of switching roles in different circumstances and using his wit to confound people.

To be nimble is to be flexible, responsive, and think quickly when you are in the fray. Nimbleness goes beyond reacting to what is in front of you. It entails a strategic response designed to ensure you are prepared to handle any future that unfolds, even though you don't know how it will develop.

Muhammad Ali teaches us the importance of fluid movement between roles that adds interest to how you present and use yourself at any given moment. So, for example, if you move from being an expert provider of information to a naïve inquirer or jester who says impertinent things, you will draw on different skills and parts of yourself. At other times, you might see yourself as the conductor of an orchestra or a gardener who is the custodian of an ecosystem. You will be less predictable, break your own patterns and keep others on their toes.

For example, Billie a new executive at a global tech company had kept a low profile and was usually controlled and polished. But when she forcefully critiqued one of her colleagues, her team were surprised and delighted at her out of character and unexpected behavior. The moment was described as electric, lighting up the meeting. As this example shows, unpredictability catches people by surprise and reinforces the impact of the point made. Billie's demeanor was usually very measured, and therefore it was easy to anticipate her moves, but it was harder to respond when she acted differently.

Being more flexible and fluid in today's complicated and pressured systems can give you an edge when you need to challenge the status quo. As a senior public servant recently said to us, "It is no longer any use being a purist and using one line of thinking. I need to be a pragmatist and use whatever I have at my disposal even if my colleagues don't expect that from me." Flexibility and agility are the keys.

4.4 Be unconventional

If memory serves us, the counterculture movement of the 1960s and 1970s challenged prevailing norms and embraced alternative ways. There remains much that we all could learn from the legacy of the hippie movement—not least, orienting yourself toward possibility, abundance, the creation of meaning out of the direct experience, and the rejection of prevailing paradigms and constraints.

Benjamin Zander and Rosamund Stone Zander have an unconventional approach to life and change, and they embody counterintuitive possibilities. We were part of a group that met with Ben in Boston—sitting in a circle, like so many other personal development activities. He entered the room with great gusto and immediately demonstrated how his multiple roles—conductor, musician, writer, inspirer, and jester—helped create an atmosphere of exploration. Ben told stories, taught us several simple methods, played music, acted the "fool," and laid out his platform for the world of possibilities.

We have carried the Zander's ideas about possibilities with us ever since, especially their response to the new or startling. Whenever we are stumped, bewildered, or simply hear something new, we also use Ben's unconventional method and throw up our arms, declaring, "How absolutely fascinating." When we use this simple but strange gesture with our groups, we are delighted by the laughter, surprise, and energy that follow.

In their 2000 book *The Art of Possibility*, the Zanders argue that humans change not because of a convincing argument but because of "a change in posture, perspective, beliefs, and thinking." Among the Zander's twelve practices, three—It's all invented, Being the Board, and Rule Number 6—are essential to provocative action. They are subversive because they run contrary to mainstream norms in the same way that throwing one's arms in the air is unexpected. By taking more unconventional stances from time to time, we have found that our clients and audiences become more open and ready to consider challenging ideas.

4.4.1 It's all invented

Provocation is designed to puncture the stories, beliefs, and assumptions we have about ourselves, as well as the behaviors that follow them. It is premised on the idea that change involves determining what we want, not what we have. As the Zanders say, "It's all invented anyway, so we might as well invent a story or a framework of meaning that enhances our quality of life and the life of those around us." Provocation often orients people to identify what is precious and should be carried forward and what is no longer serving them.

4.4.2 Being the Board

This practice is mind-bending, so hold steady for a moment, as it proposes a radical form of accountability that casts a broader frame around events, one that avoids blame and fault but asks, "What is my part in this mess?" However briefly, you internalize the problematic elements of any situation. The value of this practice is twofold: First, if your provocative action generates strong reactions, you are more likely to have empathy and compassion for those who react strongly. Second, it creates a platform for inquiry and curiosity. Being the Board invites questioning, reframing from different perspectives, and pushes you into the realm of possibility.

4.4.3 Rule #6

Rule #6 is the practice of lightening up, not taking yourself too seriously. In so doing, you may help others feel freer. This practice leads you to ask, "Which of my serious motives, motivations, and feelings could I examine and change now to modify the environment around me?" The action of saying "how absolutely fascinating" is just one example, as is the judicious use of humor and the role of the jester.

Michael likes this practice because he can, at times, be too serious and let his good intentions blind him. He forgets to watch how people around him react and then wonders why there is pushback, why people aren't with him. He will make a light-hearted comment, such as, "Well, I really did get carried away, didn't I?" wink at the group, and indicate he knows his own foibles.

4.5 Think like mangroves and act like oysters: Build a habitat of variation

At its heart, provocation helps people think more deeply, and challenges their status quo thinking, which is usually rigid, narrow, and informed by untested beliefs and assumptions. What is required are new ways of considering what is in front of you, addressing a problem from various angles, and experimenting with different approaches. But when a group is stuck, this is hard to do. The current operating system is only able to function in limited ways. More variety is needed; some new DNA will assist to create more possibilities.

Mangroves and oysters provide an apt metaphor for the power that variation plays in adaptation and change. A biological variation punctuates the existing sequence of DNA and is at the center of human survival because it strengthens the ability to be fit for purpose. In this sense, one task of leadership is to ensure variation—of thought, behavior, and problem-solving.

Mangroves are a remarkably resilient ecosystem,[4] responding for thousands of years to the pressures on them and making necessary adjustments. Oysters foster ecosystem health and, like mangroves, play multiple roles in their habitats. As such, they both have several enabling features that we could emulate.

First, they thrive in extreme environments but enhance other species' survival. Mangroves and oyster beds both filter toxins from the water, enabling other species to thrive. Removing toxicity from any situation must be seen as a valuable service. As for humans, rigid thinking is a form of toxicity as it limits our ability to explore, reconsider, and change. Provocation helps remove such limitations.

Second, they are diverse systems they provide a habitat for a variety of life, protect other species, provide food, and a formal structure for survival. The diversity of species creates higher productivity than most ecosystems. Like mangroves, the provocateur attempts to foster greater diversity—more input, varied perspectives, and provides space for the more vulnerable voices—creating a vibrant habitat for creativity.

Third, each exist between two larger geographical zones—water and land. These interstitial zones create a vibrant mixing of conditions found in only a few locations. When the best of these worlds is blended, it encourages increased variation. Variation and the selection of its best is the key to adaptation.

Fourth, mangroves, like cities that attract waves of immigrants, are nutrient-rich. The evidence suggests that immigrant drive, skills, and the desire to survive and thrive create "nutrient-rich" environments. What are the nutrients that feed adaptation and change in your circumstances?

From these four points, several principles emerge relevant to a provocative mindset:

- Variation breeds vibrancy and adaptation;
- Interactions between places and species, over time, foster transformation, and productivity;
- Space, when restricted and contained, creates environmental pressure, which creates conditions for experimentation; and
- The greater the variation, the greater the problem-solving, innovation, and adaptability.

Noel, who we discussed in the previous chapter, learned how the use of Quality Circles (QC), a well-established method in Japanese industry but new in his setting, introduced more varied and productive interactions between Capato's plant operators and their supervisors. The technique taught his teams to generate a range of interpretations to understand the source of problems and moved them away from simple cause and effect analysis which frequently resulted in apportioning blame. By introducing more varied thinking, the QC teams solved problems quickly and applied their expanded capacity across the mining ecosystem. The new working environment at Capato, like mangrove habitats, fostered a more diverse and collaborative environment, leading to system-wide growth and learning. Noel's provocative moves built an atmosphere where this could flourish.

4.6 Radical Scrutiny

Provocation almost always will be unsettling, disturbing, even emotionally destabilizing, and your good intentions are not an excuse for causing harm. Therefore, being open to scrutiny is essential.

Radical scrutiny asks that your challenging actions can be examined by those you work with. Just as you invite others to be open to learning and reflection, so must you as the disturber-in-chief.

Provocation is frequently based on your insight and judgment. You may be correct, but, equally, you may be wrong, even spectacularly wrong. You, as the change agent or consultant, are part of this system as it oscillates and moves and can become a focal point for others' concerns, frustrations, and anxiety. You serve as a lightning rod for the tensions and accomplishments of the group and need to tolerate the "heat" generated by their reactions. So, when you are open to scrutiny, you make your actions more visible, explicit, and transparent even though doing so may unsettle others, and is a risk for you.

An example of this is seen in the experience of Dr. Ken Henry, previously Secretary of the Australian Treasury and then Chairman of the National Australia Bank. During the 2018 Australian Royal Commission into Misconduct in Banking, Ken, usually a measured and thoughtful person, responded to the vigorous questioning in a argumentative and obtuse manner. He later reflected that "I really should have performed quite differently. I should have been much more open." His contrite acknowledgment stood in stark contrast to his earlier demeanor. He recognized that denying or avoiding his mistakes would only worsen a bad situation. But fessing up in the public eye is hard to do.

Provocation also requires honesty—intellectual honesty ("I don't know") and personal honesty ("I messed up here")—because your clients and colleagues will be looking to see how you model what is being worked. This is not the same as being a bleeding heart, but each person needs to ask themselves how much heat they can bear and how open they can be. In the end, if you are not willing or able to be open to scrutiny, then neither can this be asked of others. Being open to scrutiny does not mean lying down. It does, however, mean knowing when to listen to criticism, and when to defend yourself.

Radical scrutiny is, of course, not a new idea. For example, in his book *Principles*, Ray Dalio speaks of the "continual search for what is true even when the truth can be personally difficult." For instance, managers in his company Bridgewater can be asked to explore how a recent move may illuminate a self-protecting distortion in their thinking. While not for the faint-hearted, Bridgewater is held up as an exemplar of what Robert Kegan and Lisa Lahey call *A Deliberately Developmental Organization* (DDO). That is an organization whose culture is built on integrating deep forms of personal learning into everyday aspects of life. The core practices of a DDO include constructive destabilization, error as an opportunity, and rank without the usual privileges.

Radical scrutiny also requires and develops a high level of humility. If others can scrutinize you, question you, and hold you to account, you learn quickly. Staying humble means being aware of and admitting what you don't know. It means coming to love your mistakes as a source of learning and asking for help. The ancillary benefits of humility are grace and dignity. Forms of radical scrutiny are contagious and create emergent conditions that foster understanding and creativity.

At this point, a caveat. While we are proposing openness and humility, encouraging others to scrutinize your provocative actions, we are not proposing apologizing for every emotional response or disturbance people might feel. If anything, we suggest that holding steady and, at least temporarily, not responding to people's emotions is itself provocative and respectful of their capacity to live with and learn from their experience. Provocation requires a delicate dance between challenge, care, and accountability to have any real impact. However, opening yourself to scrutiny brings verifiable benefits, and increases the chances that future provocation and missteps will be tolerated, even accepted. As you saw with the example of Dr. Ken Henry, we each have to walk a delicate tightrope finely balanced between being open to scrutiny and not rolling over in front of it.

The five elements of a provocative mindset are supported by the five skills discussed in the previous chapter and provide a scaffolding for exercising provocative leadership.

In Part Three (Chapters 5–7), we explore the range of provocative action pointing to the need to use a variety of different moves.

Notes

1 https://podcasts.apple.com/au/podcast/real-risk/id1515258303.
2 See Ronald Heifetz and Marty Linsky's discussion of the assassinations of Yitzhak Rabin and Martin Luther King in *Leadership on the Line* (2002).
3 See Robert Lipsyte's report of the fight in the *New York Times* on the Web, 26 February 1964.
4 Parts of this section are extracted from an earlier article by Michael Johnstone published in LinkedIn 23 April 2019. https://www.linkedin.com/pulse/diversity-adaptation-leadership-mangroves-immigrants-phd.

References

Bridgewater Associates (no date). *Principles and Culture*. https://www.bridgewater.com/principles-and-culture. Retrieved 16 October 2020.

Csikszentmihalyi, M. (1998). *Flow: The Psychology of Optimal Experience*. Harper Perennial Books, USA.

Dalio, R. (2017). *Principles: Life and Work*. Simon & Schuster, New York.

Davis, S. (2015). *Learning to Fly: A Memoir of Hanging On and Letting Go*. Atria Books, New York, NY.

Harris, R. (2020). *Real Risks*. Podcast. https://podcasts.apple.com/au/podcast/real-risk/id1515258303. Retrieved 20 December 2021.

Heifetz, R., & Linsky, M. (2002). *Leadership on the Line*. Harvard University Press, Cambridge, MA.

Johnstone, M. (2019). *Diversity, Adaptation, and Leadership: Mangroves and Migrants Can Teach Us a Lot*. LinkedIn, 23 April 2019. https://www.linkedin.com/pulse/diversity-adaptation-leadership-mangroves-immigrants-johnstone-phd/. Retrieved 1 April 2021.

Kegan, R., & Lahey, L.L. (2016). *An Everyone Culture: Becoming a Deliberately Developmental Organization*. Harvard Business Review Press, Cambridge, MA.

Lipsyte, R. (1964). Clay wins title in seventh round upset as Liston is halted by shoulder injury. *New York Times* on the Web, 26 February 1964. https://archive.nytimes.com/www.nytimes.com/books/98/10/25/specials/ali-upset.html?scp=3&sq=robert%2520lipsyte%2520cassius%2520clay%2520sonny%2520liston&st=cse. Retrieved 29 March 2022.

Wheatley, M. (2002). *It's an Interconnected World*. Shambhala Sun, April 2002. https://margaretwheatley.com/wp-content/uploads/2014/12/Its-An-Interconnected-World.pdf. Retrieved 15 August 2021.

Whyte, D. (2003). *Crossing the Unknown Sea: Working and the Shaping of Identity*. Penguin Books, USA.

Zander, B. & Zander, R.S. (2000). *The Art of Possibility: Transforming Professional and Personal Life*. Harvard Business School Press, Boston, MA.

PART 3
TYPES OF PROVOCATION

All forms of provocation require a package of skills, capabilities, and attitudes to execute effectively. For example, if you were to share an observation with a group, you would also follow up with one or two questions and might then share an anecdote or story. Or you could equally notice a pattern of behavior and simply offer an interpretation, asking the group to comment. Having done so, some deep listening would help you deal with the responses. Other times you might challenge others to commit to one way of continuing, thereby, in effect, forcing a choice to be made.

This section takes our discussion beyond the foundational forms of provocation to indirect forms such as paradox and contradiction, stories, and counterfactuals. We also discuss several more unique and unpredictable forms of provocation, including critique and humor. These are useful because they add more arrows to your quiver, giving you more flexibility and responsiveness. In addition, their unpredictable qualities provide an element of surprise and disorientation.

By the time you have read this section, together with the chapters in Part Two, you will have a good sense of your current ability and willingness to provoke others, and hopefully will feel surer footed in your provocative efforts.

DOI: 10.4324/9781003321200-8

5 PARADOX, CONTRADICTION, AND AMBIGUITY AS PROVOCATION

The problem isn't the problem; the problem is the way you think about the problem.
Attributed to Paul Watzlawick, The Language of Change, 1973

Margaret, the Countess of Tyrol, also known as Maultasch ("Mouth Bag"), was one of the fourteenth century's wealthiest women. But following her father's death in 1335, her rivals, the Hapsburgs, seized her inheritance, the Duchy of Carinthia. She was determined to retrieve it. According to the medieval chronicler, Jakob Unrest, and later Jacob Grimm, she ordered her troops to attack the castle of Hochosterwitz in the province of Carinthia (Southern Austria). As she prepared for a long siege, she understood how difficult it would be to capture the fortress, given that it was situated 110 meters above the valley floor.

Over time, the garrison's situation became grave as food and supplies dwindled. Finally, all that remained in the castle's reserve were one ox and two bags of grain. But Margaret's status also deteriorated, as her troops became restless, and pressures elsewhere called for attention.

After many weeks, the castle commander made what seemed to be an illogical and counterintuitive decision. The last ox was killed, stuffed full of the remaining grain, and thrown over the castle walls into the enemy camp. The defenders pretended that they still had so much food remaining that it could be used as a projectile.

Margaret's increasingly discouraged troops saw this act as meaning the castle's inhabitants still had abundant food and could withstand a longer siege. As a result, Margaret abandoned the campaign and Hochosterwitz survived, against all the odds.

This story, made famous by Paul Watzlawick in *The Language of Change*, shows how common sense and logical behavior often miss the point. Actions that seem illogical and unreasonable, such as those taken by the defenders of Hochosterwitz, leverage opportunities and succeed in producing beneficial change. Occasionally, it is necessary to go far beyond what is deemed rational and sensible, unlocking new and unconventional interpretations and action. This chapter examines the use of paradox and contradiction as provocative strategies. Recognizing and amplifying the paradoxical situations people find themselves in is a good start. From there, crafting interventions that are paradoxical in nature will add to your repertoire.

DOI: 10.4324/9781003321200-9

5.1 Paradox

A paradox is a self-contradictory statement or process that runs contrary to one's expectations, can reveal a previously unacknowledged truth and often contains two opposing facts or characteristics.

Like Joseph Heller's *Catch-22*, the inhabitants of Hochosterwitz confounded their enemies by acting in contradictory ways—they could be starving and at the same time use what food remained to attack those below. Such paradox arises from the rules, understandings, or practices that people are subject to but have little or no control over because to fight the rule is to accept it. However, recognizing how you are caught is the first step, and if you can do so, you, like the commander of Hochosterwitz, can ride the energy the paradox creates and craft your own counterintuitive response.

Paradoxes are found throughout history, in both Eastern and Western philosophical traditions, and are associated with a state of not knowing or an inability to predict something with surety. Thus, a paradox becomes an invitation to cross a threshold out of the familiar and ordered into an un-normal and unknown.

We can illustrate the nature of paradox with the everyday example of a mother and teenage daughter arguing, prompting the daughter to storm out as she declares, "I just don't care anymore!" The daughter can only fight with her mother because she cares. She cares so much that she continues to argue.

For you as a change agent or someone exercising leadership, a powerful and often provocative move is to simply identify a paradox, to describe what you see. It is like casting a stone into a calm pond to create eddies and movement below the surface. Suddenly the known characteristics of the pond are disturbed, and more information is revealed. Old pictures of what the pond was are no longer relevant, old ideas are rendered unhelpful, and the view into the pond's depths stimulates different awareness and thinking. Paradox provides a portal into discovery and learning.

5.1.1 Living with paradox and contradiction

Recognizing the pressures that paradoxes create for people, especially during change, is the first step to harnessing them. Research in 2017 by Ella Miron-Spektor and her colleagues shows that contradictory tensions aren't the problem—the problem is how people think about the problem. For example, the commander of Hochosterwitz outsmarted Margaret and her troops by holding two contradictory ideas at the same time—we are starving, and we will use what food we have to confuse our enemy. A perfect paradox because the tensions generated by the contradictions created a productive energy and a highly novel response. Rather than reducing the tension and ambiguity, the commander increased them. As Miron-Spektor's work shows, embracing and harnessing discomfort increases creativity, which is needed during change.

People and organizations frequently hold contradictory commitments that compete with each other. We often hear people say they are committed to having honest conversations while equally expressing a commitment to only being kind and encouraging. As Robert Kegan has observed, "They have one foot on the accelerator and one on the brake!" But progress and resolution to our many complex challenges lie in acknowledging the multiple views, the seemingly odd perspectives, that are alive in any situation. We need to notice, even seek out, the contradictions, the ambiguous, and like the olive seller described next, have our feet firmly planted in today's reality while noticing yesterday's and tomorrow's dilemmas.

The next step, as we discuss in later sections, is to use paradox as a provocation.

5.1.1.1 An example

In 2016, we were in Jerusalem working with Israeli educators, who were keen to learn how to live and work more effectively with the contradictions they faced. They were all committed to making Israel, and the region, safer places. But being safe in Israel is no simple task, as life is full of challenges and contradictions. Residents and visitors alike live in the "in-between," constantly experiencing a range of paradoxical tensions.

Israel is a powerful military state, yet it feels vulnerable and imperiled. People are full of both hope and fear, which creates their own existential dilemmas. An olive seller at Jerusalem's Machane Yehuda market captures the sentiment in a short expression, "Machar Ain," which roughly translates as "tomorrow there will be no olives" or, more starkly, "there is no tomorrow." Yet he wants you to eat his olives!

Jerusalem attracts many people of all religious persuasions. Some of them have a deep spiritual conviction that they are in the presence of divine or messianic powers—or even possess such powers themselves. Frequently, the result is that they come to harm, or they inflict it on others. The "Jerusalem Syndrome," a psychotic state in which people identify themselves as Biblical figures, is an example of the power of holding one idea as if it were the truth in an environment where everyone believes they know the truth.

The smart and the crazy people, the committed and the zealous, all congregate in Jerusalem. The city is both a symbol and a weapon for their cause. One day, as we were wandering around a local square, a travel-worn woman approached us asking if we would help move her huge suitcase closer to the nearby public toilets. We soon noticed the large placard stuck to her suitcase, covered with uneven, barely legible handwritten polemics and pleas, decrying her father's unjust fate as a military officer. She had come to Jerusalem believing that this was a place of extraordinary power, where justice and truth could be served.

Of course, Israel is not the only country where contradictions abound. It just happens to provide many clear examples. But how do you live with such extreme polarities? Furthermore, how do you continue to grow and develop as a society, which meets people's aspirations? As the philosopher, Blaise Pascal suggests in his 1669 treatise, "We show greatness, not by being at one extreme, but by touching both at once and occupying all the space in between."

To make progress on big problems, we, like the Israeli educators, need to learn to live with and integrate contradictions into our practice, and become paradox seekers and harnessers. As Margaret Heffernan says in her recent book *Uncharted*, "the universe is far too unwieldy for mere humans to lasso it and whip it into manageable shape," which is why, for example, one never "defeats" nature, such as in pandemics. The irony is we love to try to tame nature. Witness the paradox of the oil producer, ConocoPhillips, installing chillers in the Alaskan permafrost to drill new oil wells. The permafrost is thawing because of global warming, a product of the burning of fossil fuels such as those ConocoPhillips is extracting.

These examples offer a recipe to recognize existing paradoxes and help construct them. They all:

- Bring together different elements that seem logical individually but inconsistent, absurd, and in tension when combined;
- Generate responses that embrace uncertainties; and
- Introduce a hint of humor or irony.

5.2 Paradoxical intervention

The use of deliberate paradoxical intervention was described in 1925 by Knight Dunlap in *Old and New Viewpoints in Psychology*, and later developed by psychiatrist Victor Frankl, who advised his patients to embrace their symptoms—"to do, or wish to happen, the very thing they fear."

Family therapists fine-tuned paradoxical interventions in the 1970s, especially at the Mental Research Institute in Palo Alto, California. For example, clients were asked to increase the frequency of symptoms, intensify them, or pretend they are present even if that is not currently the case. These instructions are paradoxical because the ultimate goal is to alleviate the maladaptive behavior and directly contrast with what the client initially says they want.

There are a range of paradoxical instructions, which involves some variation on the theme of inviting clients to engage in the problematic behaviors and symptoms they seek to relieve. Over the following pages, we discuss several different forms, all provocative because of the ambiguity they generate.

In its simplest form, symptom prescription involves an explicit directive that encourages a client or team to maintain their problematic behavior or symptom. This would translate in the workplace, for example, when a manager tells her team to "lighten up" during the discussion of a high-stakes issue. More often than not, their exhortation only leads to greater seriousness. Paradoxically, acknowledging the seriousness, giving it airtime makes it more likely that people can "lighten up" because they don't have to carry the burden of pretending the situation is not worrying. In the same way, it is difficult to follow a directive to be spontaneous.

In prescribing a symptom or problematic behavior, you are purposefully creating a space within which people must grapple with the contradictions of their circumstances. Your client, or group, or teenager is faced with a contradictory message: "To change, you must remain unchanged." If people comply with the suggestion and experience the symptoms, they gain some control over something that previously appeared to be uncontrollable. Or they understand something about their predicament that was once less visible, and now they have more choices.

5.2.1 Prescribe and amplify the symptom

When adaptation is needed, prescribing the symptom is provocative because of our instinctive resistance to change and possible loss. Resistance is heightened when there is tension between values or beliefs within or between people. Inviting people to slow the pace of change, or prescribe a previously unhelpful or maladaptive behavior, even though change is desired, is a provocative move.

For example, Michael recommended to Anne, a senior executive trying to overcome a slump in confidence, that she continue to be self-critical for at least one hour a day and not try to change anything, thereby learning how her self-judgment helped and motivated her. This suggestion was designed to give her time, to hold change back, until she had developed new skills.

In this way, Michael prescribed the symptom, offering an opportunity to perturb the balance of Anne's relationship with change and no change, confounding the beliefs that held her unwanted behavior in place. Further, he challenged Anne's expectations that he, as the expert, would suggest some positive strategies to build her confidence. The intervention stimulated self-reflection and self-appreciation and, at least temporarily, reordered Anne's firmly held but unexamined ideas. Though delivered with empathy, it also challenged Anne to take more responsibility for the changes she aspired to.

Prescribing symptomatic behavior is a forceful action that calls on a person or group to continue doing the very thing they want to stop, even though they claim not to have control over the behavior in question.

5.2.2 Increase ambiguity rather than reduce it

Marco and his colleague Tomaso were managers in an Italian company who were required to integrate their respective divisions. But Marco was struggling with the method proposed by Tomaso. He wanted to be seen as a team player but strongly disagreed with the proposal, which "was bad for the business and bad for me personally." Marco felt caught in between these conflicting beliefs. He was standing on unfamiliar ground. We wanted both men to expand the way they thought about this challenge; to move from either-or thinking into a both-and mindset. Therefore, we suggested that Marco spend the next week thinking about how he could satisfy both goals rather than thinking it had to be one or the other. Like many before him, he needed help to use the paradox he created for himself rather than hide from it.

Another observation we made helped him take his next steps. We said, "In order to move forward, you will need to decide how much of what you've done to prove your loyalty you are willing to put on the line to fight this battle for effectiveness." Marco described how the tension between loyalty and effectiveness required him to think deeply about what most mattered to him and how he could satisfy both.

He chose to expend some of his "being seen as loyal" capital in the service of ensuring the best outcome. The paradoxical observation nudged him to examine a less familiar pathway and, in so doing, to expand his view of himself.

In a 2000 article published in *The Academy of Management Review,* Marianne Lewis, the Professor of Management at the University of Cincinnati, explains that paradoxical tensions arise because most managers take an either/or position, creating mutually exclusive polarities rather than seeing interdependencies. Stressing one pole exacerbates the opposite extreme, often fueling defensive behavior, impeding learning, and engendering counterproductive reinforcing cycles. Managing paradox, in contrast, entails gaining understanding and developing practices that accept and integrate the tensions, in part by expanding our capacity to apprehend a larger view of reality which we previously had not imagined or had access to.

5.3 Working with resistance

We have noticed how easy it is for change agents or facilitators to be triggered by peoples' inevitable resistance. Being seen to support a change creates a barrier against which people can react, thereby fueling resistance. If you wish to challenge someone's worldview, a good place to start is to point out that resistance and loss are a precondition to change.

We have found that some clients want to assert their expertise and prove that we don't know very much about their situation. Providing more explanation or data almost always leads to a cycle of "yes, but" responses, entrenching the prevailing pattern of resistance. This common challenge to authority fits with the psychological framework that Eric Berne describes in *Games People Play,* in which "Why don't you ... " suggestions are rebutted with "Yes, but ... " responses. So, for example, you could ask for evidence of how a particular idea or solution might be suitable for an organization, only to encounter a vocal opponent who responds, "Yes, but we tried that, and it didn't work." Further explanation and the provision of more data are likely to prompt another cycle of "Yes, but" responses. The pattern continues, and positions become more entrenched.

There are different ways to utilize resistance, many of which are provocative. However, to be effective and provoke adaptation, the interventions must break or sidestep the game's prevailing rules, not through confrontation but by creating conditions in which other behavioral options become apparent.

For example, during a team consultation we facilitated, Bill, a seasoned area manager, regularly argued with us. So, we asked Bill and his colleagues to undertake an experiment. Firstly, we thanked Bill for ensuring that there was a healthy dose of skepticism in the team because the changes they were discussing were significant and shouldn't be accepted lightly. We then asked the other team members to ensure that any time Bill stopped being skeptical, one of them should take up his role to examine all possible angles of the argument. In this way, we provoked the team to look at the issue from Bill's perspective, reframing his skepticism as a vital contribution to their change process. As a result, the team enjoyed "becoming Bill" and had fun with what was less natural to them—being skeptical. The intervention also led Bill to behave in less oppositional ways, in part because he saw that others took his concerns seriously. This amplification of the resistance is another example of paradox: prescribing a "symptom."

By encouraging or reframing a pattern of resistance, more opportunities are created for the group to become responsible for it. Then, as the consultant, facilitator, manager, or parent, you hand the baton over.

Like all interventions, there is a difference between the intention and the response. All interventions, especially those that somehow provoke people, must be seen as testing a hypothesis. Adjustments are required once you have seen how people react. Not only is your intervention unpredictable but so are people's responses.

5.4 Paradox of opposites

An executive team we worked with at Google discovered that their frustrating poor performance was related to the tension between individual action and collective accountability. At an offsite workshop, the team declared, "We understand what the problems are, but just don't seem able to solve them." We put it to them that they wouldn't find any resolution until they decided how much of their autonomy and individual performance they were willing to sacrifice for the common good. As they struggled with this tension, it became clearer that the pressures to keep operating as they had (the status quo), despite being frustrating and ineffective, were still greater than the desire for change. It took a series of experiments, and some time, before the team began making any substantive change.

We often see how senior teams can overemphasize individual work and responsibility, deploying tight rules to manage people. In so doing, they signal distrust, which drives defensiveness and turf wars, resulting in more reliance on executive oversight. Creating a paradox helps you look below the surface of habitual thinking because temporarily, you can be confused, in a liminal space. You have an "ah-ha" moment where light squeezes through the cracks of your worldview, and what was invisible and routine becomes visible.

A paradox is a bit like looking at an Escher painting as it helps you cross the threshold behind the ordinary observable reality to glimpse an unexpected and incompatible image. Thus, paradox becomes a means to lift the lid on what we prefer to ignore, and helps identify the contradictions and tensions that hold us and the problems we face in place.

Borrowing from Michael Raynor's, *The Strategy Paradox*, you can see how most successful teams or businesses are based on making firm commitments now to a pathway into an uncertain future. No one knows what the conditions will be next year, let alone in five or ten years. Yet, they take the risk and commit wholeheartedly. A paradox, then, arises from the collision of commitment and uncertainty—certainty and unpredictability. We explore these tensions in a large US bank in Chapter 11.

In another example of provoking people by prescribing symptomatic behavior, we worked with an executive team who complained about the bad habits they had developed regarding timeliness. People were regularly late to meetings, and those who arrived on time felt disrespected. We suggested they undertake an experiment whereby they all agreed to be late to all sessions on Tuesdays and Thursdays but continue to come as usual on other days. After some initial hesitance, the team committed. Two weeks later, we were informed that no one had been late to meetings despite agreeing to be so.

Here we took the "side" of the problem and argued for continuing with lateness to experience the contradiction inherent in their situation. By arguing for more lateness, but under controlled conditions, the team members were free to consider the respect contained in being punctual. The frame of reference had changed, and people began to feel in charge of the very behavior that seemed out of control.

Paradoxical interventions can be a cheeky and humorous assault on entrenched symptoms, client resistance, or ambivalence. For example, we ask people not to change symptoms (behavior, thought, feeling), increase them, or pretend to have them. Paradox is an invitation to experiment with the restraints of change because it grabs people in unexpected ways, allowing new thinking and information to go beyond the ingrained thresholds. People then start talking in more focused ways about issues that were previously not visible to them or, if visible, not open to discussion.

5.5 The double bind

A more complicated form of provocative intervention is the double bind, made famous by Gregory Bateson. It is a form of paradoxical communication in which conflicting messages are received, each negating the other. In his book, *Catch-22*, Joseph Heller offers what has become one of the most famous double binds. Heller's characters were crazy if they flew combat missions and therefore didn't have to, but if they didn't want to fly, they were sane and consequently had to. Like Captain Yossarian, Heller's main protagonist, if you respond to either statement, you will fail or, at best, feel stuck.

For example, a manager can demand honesty and transparency from their team but undermine this by using covert methods that punish honesty. If you act honestly, you risk punishment, and if you don't, you risk disapproval, a form of punishment. Double binds explain why developing a culture of honest feedback and transparency is so complicated. You are dammed if you do, and dammed if you don't.

Another team complained that they felt caught by their value statement, which said, "We will be responsive and flexible," leading to an unrelenting demand from their (internal) clients. The team had interpreted this value literally and, as a result, found themselves saying yes to every customer request. They were caught in a bind—if they said yes, they honored their values but exhausted themselves, but if they said no, they would disappoint and lose clients, which would stress them and lead to criticism. Among our interventions, we asked, "How can you learn to withstand your client's disappointment as you make firmer choices about what you do and don't do?" The question invited the team to live in the grey zone between yes and no, between their stated value and their tacit values (of being healthier and prioritizing their work), and to understand that their problems weren't fixable, but they were learnable. We provoked them out of their usual way of resolving problems and developing more of an adaptive mindset. They now understood that progress would be measured by how they learned together and reinforced hidden behaviors such as making and keeping priorities. It was hard work for them, given their history of pleasing others and seeing their exhaustion as a badge of honor.

When she was a therapist, Maxime worked with a family whose sixteen-year-old daughter had attempted suicide. After a session where the parents had complained about the daughter not helping with the housework, all the family agreed to experiment with household tasks. The daughter agreed to do the dishes after dinner, and the mother agreed to notice. The following week, when reporting back on their tasks, the mother commented, "She did the dishes, but she didn't mean it." The double bind for this girl was made chillingly evident. By agreeing to the task of doing the dishes, she was bound to fail as it became apparent that her mother wanted her to wash the dishes and appear as if she liked doing it. Thus, the daughter could not be judged as successful at the secret test of being seen to enjoy housework. The double bind was visible, revealing the conditions in the family that made it impossible for her to succeed. Maxime's response was to ask the parents to continue to believe their daughter was not complying while also encouraging her only to comply if she didn't mean it. The intervention was a counter-double-bind designed to catch the parents in their own pattern of disappointment. Like all interventions, this therapeutic stance was not a solution but a provocative move to push the family system into a more productive cycle—one step toward the family finding their way out of a dangerous situation.

5.6 Paradox in practice

In addition to being a tool for leadership practice, paradoxical interventions are now used in various settings beyond their roots in family therapy. One example comes from Boaz Hameiri, an Israeli social psychologist, who experiments with different forms of "symptom prescription" to influence how Israelis think about current social and political dilemmas, including Israel's relationship with Palestinians. A 2018 research paper shows that mid-level provocative messages exaggerating extremist views can help unfreeze anti-refugee attitudes and anti-Palestinian beliefs.

The provocations prompted heightened levels of surprise, tested participants' sense of identity, and led to re-examining long-held beliefs. Hameiri's participants exposed to paradoxical interventions "expressed more conciliatory attitudes regarding the conflict, even one year after the intervention, and also tended to vote for more dovish parties than previously."

From a practice standpoint, paradoxical messages should not be too extreme or absurd since overly "heated" people raise more vigorous disagreement. There is a sweet spot to be found between insufficient and excessive provocation, a place where you will grab people's attention and increase the chance of learning, as well as of changes in attitude and behavior.

Several conditions seem to increase the likelihood that paradoxical actions will have some beneficial impact. You should, however, recognize that these are not ends in themselves, instead, they are a means to stimulate reflection, learning, and cognitive and emotional ambidexterity. You must:

1. Demonstrate your care for recipients and have their best interests at heart;
2. Use non-judgmental language and indicate you understand people's perspectives;
3. Make the message consistent with the beliefs and attitudes of the recipient. It should target the recipient's tolerance of acceptance, even though the statement is exaggerated or even absurd;
4. Allow for some surprise or confusion; and
5. Undertake the work with an experimental mindset, where you might be on-target but equally might be off-target.

Here, we have looked at how everyday dilemmas often contain a paradox that acts as a type of transformational window, a crevice in our own thinking and belief system that leads to temporary confusion and a reassessment of what is known. The liminal zone encourages a crossing into different awareness and perspective, where the familiar stepping-stones are less useful and, therefore, we, or the group we are part of, have to draw on other latent capacities.

The next chapter focuses on stories as provocation, providing examples of how well-crafted narratives can stimulate, evoke, and challenge people into adaptive action.

References

Bateson, G. (1972). *Steps to an Ecology of Mind: Collected Essays in Anthropology, Psychiatry, Evolution, and Epistemology*. Part V, Chapter Four, Substance and Difference. The University of Chicago Press, Chicago.

Berne, E. (1964). *Games People Play*. Ballantine Press, New York.

Dunlap, K. (1925). *Old and New Viewpoints in Psychology*. Wolfe Publishing, Mosby Europe.

Frankl, V. (1975). Paradoxical intention and dereflection. *Psychotherapy, 12*(3), pp. 226–237.

Hameiri, B., Bar-Tal, D., & Halperin, E. (2018). Paradoxical thinking interventions: A paradigm for societal change. *Social Issues and Policy Reviews, 13*(1), pp. 1–17. https://spssi.onlinelibrary.wiley.com/doi/10.1111/sipr.12053. Retrieved 12 May 2021.

Heffernan, M. (2020). *Unchartered: How to Navigate the Future*. Avid Reader Press, Simon & Schuster, New York.

Heller, J. (1995). *Catch-22*. Simon & Schuster, New York.

Lewis, M.W. (2000). Exploring paradox: Toward a more comprehensive guide. *Academy of Management Review, 25*, pp. 760–776. https://journals.aom.org/doi/10.5465/amr.2000.3707712. Retrieved 5 November 2020.

Miron-Spektor, E., Ingram, A., Keller, J., Smith, W.K., & Lewis, M.W. (2017). Microfoundations of organizational paradox: The problem is how we think about the problem. *Academy of Management Journal*, *61*(1), p. 2017. Published Online: 16 March 2017. https://www.researchgate.net/publication/315078722_Microfoundations_of_Organizational_Paradox_The_Problem_Is_How_We_Think_about_the_Problem. Retrieved 17 August 2021.

Pascal, B. (1966). Pensées, transl. Krailsheimer, A.J. (Penguin, London. The Thoughts of *Blaise Pascal* [1669]). https://oll.libertyfund.org/titles/pascal-the-thoughts-of-blaise-pascal. Retrieved 1 May 2021.

Raynor, M.E. (2007). *The Strategy Paradox: Why Committing to Success Leads to Failure and What to do About it.* Crown Business Publishers, New York, NY.

Watzlawick, P. (1973). *The Language of Change: Elements of Therapeutic Communication.* Basic Books, New York.

6 STORIES AS PROVOCATION

Maybe stories are just data with a soul.

Brené Brown, 2011, The Power of Vulnerability

6.1 Introduction

It is April 2018, and we are sitting in a small room overlooking the Old City of Jerusalem. It is a hot, dry day, and people are restless. We are here to work with a team that has recently learned that it will be disbanded. They are in shock, subject to a decision made by executives who no longer see their work as central to the organization's mission. It is a hard pill to swallow, especially for Sarah Mali, the unit's founding director, but also for her colleagues. These eight people committed themselves to develop better leadership in their community. For them, "it was not a job but rather a connection to a purpose and a group of people who all care beyond the job."

Finishing something that is a vocation, a calling, rather than a job, is difficult because of the degree to which they infused the work with heart and soul. So, we invited the group to share their collective story, and what it meant to be together as a team for the last time.

Sarah begins:

> *I had a dream last night. They had taken my office and subdivided it, placing twenty desks around the room where there had been only one. Mine. Twenty people in tiny spaces, each closed off, with no room for movement. Someone came into the crowded office and said, "This is your space. Make the most of it!" Then they left. The twenty people were alone and in the dark.*

Sarah paused and looked at her colleagues. Most of them had tears in their eyes. She continued:

> *I still really believe in our purpose, what we set out to do. But I don't want to do it in a place that doesn't believe. I won't do it! Even though it feels hard, I realized that we all fulfilled something grand. I feel fulfilled.*

At this point, Sarah spoke in Hebrew and explained that the Hebrew word for fulfillment was "hagshamah," which has its root in the word "geshem," meaning rain. Holding herself steady, she continued:

DOI: 10.4324/9781003321200-10

> *We all deserve opportunities to continue this for ourselves even though we won't be together. Our rain can and will continue to fall but in different places. I hope there might be an opportunity to be together, but it might not happen. So, let's continue to fulfill what we all started to do.*

She paused, looked down, and then held her colleagues' gaze, taking in the strong feeling in the room. She was finished, and it was finished.

There was a long silence before Maya spoke, her voice trembling as she looked directly at Sarah, then at the rest of her colleagues.

> *I haven't been able to feel my grief before. I've been denying that this is happening. It feels like being in a vehicle that is immediately behind a car crash. You can see it happening but at a distance. You want to call out to the driver in front of you and say, "Given that you are in the driver's seat, how can we be there with you, so you don't feel so alone?"*

For several hours, the group shared their recollections of being together and the value they had created both for their clients and community and, perhaps more importantly, for each other. Their stories continued, ranging from anecdotes about crucial decisions that had been made through to their appreciation of Sarah and the job she had done.

As they started to wind down, it became clear to us, as their facilitators and witnesses, that the team had begun meaningful adaptive work—they confronted an unwanted reality, full of grief but also tinged with hope. They grappled with an essential question: "How do you find other means to create connection and meaning when what you have stops?" In Chaim Potok's novel *The Chosen*, a father advises his son who is leaving home, "sometimes you have to go a long way from home in order to decide how far you want to come back." Similarly, this group had to explore how to find meaning in a variety of different contexts so that they could come back to what they believed.

The goodwill and grace the group showed one another have stayed with us and stands in stark contrast to how most endings occur. There are usually many "thank yous," some reminiscing, and a few random hopes for the future thrown into the orphan abyss of loss. In this case, Sarah's team took the time to feel the loss, speak to it, and use it to see other possibilities.

The day also demonstrated the power of creating an environment in which adaptive work can be done. The conversation we witnessed that day was highly charged and provocative, not because anyone was directly challenging anyone else but because of the way each of the stories told, starting with Sarah's, pushed those present to confront an unwanted reality.

Sarah recognized the nature of the occasion and used it to tell her own story and trigger stories in her colleagues, as we saw with Maya. Sarah's clarity and vulnerability were core ingredients in the provocative mix and, had she held back, it is less likely she would have had such a deep impact. The stories were provocative because they activated those present, mobilized them to be brave, and acknowledged the meaning of what was happening to them while they were together, exposed, and unprotected.

The stories told also remind us that provocation comes in many forms. Stories that call us to be seen and heard, evoke memories, connection, and emotion, provoke us to reconsider how we see each other and the world we face together. But the provocation is less direct, less in your face. As you tell a story, you do so knowing that as it leaves your lips, it takes on a life and meaning in each listener that you cannot control. You are the archer, releasing the arrow, which then pierces and provokes each person differently. What lands and our response is unique in each of us.

In this chapter, we examine how stories are a provocative device, one that can be used in a wide variety of settings. We show how stories:

- Help confront difficult challenges in a way that makes them accessible;
- Activate and encourage people to take risks and to talk plainly about complex issues;
- Help get people ready for the confronting work of change; and
- Can be gentle and loving, but also provocative.

6.2 Stories and leadership[1]

Current thinking about storytelling as a leadership method suggests that using personal and business stories can help open people up to change, can provoke and stimulate thinking, and free people up to themselves and new possibilities.

There are several reasons you would choose to draw on stories and narrative, most of them eloquently outlined in the plethora of books on business storytelling. In summary, stories are valuable because they:

1. Connect people with themselves, their history, and their aspirations;
2. Are a means to bypass the usual, rational, data-driven arguments used to justify change;
3. Help overcome people's instinctive resistance and skepticism, especially when they have strong beliefs and values;
4. Stimulate people by generating emotion, allowing us to reveal more about ourselves, our struggles, and our vulnerabilities;
5. Allow teaching without being didactic or pedantic;
6. Create a time and space for reflection, exploration, and dialogue; and
7. Help us remember, honor what has occurred, utilize lessons learned, and inspire people.

Stories help direct our attention to critical issues. They involve us, especially emotionally, helping to build commitment and a platform for action. By connecting to our feelings, a story will activate and appeal to our more trusting, empathic, and altruistic selves. And a story will mobilize us to act, to feel connected to purpose, and, as we saw in Sarah's story, to behave in a manner consistent with their beliefs.

Paul Zak, the Founding Director of the Center for Neuroeconomics Studies at the Claremont Graduate University, has proven the causal effect of oxytocin on prosocial behavior, and the link between emotional stories and increased commitment to learning and action. He shows how stories enhance empathy and trust. Hollywood movie directors also understand this link in developing an emotional arc and trajectory, providing what is sometimes referred to as a "surprising familiarity." That is, they appeal to universal themes and an audience's emotions in ways that transports them into the story. An audience becomes temporarily part of the story. As our editor and friend Richard Martin explains, an audience is always part of the story. The viewer of a film or a reader of a novel become co-creators of the story. They fill in the gaps, the back story, the meaning. Listening, viewing, and reading, in this way, are subjective and emotive. The intent of the filmmaker or novelist bumps up against the meaning-making of the viewer/reader. Between storyteller and listener, there is a space where new narratives happen.

Overall, a story can create an indelible message, a container for collective wisdom, and important life lessons. Stories can entertain, teach, delight, frighten, or inspire. They are leadership tools used to draw and hold people's attention, directing them to critical issues.

6.3 Crucibles as provocation

In our work, we regularly invite leaders to tell Crucible stories—critical moments in their lives, which forge their identities and values as leaders. We adapted this idea from Warren Bennis and Robert Thomas, who show in *Geeks & Geezers*, how unplanned, often traumatic, experiences transformed leaders and became the source of their distinctive leadership abilities. The work shows how full potential is activated only after reflection, meaning-making, and learning.

For example, as part of a residential leadership program for health professionals, Maxime asked participants to share crucible moments, and people shared profound stories of loss, failure, and shame. The group had an emotional experience. As we finished for the day, the Director (Ken) asked to speak to Maxime privately. They walked outside together, and he began to tell her how dismayed he was that she "had been so irresponsible as to expose colleagues to each other's personal experiences." Maxime listened as she tried to understand what it was that had perturbed him.

Ken objected to being exposed to other people's lives, their triumphs, and struggles. He became outraged, speaking fast and loudly, his face dark and contorted with rage. He was a big man, and Maxime is quite small, and he loomed over her, beating the air with his fists, apoplectic at the imposition. Maxime understood that Ken felt exposed, he hadn't signed up for the activity, and his emotions were confusing.

Suddenly Ken stopped, stepped back, and as Maxime looked up at him, for a moment, it was as if his features fissured, splintering like glass. In this moment of metamorphosis, his arms dropped to his sides, and he held his hands to his head. He gasped as the rage suddenly ran out of him. His face softened, and he breathed, "Oh, oh, oh, I get it. I get it." And after a pause he said, "I had no idea what was going on for any of them. I had no idea at all. And I should know. They're my people."

Maxime had never before, nor since, seen in the space of thirty seconds, the physical manifestation of a powerful new idea taking hold, and sweeping aside firmly held beliefs. Ken began to consider the value of knowing his staff on a personal level. It was a revelation. Maxime and Ken stayed outside together for a long time, and the man who returned to his people was very different from the one they had known.

Here you see how provocation can challenge and perturb an existing limiting pattern. If no provocation is forthcoming, then help may be needed from an outside agent, and that could be you. Although you will have ideas about what an individual, team, group, or organization may need to develop or change, you cannot know. And so, seeking to do good, you need to breathe deeply before you take a risk to provoke others out of their stuckness. And then, you must observe the impact and arc of their response so that you can determine a helpful level of pressure and support. Your job is to support the emergent tendrils of learning to take root.

Maxime had previously seen a range of responses to the crucible activity, so, she knew what to expect. Except for this time. As Ken felt disturbed, Maxime continued the provocative moment with a combination of deep listening, validating his feelings, inviting him to consider the effectiveness of his beliefs, and through the simple act of hanging in there with him. Although Ken was shaken and shocked, he felt gratitude for the discovery he had made, and wrote later about the lifesaving impact that the experience had on his work and home relationships. For example, he began a routine of asking his staff about their lives and personal interests, something he had never done before. But it doesn't always work out that way.

The work of provocation requires you to find a way to trust others to adjust themselves when you have nudged them out of their beliefs and assumptions of the familiar but unproductive holding pattern. Although you will build a body of experience that allows reasonable prediction, you cannot know how someone will react. Hence, you need the reciprocal muscle that enables you to hold steady so that you can be a witness to adaptation and development, not the architect.

6.4 Stories as a pattern interrupter

"Jade," an experienced executive at a technology company, found herself leading a fractious team, many of whom were there because of a recent restructuring. She was at her wit's end because there were frequent arguments, stakeholder criticism was increasing, and because all the tactics and strategies she applied were not working.

As part of our coaching work, Jade wrote about her experience to see it more clearly and objectively. She relayed the story to her team as if it were a tale from her past, to create emotional distance between herself and the team's distress. She spoke of how incompetent she felt and how hard it was to ask for help. She explained that even with a reputation for being an "ace leader," she wanted and needed the team's guidance on moving forward. At the heart of the story, she revealed that, she felt out of her depth, didn't know what to do, and asked for their help.

Some members in her team were shocked, not expecting her to be so open and exposed, given her reputation for toughness and success. Her story, and the vulnerability it contained, did not solve the team's problems, but it was a key that unlocked a series of different team conversations. The storytelling provoked people because it surprised them and appealed to their compassion.

Jade's intervention broke the team's pattern of argument, bypassing months of bad feeling, eliciting a different response. Her story was a pattern interrupter. In this way, it epitomized what provocation could be. Jade's storytelling was neither fierce nor strongly expressed. But, by appealing to the compassionate side of her team, she challenged how people saw her, thus unsettling the status quo. By revealing more of who she was, Jade encouraged her colleagues to see her more fully, less as a powerhouse, all-knowing boss, and more as someone who didn't know how to solve all problems. She broke the impasse, and the team began a series of more productive discussions. Paradoxically by being more vulnerable in her story, she had more power. As Brené Brown declares in a 2011 TED talk, "vulnerability fuels our daily lives and is the birthplace of innovation, creativity, and change."

6.5 Provocation as revelation

Maxime recently worked with a group of Defence officials where one participant revealed that he had left the service three times during his career, returning each time. He was now sure being in uniform was right for him and knew he was bringing his best to work. The others seemed struck by this disclosure, and there was a thoughtful silence. Then a quieter member spoke about his own aspirations and how he had always held himself back, especially from asking hard questions. He spoke at length of his admiration for his colleague, recognizing the courage it must have taken to leave and come back, and now tell the group. It seemed like a sacred moment, where one man acknowledged his colleague, and showed he had just learned from the example. He talked about his own lack of imagination, having never allowed himself to consider this possibility, and how much more he wanted for himself. He owned up to finding his courage lacking in the past but not his hope for himself and his work. While Maxime and her co-facilitator orchestrated the creation of the opportunity for self-disclosure, the actual moment was a personal revelation that commanded attention.

The story highlights how leadership is both an action and revelatory art. Just as an artist, poet, or author tries to reveal something about the human condition, stories can provoke people to discover something about themselves and their collective stuckness. Your efforts to mobilize people to embrace change, even when they suffer some form of loss, require you to ensure deep engagement and commitment to a process where the end is uncertain, and the timeline unclear. Stories are among the tools in a leader's repertoire that help create engagement and to have others be part of the story. Sarah included her colleagues in the story. They appeared in her dream and her reimagining their future.

The reason stories are so powerful is complex. Simply stated, stories activate all three sensory modes: visual, auditory, and kinesthetic. As humans, we want to be engaged, to feel, joining with others in their joy and sadness. A story wakes us up, and we identify with the storyteller, activating mirror neurons, cells in our brain that allow us to feel and understand others' actions. Our colleague, Nancy Houfek, points out that we don't need to try to understand what others are feeling in a story; we can actually feel what they are feeling. In this way, stories serve as an "empathy bridge."

By making emotional connections, stories pull people toward their common purpose. They avoid, therefore, the effort required to persuade people with more rational "push" arguments. It is not unusual to be in the Sisyphean position of trying to convince people to agree with something or make an operational or behavioral change, and finding that the experience feels like pushing a rock uphill. People are comfortable, content with the familiar, stubborn in their resistance. They don't like to be compelled. But they are far more likely to join you if they feel pulled toward your message. When mirror neurons are switched on, the audience both pictures the possibility of change and feels it. A story becomes a means of connecting people to a shared truth in a short space of time.

Maxime's exchange with Ken illustrates how initially he was not persuaded about the value of the exercise, exactly the opposite. But by holding steady in the face of his fury and listening to him, he made the connections himself. Thus, Maxime fostered conditions in which he could ride his own wave, and arrive at a different location than that he departed from.

6.6 Gentle but confronting provocation

Some stories we encounter are at the most opportune moments, precisely when we are most open to reflection, change, and difference. Stories can be relevant to the situations in which we find ourselves, conveying emotion and sentiment in ways that can take us by surprise. As such, stories can perform a preparatory role, warming us up for the challenges ahead. They prompt us to action by appealing to our values and beliefs, creating a context for openness.

Such stories strip away convention, inviting us into a zone of emotional readiness. This is a form of productive unsettling.

Early in 2021, we had such an experience when attending the memorial ceremony for the singular Lotte Weiss, a family friend who died aged 97. Lotte, who authored *My Two Lives*, made it her life's work to recount her experiences as a Holocaust survivor, ensuring that the horrific lessons of this time were never forgotten while also expressing hope for the future.

The ceremony marked the end of "shloshim," the thirty days of Jewish mourning that follow the death of a loved one. Many of the rituals of shloshim create time and space for reflection, serving as a guide for the living. Mourners share the burden of loss, and provide one another with relief and restoration through shared grief and deep emotion.

Grief is deeply provocative because it takes us to unexpected places and momentarily renders us helpless. It forces us to take stock, examine what is, and reflect on what could be. The novel, challenging, and disorienting experience of grief can help us all consider new options. At Lotte's memorial, many people spoke and shared their recollections, including her two sons. However, nothing quite prepared us for the story told by Fay Sussman, a Sydney-based musician and singer who recounted her relationship with Lotte.

> *I met Lotte by coincidence at Cadry Carpet's Christmas party in Sydney, where she worked. I told her about my own tragic history and how I began my life as a musician. Lotte was interested in my love of Yiddish music and how I used it to unite people and break down barriers. After some time, Lotte mentioned the Yiddish song, "Papirosn" (The Cigarette).*
>
> *Lotte spoke in hushed tones and said to me, "I remember this song because it was sung by Flora, a girl I knew, from the wagons that took us all, young Jewish women, to Auschwitz in 1942. I will never forget that song, nor dear Flora who perished soon after in Auschwitz."*
>
> *The song has a plaintive melody and is about an orphan forced to sell cigarettes in the street. It seemed so appropriate to Lotte's journey. Lotte and I sat there for quite some time. Her eyes were moist. I took a deep breath before she asked me, "Do you know this song?" I replied that I did and asked if she would like me to sing it.*
>
> *Lotte replied haltingly, "Yes, I would." So right there, in a roomful of people celebrating Christmas, I sang "Papirosn," depicting a boy's tragic fate, losing hope after having lost his parents and seeing his sister die.*

Fay held the audience spellbound as we anticipated what would happen next. She had carried us not only to that Cadry's meeting but to the wagons that had transported Lotte and so many others, including Michael's Aunt, Lilly. Fay had reminded us of Lotte's desire not to forget the past but to work together for a better future.

The room was still while Fay began to sing in Yiddish. As the words enveloped us, we marveled at Lotte's life, at her fortitude, at her willingness to listen again to a song that was associated with so much pain and loss, finding hope where others could only see despair.

We left the ceremony deeply moved, having reconnected with Michael's old friends and their shared history, and determined to model in however small a way the good that Lotte had done.

As we learned so powerfully at Lotte's memorial, stories can mobilize people to action in a variety of ways. On this occasion, the provocation was gentle, although there was something disconcerting about Lotte's link to a song that had such a strong association with transportation and death. However, the way Fay told the story was evocative, folding her own story into Lotte's, collapsing the boundaries between time and place and people. It became a story of now, of us, Jewish history, of suffering and hope, of life's affirmation. Like Lotte herself, it was filled with energy and compassion, gentleness, and courage. An inspiration to us all.

The experience shows how provocation can strip away the veneer of convention and pretense but also push us to consider change despite the obstacles. This moment, and the multi-layered story in it, remind us how stories can prepare us to confront a challenge we face even though it is painful to do so. And how provocation can also be gentle and loving.

6.7 Crafting a provocative narrative

While teaching at Harvard University's John F. Kennedy School of Government, we worked with Nancy Houfek, who helped students learn how to bring themselves more to the "stage" of teaching and has run sessions on storytelling for leadership educators. She teaches techniques from the theater that leaders can use to prepare for and deliver an impactful story, including connecting with the audience, having a presence, knowing your objectives, and "landing your message." And she teaches how to use verbal and nonverbal language more effectively, noting how both modalities increase the impact of a story.

In effect, Nancy encourages us to bring ourselves and our life experiences as stories into our work, whatever that may be. These stories are a direct means of activating people, their joy, and their energy.

Learning to tell powerful stories involves a combination of technique and inspiration. Indeed, most teachers of this craft emphasize how vital the mechanics and methods are to enact the narrative. As with any craft, with good technique under your belt, your stories will feel fresh, allowing it to have an impact and affect the listener below the neck. It stimulates, engages, evokes, and provokes.

Leaders and innovators are usually impassioned by their ideas for change. All too often, however, there is no story offered to support their visions, hopes, or aspirations. This omission diminishes the chances of success. We have seen how people need to feel the issues they confront, to experience the problem to take action on something that matters to them. Sarah's example illustrates what happens when people begin to feel the story, when the challenge described moves them to care and support what is required. Sarah didn't need to rally her people to the cause or ask them directly to do the hard work required. Her story helped them draw these conclusions themselves.

In his 2011 essay "Public Narrative, Collective Action, and Power," Marshall Ganz describes three overlapping narratives, each of which creates an emotional link and builds a compelling case for change, a link between themselves and the collective action required. They are:

- Stories of Self that tell our personal journeys of learning and growth;
- Stories of Us that narrate why we are drawn to the challenge and what values we share; and
- Stories of Now that describe the gap between the current reality and what ought to be.

Ganz's three narrative elements are at the heart of provocation, especially when used together.

In Jade's case, her portrayal of herself resonated with her colleagues partly because they could identify with her struggle. She embodied the contradictions she felt, strong and vulnerable, in charge and out of control, and a risk-taker as well as cautious. Jade's story was provocative precisely because it was simultaneously recognizable, remarkable, and yet unpredictable (Jade's "story of self"). Jade's risk-taking stimulated, aroused, and elicited a range of reactions from her colleagues, which led them to consider how they were all implicated in the problem (the "story of us"). Any way forward required them all to be involved (story of "now"). A hallmark of a compelling story is that its provocation is productive.

Shawn Callahan, a master storyteller, and author of *Putting Stories to Work*, says, "We only get the benefits of a story when one is told." If you want to start being a better storyteller, you could become what Shawn calls a story "spotter"—someone who can hear the seeds of a good story around them or who notices others' haltering beginnings at locating an experience in a particular place and time. To generate stories, you can simply ask others to relate a time when they felt under pressure and reflect on what they learned from it, or a time when they made a mistake, or an intervention that didn't work out, and to consider why. Equally, telling a provocative story requires a keen eye for the pressure points in a group or organization and the ripest issue. Setting stories up requires an invitation into shared intimacy and vulnerability or a common cause.

In summary, there are five elements to an impactful story:

- It is vivid and full of detail;
- It matters to the listener;
- Something unanticipated is expressed;
- It expresses emotion; and
- It provides insight, challenges beliefs.

To this list, we would add two features of a provocative story:

- It helps name, describe, and respond to a challenge; and
- It prepares people for learning, disturbance, and change.

If you also want to challenge the status quo, your stories need to have provocative qualities that go to the heart of the challenges faced. In addition, part of your job is to create the conditions for stories to be heard, found, and told by others. These conditions allow you and your group to identify moments that reveal something about the barriers to change, people's wisdom, and ultimately about their capacity to live with disturbance. (See a summary in the Application Box 6.1.) So, you can be a storyteller, a story listener, or a story finder.

How will you use stories to provoke people, to stimulate, arouse, and mobilize them? What life lessons have you learned that might assist others if you used them to create a powerful story?

Application box 6.1

When is it useful to tell provocative stories? What to look for.

- When people are stuck, or conversation becomes circular.
- When unexpected reactions or feelings are expressed.
- When your plan (as facilitator or change agent) becomes less relevant or is derailed.
- When you have a powerful message, but the setting requires respect and delicacy, or need to back up a logical argument.
- When people are stuck in their heads—you want to move the focus from abstract and intellectual to emotion and concrete.
- When you hear your client group tell their own stories.
- When you want to highlight your purpose (of the group's).
- When there is a history of hurt, loss, and confusion.
- To mark the beginning or end of something meaningful, and to mark progress.

Note

1 The ideas in this chapter have been synthesized from listening to many great storytellers, and from conversations with several experts in the field. We particularly acknowledge the work of our colleague Nancy Houfek, previously head of Voice and Speech at the American Repertory Theatre, with whom we had the pleasure of working with, and learning from, at Harvard's Kennedy School of Government.

References

Bennis, W.G., & Thomas, R.J. (2002). *Geeks & Geezers – How Era, Values and Defining Moments Shape Leaders.* Harvard Business Review Press, Cambridge, MA.

Brown, B. (2011). *The Power of Vulnerability.* TED Talk, 3 January 2011. https://www.ted.com/talks/brene_brown_the_power_of_vulnerability/transcript. Retrieved 10 October 2020.

Callahan, S. (2016). *Putting Stories to Work: Mastering Business Storytelling.* Pepperberg Press, Melbourne, Vic.

Ganz, M. (2011). *Public narrative, collective action, and power.* In Odugbemi S. & Lee T. (eds.) *Accountability Through Public Opinion: From Inertia to Public Action.* The World Bank, Washington D.C, pp. 273–289. http://nrs.harvard.edu/urn-3:HUL.InstRepos:29314925. Retrieved 20 October 2020.

Houfek, N. (2007). *The Act of Teaching.* Video from Derek Bok Center for Teaching and Learning, Harvard University. https://www.youtube.com/watch?v=6ssHzyVn3HY&feature=emb_logo. Retrieved 20 October 2021.

Potok, C. (1967). *The Chosen.* Simon & Schuster, New York.

Weiss, L. (2003). *My Two Lives.* Griffin Press, Sydney, NSW.

Zak, P.J. (2015). *Why Inspiring Stories Make Us React. The Neuroscience of Narrative.* Cerebrum, February. https://www.ncbi.nlm.nih.gov/pmc/articles/PMC4445577/pdf/cer-02-15.pdf. Retrieved 29 December 2021.

Zak, P.J. (2019). *How Our Brains Decide When to Trust. Harvard Business Review*, 18 July 2019. https://hbr.org/2019/07/how-our-brains-decide-when-to-trust. Retrieved 29 December 2021.

7 UNIQUE FORMS OF PROVOCATION

The most effective person in any situation is the one who is most flexible, who has the widest range of behaviors.

Commonly used idea—probably a simplified version of Ross Ashby's Law of Requisite Variety.

7.1 Being caught unawares

Several years ago, we visited our son Guy in London. It was a rainy, cold day, and as we prepared to leave his house, Guy recommended that Michael take an umbrella. Unthinkingly, Michael replied, "It's not far to the car; I will be alright." As we climbed into the car, Guy said to his father, "Gosh, it is really hard to get your attention. You don't listen, and therefore are impossible to help!" At first, Michael was stunned before realizing that the unexpected feedback was a wake-up call. Guy had spoken directly, and truthfully. What had appeared churlish or defiant was, in fact, an adaptability test, its message by-passing rational thought, and landing straight in the heart. Guy's feedback was potent precisely because it was totally unexpected, truthful, and challenged how Michael thought of himself. The status quo was unsettled, prompting him to think about his attitude to accepting guidance, and being less sure about his own ways.

The beauty of surprise is that your whole being is activated, opening an opportunity for creating news of difference and learning. We have discovered five distinctive forms of provocation—unpredictability, critique, subversion, counterfactuals, and humor, in a variety of ways: watching comedians and satirists, studying the counterculture and protests, and being caught unawares on numerous occasions throughout our lives. Adapting Ross Ashby's notion of the Law of Requisite Variety, which he outlined in his 1956 book, *An Introduction to Cybernetics*, we believe that the most flexible person or group in a system are those with the widest range of possible choices and responses. They are more able to respond to the complex situations they face. Like the victorious chess player who wins through having more moves available to them, if you have a wide and deep toolbox, you can respond more effectively and frequently to whatever you face.

In this chapter, we examine these unique and less predictable forms of provocation.

More conventional and comforting, or inspiring, interventions are helpful when your audience or organization is ready and committed to the work of change.

DOI: 10.4324/9781003321200-11

The status quo has its own predictable, self-perpetuating mechanisms, creating tradition, compliance, and loyalties that are hard to resist and overcome. However, less familiar, and unforeseen strategies are helpful when you are trying to prepare the ground or ripen an issue. Indeed, the power of provocative moves lies in the element of surprise, activating the benefits of discomfort and creativity. In addition, our five unique forms of provocation exemplify the power of dissent, confusion, and unpredictability. If you want to change, you will need mechanisms that build people's capacity for resistance and non-compliance. These left field approaches are an alternative but captivating way to help people see the nature of the problem they face and their part in its creation.

7.2 Unpredictability as a virtue

A surprise is part of the power of provocation. The ability to catch people unaware, prod a belief system, or simply state something many think but have not vocalized is central to a provocative mindset. Unpredictability takes many forms, including the nature, timing, or situation of your comment or question. For instance, Michael was surprised by his son's comment, which came out of the blue, and created a provocative moment.

There are many ways to be unpredictable. For example, you can use a variety of roles and, like a chameleon, change them moment by moment. Guy's shift from son to truth-teller, for example, had an impact on his father. The use of multiple roles is a means to confound expectations, question patterns of communication, and highlight unhelpful behavior. You can play many different roles, some formal (facilitator, convenor, and chairperson) and others informal (concerned citizen, devil's advocate, and gardener).

Bringing unexpressed sentiments, and invisible feelings into a conversation, as if they were a role or person, helps voice what is often left unsaid. It can unlock an exchange, making it possible for people to talk freely. In our work, we often use methods from psychodrama to show different roles and feelings in real time. During change, many are subject to fears about what will be lost, but such matters are often hard to discuss without the adoption of different roles to tease out the issues.

Consider the difference between talking about how a team leader inadvertently silences and marginalizes one of his colleagues, and how the team colludes with this, and helping them feel it in real-time. You could use a dramatic role to illustrate what it feels like to be silenced and ignored. Step to the side and talk as if it were you that had been ignored and play this role: "When you cut me off in the conversation, I thought you didn't want to hear my opinion, and I felt sidelined." Such mini dramas involving different roles create powerful moments and provoke more in-depth reflection.

When Muhammad Ali used his unusual rope-a-dope strategy[1] in the ring, he confounded his opponents, disturbed their rhythm, and gave himself an opportunity to win.

In a world where predictability is considered a virtue, unexpected behavior and actions help secure people's attention and break established patterns. Certainty lowers the need to be vigilant, but predictability also means others know what is coming. Ali would not have won so many fights if he had relied on the same routines of attack and defense. His secret weapon—other than his wit—was the variety of unusual and unexpected ways he approached each fight.

7.2.1 Unpredictability as a resource for change

Joel, a senior executive, came to us for coaching, describing himself as quiet, reliable, and risk-averse. His manager saw him as capable but not of great things. While Joel knew that others valued him for his reliability and consistency, he knew that his career was plateauing. He felt stuck, and believed that he and his work were dull. On the back of our conversations, Joel decided to introduce some variation into his ways of operating to challenge his relationship with predictability.

Joel began experimenting. He believed that his team would achieve better outcomes by building a more risk-tolerant environment. To this end, he introduced some randomness into the format of his executive team meetings. For example, every second meeting, he adopted a different format, changing the rules of engagement, spontaneously asking one of his team to take on a different role.

In this way, Joel created some confusion and uncertainty among his team, moving away from the familiar, well-established routine. On one occasion, Joel informed his team that there would be no meeting that week, thereby breaking a longstanding pattern. However, he then instructed his colleagues to come and see him if they had any significant issues to discuss, but only after they canvassed critical stakeholders' views. This was atypical as people were used to going directly to Joel whenever they wanted.

Two months later, Joel gathered his team members and reviewed their reactions, which both surprised and delighted him. This, too, was unforeseen as there was rarely an occasion for delight given the way that Joel usually kept things very rational and ordered. Among the reactions his team reported were the following:

- We needed to work things through ourselves without structure or guidance, and, as a result, we were more engaged with each other;
- We found ourselves disagreeing with each other, which meant we also had to work through these differences to find a common position; and
- We spoke with a broader range of people, as we weren't sure how to proceed, with the result that we arrived at a better solution.

Subsequently, Joel implemented a wide range of changes to his team's operating practices. Although some of his experiments failed, overall, his increased nimbleness resulted in significant changes in how he thought about himself, his role, and his understanding of what it means to change. In addition, the experiments positively impacted the attitude, behavior, and capability of his team. Joel began to see himself as a capable innovator, and continued to delight in surprising his team with other experiments. Today, while he still sees the risk in unpredictability, his team now expects the occasional left-field initiative from him.

Why would someone like Joel find the virtues of unpredictability so thrilling yet challenging?

First, when you become aware of your predictable routines and ways of thinking, you expose the coding and rules that drive your daily actions and the assumptions you make about yourself. Then, you can examine just how useful they are.

By staying in a relationship with both predictability and unpredictability, Joel discovered that he could question his own need for security, certainty, and being seen as safe. He learned that safety comes in many forms, including tolerating more of organizational life's reality, which is uncertain and at times random. He also learned how to allocate his energy better. It takes a lot of willpower to keep things consistent and buttoned-down, but the oscillations created through even small random acts also can generate energy.

Second, when you are predictable, it is easy for other people to have your measure, and plan their reactions to you in various situations. The mutually reinforcing nature of predictability creates overfamiliarity, and is the enemy of creativity and novelty. Conversely, the atypical allows you to access new and emergent knowledge. In the case of Joel and his team, their usual behaviors ensured that they operated within what they currently knew, and helped explain some of their inability to respond effectively to new demands. That changed when he opted to embrace other ways.

Third, unpredictability allows you to test norms and the status quo. The status quo is just a fancy name for all those personal or organizational routines you use because they orient you toward what you know how to do and what is expected. However, the unusual introduces variation, gives you scope to highlight critical issues, and confound expectations. Introducing a point about which you have had reservations, or haven't raised before, takes people by surprise, even temporarily, and creates a low level of disturbance as they reorient to you. This has the effect of drawing focused consideration to the issue.

Regardless of the context, unpredictably helps you grow and learn because the process requires you to live and work at the edge of your capability and self-image. Joel certainly never saw himself as a risk-taker or natural experimenter, valuing his reputation as a steady hand instead. But he has learned to become a risk-taker by introducing more variety into his work repertoire.

A surprise is the archenemy of predictability and control, so stretching yourself helps ensure that you challenge yourself regularly. How can you ensure that old habits and assumptions aren't tested if you don't surprise them and yourself some of the time?

7.3 Critique as provocation

Rex and Morgan, two senior executives in a bank, were committed to their organization's new leadership behaviors. However, they still regularly intervened to direct their subordinate Martin's efforts despite agreeing to delegate, and trust others more. When they discussed this dilemma with their coach, James, he suggested that their behavior would distort accountability in the business. James explained that if they rejected Martin's ideas, not only would he (Martin) be disheartened, but also they, as managers, would have assumed accountability, removing any sense of responsibility, independence, or trust in the judgment of those staff who reported to them. James's feedback went to the heart of the bank's cultural challenge—they wanted responsibility and accountability to be spread more widely in the business. Still, the two executives continued to act as if they were responsible for everything. First, James provoked by critiquing their commitment to their stated goals by describing the contradiction between his clients' actions and intentions. Then, he held them to account in more direct and challenging ways. The provocation started a deep conversation, whose implications continue to this day.

Feedback, such as that Rex and Morgan received, is unsettling for people because our wiring makes us all process stimulus deeply. Everyday critique is provocative, and often is helpful if we can listen to it. James helped his clients do so.

Rahel Jaeggi, a German philosopher, helps us think about critique as provocation in a 2018 paper by identifying three types of scrutiny, each challenging a different aspect of a human system.

First, internal critique occurs when you describe the discrepancy between norms and reality. You might hear this provocation, for example, when a teenage son says to his father, "I don't recognize this family anymore. What you are doing is not what you say we should do. You're a hypocrite." Or, when a subordinate says to their manager, "That is not what you promised and committed to." The focus is on the disjuncture between a stated intention, and what is happening now. It highlights an adaptive gap.

Second, day-to-day criticism is an example of external critique, and happens when you use your judgment, as an outside observer, to suggest something is wrong and needs fixing. But such criticism is risky because it separates you, the observer, from others. Guy, for example, took this risk with Michael, and because he had skin in the game, it was a worthwhile risk to take. But often, others won't thank you for interfering.

With the third and perhaps most disorienting form, immanent critique, you would observe and challenge the inner contradictions found in the standards and rules of the system you think need changing. You are not trying to modify or refine a norm or value but to change them totally. The provocation helps identify how the norm, and the behavior that follows, contribute to the ongoing problem or crisis faced. When James gave Rex and Morgan feedback, he invited them to change the rules that guided their behavior.

A critical distinction between these three forms of provocation is that, unlike external and internal forms, an immanent critique does not suggest what is right or wrong; instead, you point to a piece of coding that needs rewriting. As Jaeggi emphasizes, adaptation and change are not predicated on "a premade ideal of how the order of things ought to be." As such, this form of critique is more provocative and unsettling.

Medieval history professor and devout Christian, Dr. Beth Allison Barr, uses historical analysis and personal experience to challenge the historical ideals of her Church which encourage women's submission to men. In her new book *The Making of Biblical Womanhood*, she questions "complementarianism," saying the narrative "that men carry the authority of God is frightening, and it's not Christian!" Barr sees herself in a long line of Christian activists who are trying to change a fundamental premise of their belief and who use all the means at their disposal to critique the inner contradictions of their church. Barr sheds light on the #ChurchToo movement, abuse scandals in Southern Baptist circles, and the broader evangelical movement.

Barr surprised her community with her powerful critique, pointing to the contradiction between her church's teaching and historical evidence. In so doing, she encouraged a more overt discussion of the current attitudes to women. Her provocative book and the church's reaction to it have created an alertness, energy, and urgency, a catalyst for creativity. Provocation affords us the opportunity to redefine reality, establish new learning conditions, and identify an alternative, counterfactual means of moving forward.

These distinctions about critique are essential because they recognize that purposeful provocation can only start the process of inquiry and exploration. We all need to understand how our system functions, and see where predictable actions and inner contradictions are revealed. Beth Allison Barr knows that her book is a way to start a conversation, but she is playing a long game.

Following is a further example that illustrates the difference between criticism, and immanent critique.

If you are a farmer and believe that climate change does not affect ongoing severe drought in your country, then you are likely to address the symptoms of the problem by taking short-term action. You will, for example, buy extra animal feed, conserve water for essential purposes, and await better conditions to purchase new livestock. However, these responses do not question any of the established practices or institutions involved in reinforcing the existence of climate change, and whether it affects your ongoing behavior. Nor do they question your assumptions about drought. Doing the same thing over and over will have no impact on the underlying issue. But immanent critique would pose provocative questions that target your beliefs about climate change, and might prompt you to consider how to transform and redesign key components of agriculture and those institutions that support it. For example, as we discuss in Chapter 8, you might think about how repeated fertilizer use contributes to the degradation of soil quality on your farm.

Immanent critique starts from the internal contradictions of a group or institution. It aims to activate the adaptive potential of the system in question by raising awareness about its self-reinforcing patterns and behaviors. Therefore, social change is the product of provocative critique leading to a confrontation of a group with its problem.

7.4 Subversion and truth-telling

The Guerilla Girls are a feminist collective that created a billboard in 1989 portraying a naked woman wearing a guerilla mask. The text reads, "Do girls have to be naked to get into the Met Museum? Less than 5% of artists in the Modern Art sections are women, but 85% of the nudes are female." The facts speak for themselves, challenging us to deny that women are still subject to social and political oppression, by appropriating the visual language of advertising. Their billboards use facts to subvert what they see as oppressive practices.

Political activists use rhetoric, writing, art, satire, or mass protest to provoke by subverting dominant narratives, and in the tradition of philosophers such as Simone de Beauvoir and Michel Foucault, they show how the values and institutions of the powerful restrain change.

Subversive tactics are part of the long tradition that Michel Foucault called *Parrhesia*, based on the Greek practice of truth-telling. In his 1984 lectures, Foucault describes *Parrhesia* as a radical method of provocation because "it involves some form of courage, the minimal form of which consists in the 'parrhesiast' taking the risk of breaking and ending the relationship to other people which was precisely that which made his discourse possible." The truth-telling of provocateurs like The Guerrilla Girls and Hannah Gadsby is risky to both teller and listener because courage is required to hold steady and consider the provocation even though it may threaten some part of who we think we are.

The 2021 Australian of the Year, Grace Tame, provoked the public by telling the truth about sexual abuse. She opened the lid on government inaction when she informed the National Press Club in Canberra, "It shouldn't take having children to have a conscience." Her comments alluded to the Australian Prime Minister Scott Morrison's lukewarm response to allegations that a young woman had been raped in Parliament House, offering his role as a father to indicate he understood the gravity of the situation. "On top of that," Tame added, "having children doesn't guarantee a conscience."

Provocateurs like Tame remind us of critical facts and continue to constructively subvert beliefs that restrain progress and are seen as oppressive. Activists usually speak for others, attempting to represent ideas that are unpalatable and uncomfortable to the mainstream. They point to what a future could and should look like. We have seen protest movements gather global momentum in recent years, from Black Lives Matter, #MeToo, and the #FeesMustFail protests in South Africa.

History shows us that carefully orchestrated protest over time has effectively contributed to changing both law and culture. By their nature, the frequency and persistence of protests erode elements of the established order and increase public awareness of the need for change. Those who provoke through protest are in effect saying to the powerful that they insist on having an equal voice in determining how society is structured and who it benefits. The provocation of a protest is based on the idea that resolution requires a reordering of society, and a change in how certain, often marginal, groups are seen.

Effective protest always uses the critical skills of provocation. There is always a need to assess the readiness of the broader population to consider the issues at hand and to regulate the disequilibrium, pulling back when there is a risk of explosion and delegitimization of the protesters. When that happens, there also needs to be a willingness to find other ways to put pressure on the system.

In Part Four, we will consider the work of several of the people who fomented protest-like movements at a local micro-level. They saw a clear need, mobilized their communities or organizations, and provoked persistently over several years.

7.5 Counterfactuals and provocation

Every day during the Covid-19 pandemic, someone, somewhere, might be heard to say, "If only I hadn't entered that store, I wouldn't have caught the virus." They are using a counterfactual—a form of thinking that focuses on how the past might have been, or the present could be, different.

But counterfactuals are also another means to provoke, addressing entrenched habits and beliefs because they provide alternative constructions of the past or future. Counterfactuals test dominant narratives that define shared experience and help overcome the tendency to see the future as an extension of the past. And they create possibilities for future action. When you ask, "What would happen if …", you initiate a different way of seeing something.

Philip Tetlock and Aaron Belkin demonstrate in their 1997 book *Counterfactual Thought Experiments in World Politics*, how counterfactuals force you to grapple with the consequences of your choices and to become more open to your own biases or alternative paths. The provocation of contrarian views forces you to ask more "what if" and "how come" questions about current reality. It generates deeper curiosity and avoids doing more of the same.

Counterfactuals, subversion, and truth-telling are all critical components of effective human adaptation. They spark debate, force dominant voices to pause, and encourage other views to emerge. A variety of provocative methods helps create new data on which to formulate problem definitions and resolutions. They all stimulate ongoing inquiry and even controversy.

Satirists such as Stephen Colbert, Samantha Bee, Tim Minchin, and The Yes Men Collective use counterfactuals to highlight the double standards in society, and help us consider social and ethical problems. For example, in response to the criticism he received for using the N-word during a performance, Tim, a white performer, and composer, wrote the counterfactual song *Prejudice*, testing his own invisible racism and his audience's. He begins by setting the scene.

> *This is a song about prejudice, and the language of prejudice, and the power of the language of prejudice. It's called "Prejudice."*

He continues by teasing the audience, inviting us to think he will say the unsayable and cross forbidden boundaries, causing offense. Thus, he moves into the ambiguous territory between intended and unintended provocation.

> *A couple of Gs, an R and an E, an I and an N*
> *Just six little letters all jumbled together*
> *Have caused damage that we may never mend*

And it's important that we all respect
That if these people should happen to choose
To reclaim the word as their own
It doesn't mean the rest of you have a right to its use.

Tim then arrives at the chorus, tantalizing the unsuspecting audience.

Only a ginger can call another ginger, Ginger
So listen to me if you care for your health
You won't call me Ginger 'less you're ginger yourself yeah.

Prejudice (or *The Ginger Song*) is a masterful example of the use of a counterfactual. He asks us to think about race by considering our attitudes toward redheads. While he intends to explore racist language and who can use certain words, his subject matter is redheaded people. The satire is multilayered, however, as *ginger* is an anagram of the N-word. By taking us into the humor of *gingers*, Tim bypasses normal self-censorship and invites his audience to think about what can't usually be discussed, especially among white and privileged groups.

Imagine a politician trying to have the same conversation. It would be hard and likely would fall flat. Tim, though, as a humorist, songwriter, and counterfactualist, can use this form of provocation. In so doing, he helps us see how provocation can come from unexpected and indirect places.

7.5.1 Blindsiding people: Provocative interpretations

Once while working with senior university administrators, we noticed one prominent man who spoke frequently and often across his colleagues. We asked him, "Do you realize the opportunity costs you are inflicting on your colleagues when you hold the floor so much?" He was offended by the unusual comment, but subsequently said he hadn't realized how he was "hogging the airwaves." He also told us that the unexpected timing of the comment was as powerful as the comment itself.

A part of the risk and beauty of provocation is the unpredictability of your actions, and others' reactions. People can respond atypically because a deeply held belief or value has been tested, and it may feel like a violation, something threatening. A piece of hard wiring, a moral code, will be breached if the receiver believes that something should remain as it is.

Like the invisible rules of a team or organization, our personal coding represents the correct arrangement of the world even if they don't help us anymore. When the loud university administrator was confronted, his coding was more visible to him. Similarly, bank executives Rex and Morgan were forced to see how their actions made their subordinates less accountable; their good intentions stood in stark contrast to the impact of their actions. They could no longer deny how implicated they were in the business' lack of initiative and independent decision-making.

In this sense, provocation can be seen as necessary subversion, prompting a shift in behavior, and thinking. Provocation wrapped in good humor, care, and even love, will be easier to accept, however challenging it may be.

Well-targeted provocation will usually elicit a response to the challenge inherent in it. Nevertheless, there is always some uncertainty about where it will land, and what nerve it will touch. A sharp interpretation is, in fact, one of the most effective forms of provocative action, as it can take a group by surprise, bypassing habitual ways of thinking and responding. Predictability and consistency are comforting to people, and comfort is something that most of us crave. When interventions are unpredictable in range and tone, it makes it easier to hold people's attention while they experience discomfort.

7.6 Humor as provocation[2]

Humor is defined by the psychologists Eliyahu Rosenheim and Gabriel Golan in a 1986 article "as an approach to oneself and to others that is characterized by a flexible view enabling one to discover, express, or appreciate the ludicrous or absurdly incongruous." This could equally be a definition of provocation—acts that enable people to discover how their problematic, absurd behavior constrains progress.

In the middle of her show *Nannette*, for example, Hannah Gadsby speaks about her identity. She says:

> *I don't identify as transgender. But I'm clearly not normal. I don't even think lesbian is the right identity for me. I really don't. I might as well come out now. I identify as tired. I'm just tired.*

In just thirty seconds, with this joke, Gadsby inverts comedy tropes, takes a risk with her disclosure, and has the audience laughing and thinking at the same time. She puts the audience at ease, and socks them between the eyes. Like the jester, Gadsby provocatively subverts what is familiar and, in so doing, uncovers the unspeakable and the hidden.

We use provocative humor to build an environment of trust, and owing to its inherent ambiguity, it enables us to achieve several goals simultaneously: building bonds, fostering risk taking, and experimentation. As a result, people are more open to being challenged. If humor leads to a breakthrough or cracks open an impasse then it can be considered a provocation because it enables us to shift from the status quo, however temporarily. Humor can also provide a very different perspective on a situation and focus attention. For example, James, a senior engineer told his colleagues during a recent meeting that they often "come close to having a frank but more difficult conversation, but almost always step back when the atmosphere feels too hard." He continued by describing the team "as a group of chimpanzees teasing a tiger, but never getting too close." James seized a moment to comment on a pattern that held his team back, and did so in a provocative but light-hearted manner.

7.7 Lessons from comedy: Hannah Gadsby

Hannah Gadsby burst onto the international stage, confounding expectations, with her breakthrough show *Nanette*. She enticed her audiences into thinking it was a standard stand-up comedy routine, something she was well-rehearsed in, and then subverted all these hopes by deconstructing comedy, and launching a blistering attack on misogyny, hate, and violence against women.

Comedy, she suggests, relies on creating tension and providing release with a humorous punchline. "When I tell jokes, we laugh, and it is good medicine," she observed. "I relieve others of the tension." With *Nanette*, though, she began to tell raw stories of her pain and shame growing up as a gay woman in Tasmania, detailing the illness and trauma she suffered. "Telling my own truth," she explained, "I am putting anger into the room and not relieving you of it." Now, she keeps telling jokes and keeps the audience on the hook.

"This tension is yours," she tells a stunned Sydney Opera House audience. "I am not helping you with it anymore. You need to learn what this feels like." Gadsby describes how she would no longer pay the price for the lessons Australians and others had not learned.

> *I have built a career out of self-deprecating humor, and I don't want to do that anymore. Because do you understand what self-deprecation means when it comes from somebody who already exists in the margins? It's not humility. It's humiliation.*

In breaking away from standard comedy practice, Gadsby attempted to reshape the medium. She pushed herself and her audiences to the edge. In so doing, she used her own stories to challenge and rechallenge prevailing attitudes. She continued a long tradition of comedians from minority and marginalized groups such as Lenny Bruce, Richard Pryor, and, more recently, Margaret Cho, who have used provocation to disturb while holding audiences in the arms of laughter.

Gadsby, though, has gone one step further in her provocation. She uses familiar comedic tools such as repetition, irony, amplification, and hyperbole to create an in-between space where the audience is captured in the moment while also being pushed into thinking about the need for change in the future. She is a truth-teller, who is forcing the audience to confront its own biases and shortcomings. She achieves this by making use of painful, personal truth. But Gadsby also does not treat her audience as fragile or in need of protection. As she puts it, she does not wish "to escape from the storm but to face the eye of the storm," designing her performative narrative to accomplish this.

Gadsby builds the audience's capacity to sit with the pain and disturbance, encouraging its members to think and feel simultaneously. Then she will tell another joke, reducing the disequilibrium, providing some breathing space and time for reflection, before returning to the work at hand. Gadsby forces us to consider how "the toxic culture that enables abuse and misogyny needs to change," ensuring that people cannot turn their gaze away from the issue for the duration of the show.

Ultimately, Gadsby's gift is to encourage us to rethink the stories we tell ourselves. She wants us to question who we truly are. She also demonstrates five techniques that are at the heart of your work as a provocative facilitator, change agent or leader:

- Disequilibrium;
- Paradox and contradiction;
- Exaggeration, irony, amplification, and absurdity;
- Building and breaking tension; and
- Truth-telling, reframing.

7.7.1 Reflections on humor as provocation

Humor is a valuable addition to the repertoire of leadership tools because of its inherently ambiguous quality. It performs several functions at once and, therefore, requires a group to operate on more than one level. Humor creates a holding environment where the bonds, connections, and shared values are strengthened between people so that critical issues can be explored.

In this way, humor, which goes beyond the creation of light relief, offers you greater flexibility to support provocation, which tests and challenges the status quo—the heart of leadership work. Humor also reminds us not to take who we are too seriously. It mitigates the excesses of power that you hold as a change agent. Humor reminds us to use our power lightly. As journalist Eric Sevareid observed in his 1964 essays, "Next to power without honor, the most dangerous thing is power without humor."

Humor, in whatever form, reminds us all to surround ourselves with people who can, and will, playfully cross the boundaries—testing conventions, challenging assumptions, and ensuring we can make smart decisions with compassion, given the impact we can have when exercising leadership.

Whether gentle or shocking, any provocation is unexpected because most people don't ask to be challenged or unsettled. The experience can be unique because of the form of provocation, the feelings generated, and because learning happens. What is special about the forms of provocation considered in this chapter is that they are not part of the conventional leadership toolkit, adding to their surprise value when deployed in an organizational setting.

Notes

1 A boxing tactic of pretending to be trapped against the ropes, goading an opponent to throw tiring ineffective punches.

2 All quotes from Hannah Gadsby are taken from a variety of interviews, presentations, and performances, including an appearance with Leigh Sales on the ABC *7.30 Report*

(17 September 2017), her speech to the Hollywood Reporter's *Women in Entertainment* (6 December 2018) reported by Linda Xu, her TED talk (10 September 2019), and the Netflix recording of her live show *Nanette*.

References

ABC (2017). Comic Hannah Gadsby. *Forcing the Audience to Look Beyond Laughter*. Interview with Hannah Gadsby. Leigh Sales, 7.30 Report, ABC Television, 14 September 2017. https://www.abc.net.au/7.30/comic-hannah-gadsby,-forcing-the-audience-to-look/8947186. Retrieved 23 August 2020.

Barr, B.A. (2021). *The Making of Biblical Womanhood: How the Subjugation of Women Became Biblical Truth*. Brazos Press, Ada, MI.

Foucault, M. (1983). *Discourse and Truth: The Problematization of Parrhesia*. Six lectures. https://foucault.info/parrhesia/. Retrieved 30 June 2020.

Gadsby, H. (2018). *Nanette*. Netflix Special. Recorded at Sydney Opera House. https://www.netflix.com/watch/80233611?trackId=14277281&tctx=-97%2C-97%2C%2C%2C%2C. Retrieved 1 June 2021.

Gadsby, H. (2019). *Three Ideas. Three Contradictions. Or Not*. Ted Talk. https://www.ted.com/speakers/hannah_gadsby. Retrieved 30 August 2020.

Jaeggi, R. (2015). Towards an immanent critique of forms of life. *Raisons Politiques*, *57*(1), pp. 13–29. 10.3917/rai.057.0013. Retrieved 10 June 2021.

Minchin, T. (2010). *Prejudice*. (The Ginger Song). Ready for this Live Tour. https://www.youtube.com/watch?v=KVN_0qvuhhw. Retrieved 1 January 2022.

Rosenheim, E., & Golan, G. (1986). Patients' reactions to humorous interventions in psychotherapy. *American Journal*. PMID: 3963269. https://psychotherapy.psychiatryonline.org/doi/abs/10.1176/appi.psychotherapy.1986.40.1.110. Retrieved 12 November 2020.

Sevareid, E. (1964). *Eric Sevareid Essays*. McGraw Hill, New York.

Tame, G. (2021). Grace Tame's Press Club Speech in Full, National Press Club, Canberra, 3 March 2021. https://www.news.com.au/national/politics/grace-tames-australian-press-club-speech-in-full/news-story/2f641d003254955a25d754a6a59b1926. Retrieved 30 September 2021.

Tetlock, P.E. & Belkin, A. (1997). *Counterfactual thought experiments in world politics*. Chapter 1 In Tetlock, P.E., & Belkin, A. (eds) *Counterfactual Thought Experiments in World Politics*. Princeton University Press, Princeton, New Jersey, pp. 3–38.

Valentish, J. (2018). *'I Broke the Contract': How Hannah Gadsby's Trauma Transformed Comedy*. Interview, The Guardian, 16 July 2018. https://www.theguardian.com/stage/2018/jul/16/hannah-gadsby-trauma-comedy-nanette-standup-netflix. Retrieved 5 November 2020.

Xu, L. (2018). *Hannah Gadsby Blasts "Good Men" at Hollywood Reporter Women in Entertainment Event*. Speech to Hollywood Reporters Women in Entertainment Event, 6 December 2018. https://www.hollywoodreporter.com/news/general-news/hannah-gadsby-blasts-good-men-at-hollywood-reporter-women-entertainment-event-1166569/. Retrieved 30 August 2020.

PART 4

APPLICATION—PRACTICING PROVOCATION

The eight chapters that follow each show how provocation was used in one situation where people faced their fears and overcame the constraints of the status quo by embracing an opportunity. Each chapter is based on conversations we have had with a client, a community activist, a friend, and someone we discovered through our research.

Each of the protagonists has identified a need, a fundamental challenge, in their community or organization and has set about addressing it. They have done so without calling themselves provocateurs or leaders. But they all have provoked people in some ways though in each case the circumstances required something different.

We have selected these case studies because they each highlight one or two of the provocative schemas described in Chapter 1, and show the advantages and risks of the approach chosen.

Many of our examples are Australian because this is home ground for us, and also because Australia has become one of the most connected and interdependent societies in the world. In some ways, this small, distant country is both a microcosm and reflection of the global world, and is used as a petri dish in which to try things out. Australia has been in the forefront of social change, economic liberalization, and scientific discovery, yet it is also greatly affected by trends and pressures occurring elsewhere. For this reason, the case studies used in the book reflect much of what is occurring elsewhere—be it environmental change, water security, offshoring of manufacturing, changes in family life and social norms, transforming a business in response to changing customer needs, or the challenges of integrating immigrants and refugees. Our case studies provide insights into what is happening or could happen elsewhere. The issues and implications that flow from the next chapters are generalizable across continents and settings.

There are four categories of examples. First, the specific local experience, on a farm, in a school, or a small community where provocation was required to shift attitudes and behavior.

Second, there are two examples of significant change within a single organization, a bank or government agency, where a choice made to reinvent itself.

DOI: 10.4324/9781003321200-12

Third, an example of national change across a whole system where only the government can take the first steps, using policy to provoke, even insist, on necessary adjustments in water policy.

Finally, we describe the experience of several unique individuals who took calculated risks for something they believed in even though their jobs and status were at stake and where life transitions generate provocative moments from which we can learn, grow, and adapt.

8 PARADIGM CHANGE—BREAKING WITH TRADITION IN AGRICULTURE

We have to change our mindscape in order to change the landscape.
Comment in interview with Charles Massy

In 1976, twenty-two-year-old Charlie Massy, a recent science graduate, returned home to run the family farm, Severn Park, near Cooma, New South Wales in Australia. Although Charlie had grown up on the land, he knew very little about farm management. He loved the property with its sweeping fields and the wildlife but also came to see that he was maltreating it through the overuse of chemicals and fertilizer. But he knew nothing else. By 1982, following a devasting drought, Charlie was exhausted, depressed, and deeply in debt. Standing on a hill near his homestead, watching the fields denude their soil, Charlie felt viscerally that he had to change his farming practice because it simply did not work. He needed transformative change.

Paradigm change in agriculture is ambitious because it targets a way of life and a deeply entrenched institutional and economic power system. This chapter describes how Charlie and another farmer, Colin Seis, began to challenge a century of farming practice, shifting the paradigm. To paraphrase Thomas Kuhn's theory of paradigm shifts, over time, they offered compelling arguments, a willingness to try anything, the expression of explicit discontent, and a willingness to challenge the fundamentals. Charlie and Colin experienced how provocation was pivotal in bringing difficult issues to the attention of farmers and a very conservative sector like agriculture. They spoke out, asked hard questions, experimented, and were persistent—critical features of provocative action. In the following pages, we will examine the key principles Charlie and Colin followed, the tactics they used, and how they navigated a highly emotional and political landscape. First, Charlie and Colin transformed themselves, then their farms, and then they directed their efforts to influence others. Each phase involved a sequence of increasingly provocative experiences and actions.

8.1 Start with the problem

Charlie Massy's vision and drive arise from decades of work on his farm, but the turning point was the drought that devastated his farm. This was the shock that opened his mind, catalyzing a lifelong learning journey, the transformation of his worldview, and a willingness to experiment with new ways.

DOI: 10.4324/9781003321200-13

Colin Seis's story has a lot of similarities with Charlie's. His family has been farming their Winona property on the Central Tablelands of New South Wales since the 1860s, building the enterprise by following established methods, including plowing, and steadily increasing the use of fertilizers and herbicides. By the 1980s, Colin had identified signs of an unhealthy and suffering system, including "loss of land to salinity, declining soil structure and quality, soil carbon loss, a variety of diseases, plus the high cost of fertilizers and other inputs." The farm began to fail while costs rose.

The tipping point arrived with a devastating bushfire in 1979. Colin lost most of his flock of sheep, and all his buildings, and suffered severe burns. He had hit rock-bottom, and there was no money left to help with the recovery. Comparing his experience with the impact of the Australian bushfires of 2019–2020, he remembers, "It was basically like an atomic bomb going off on this place and destroying everything."

In both cases, the problem had developed over time but became more immediate because of a crisis. The severe droughts and fires were the external push that woke Charlie and Colin up. Something fundamental had to shift. The crisis provoked them to reimagine who and what they were, and led to two modest, mild-mannered men becoming paradigm breakers who challenged other farmers as well as the agricultural establishment. They began using Regenerative methods, which seek to rehabilitate and enhance the whole ecosystem of their farms by placing a premium on soil health, maintaining year-round ground cover, and reducing chemical inputs.

8.2 Provoke yourself

After the drought, Charlie realized that he did not understand how his farm's ecosystem worked, how the biophysical functions of soil, water, climate, and animals interacted and affected one other, let alone what he and other humans did to affect them. But he did see that if "one part was messed up, then all parts were." During the drought, he had fed his stock with purchased grain, increasing his debt, while the landscape became catastrophically damaged because of his actions.

To address the fundamental challenge he faced, he had to make a radical shift in mindset, values, and practice, starting with "the one square foot of real estate between my ears." Charlie had to become active in the farm's regeneration rather than complicit in its difficulties, even if that meant breaking with tradition. This realization was the first major self-provocation: he was part of the problem, if not the problem.

Charlie had to look, sense, and act differently. This entailed a significant transition, temporarily diminishing his competence. He didn't want to use the old industrial farming language he was familiar with, let alone its techniques, but couldn't yet express himself in the emerging vernacular.

On the other hand, Colin had a forced period of reflection and soul searching while he was in hospital recovering from the fire that destroyed his property. He wondered how his family could recover and survive after this devastation. Colin had to rethink his way out of the calamity, questioning himself and the farming methods he relied upon, appraising what was precious and essential, and what could be let go. He wanted to honor the legacy of his grandparents and father, not to criticize them. But, at the same time, he needed to interrogate and dismantle the old farming system that had endured for over a century. Radical change was necessary to enable a new form of farming to emerge.

Like most farmers of his generation, Colin hoped in vain that things would improve, applying what he subsequently termed the "moron principle," pretending that everything would be OK if he only persisted. As happened with Charlie, though, he came to realize that he was doing nothing more than treating symptoms rather than remedying issues, and making realchange.

At first, he had to rely on standard methods to rebuild the farm and simply survive. However, when local agronomists advised him to use more pesticides to counteract disease, not only could he not afford to buy the chemicals but also he saw that he must address this long established approach which was part of the problem. Fueled by his curiosity, Colin began to challenge conventional wisdom by asking questions, and then radical experimentation. He explained

> *I started to search for ideas. That's when it opened my mind up. I truly started to search, to dig for things. Then it was not necessarily about innovation, only about survival to start with. In the beginning, I was the only one doing this. I didn't even tell my father, though he was quite supportive. Then, I realized that the answers lay in natural systems—in Mother Nature. The answers are always there. What would happen in natural systems? So, I started to think about mimicking the natural ecosystem. That really fascinated me.*
>
> *I remember sitting on a tractor going round and round in ever-diminishing circles sowing a new oats crop because there was no feed on the farm, and realizing that I would be doing the same in six months. So, I started to ask myself, "Why do we have to sow a crop to feed the sheep? Why can't the land do it on its own? Why do we have to interfere all the time to be productive?"*

Charlie on the otherhand, now an academic and communicator, began the process of constructing what he stood for, and deconstructing what he could not abide. He spent many years developing himself and his ideas, culminating with a Ph.D. thesis and his 2017 book *The Call of the Reed Warbler*. Once he became clearer about himself, he began to provoke others.

8.3 Build the conditions for change

Provocation is designed to disturb and unsettle human systems for a positive purpose and help them progress on the fulcrum of change. Therefore, the decision to provoke is serious because others may not agree with your diagnosis, and may contest the need for change. Farmers worldwide who have been fighting for change in agricultural systems have learned this the hard way.

Often, the "real" issue is not what is initially faced but rather the people associated with it. To effectively transform problematic agricultural practices, such as grazing methods and soil management, the leadership challenge is to persuade people that there is an issue in the first place, and then to change their ways, accepting the turmoil that will ensue. Of course, it is much easier to mobilize people when there is an emergency, and something needs to happen quickly. But in farming, a crisis may emerge slowly, inexorably, only becoming evident when there is a loss of livelihood, property, pride, heritage, or esteem. Here, change is existential.

Charlie's and Colin's love of the land inform and fuel their ongoing provocative action. Neither likes to confront, judge, or offend. Equally, however, neither "can tolerate stupidity." They will take on established structures and institutional foolishness where they think it exists and when it damages the well-being of their farming colleagues and neighbors.

Early on, both established some fundamental conditions that made their provocative action safer and more likely to be effective. They began small and locally, experimenting in various ways on their own land before recruiting others. They used themselves as guinea pigs. However, while they acted alone, they tested their ideas with a range of people before trying them out. Charlie and Colin also educated themselves and worked on their own attitudes and behaviors. They worked on what Otto Scharmer and Katrin Kaufer refer to in *Leading from the Emerging Future* as "openings." That is an open mind, heart, and will. In this sense, they saw the necessity to live and feel a new paradigm before changing the old one.

In a 1999 paper, Donella Meadows outlined how specific actions can produce a valuable change in everything, creating pivotal moments. A leverage point is like an acupuncture node—a place where targeted pressure can start a beneficial ripple effect across the whole body. In Colin's case, he decided to stop fertilizing his property, and allow natural grasses to become a resource. Similar ecological concerns prompted Charlie to sell his Merino stud. Charlie realized that the flock and its grazing needs prevented him from caring for the land, thereby disturbing the local ecosystem. Paradoxically, his success in Merino breeding became an impediment and distraction to his commitment to a different form of agriculture and his ability to develop the necessary ecological literacy.

As they adapted, Charlie and Colin set themselves new rules and guiding values. If an action was not consistent with their new frameworks, they would not use it. Instead, they tried to work outside the established paradigm, standing apart from other farmers. In the first instance, this was only an indirect provocation because they were trialing new ways in private. Eventually, however, they took the new rules on the road, and became advocates of Regenerative Farming.

8.4 Think systemically

A core principle of provocative practice is to take a whole system view. Both Charlie and Colin came to the same conclusion primarily by watching what happened on their land and how it responded to different actions. Charlie and Colin relied on their curiosity, observation, and systems insight to find new ways to respond to their land. Charlie summarizes:

> *The driving systems of the landscape and its interrelated networks are invisible until evidence of their functioning or malfunctioning is physically expressed. Until one's understanding and perception change, and therefore one's mind changes, we can be blind to what is all around us.*

Crisis catalyzed greater attunement with landscape and ecosystem, enhancing their ecological literacy and fomenting changes in their practice and mindset. What was critical was the realization that the established agriculture rules no longer supported healthy farming, including a healthy ecosystem.

While he did not have formal academic training, Colin had a gut feeling about what he should pay closer attention to on his property. His greatest insight was that he and his father had been destroying perfectly good sheep feed in removing naturally occurring grasses while sowing crops. They now understood "that natural grasses were not weeds but valuable, not only as feed but also as soil stabilizers." Colin saw that allowing the ecological systems to regenerate would activate natural forms of self-organization.

8.5 Ask impossible questions

Colin developed his innovative cropping approach over a beer with his friend Darryl Cluff when they questioned the assumption that two different farming systems were incompatible. Until then, it was commonly accepted that you couldn't have pasture and crops simultaneously. They examined the possibility of two types of plants coexisting to the mutual benefit of ecosystem and production.

Colin had noticed how the native grasses became more established on his property once he started regeneration, which prompted him to question whether "nature didn't intend for annuals and perennials to coexist." As their conversation progressed, Colin and Darryl asked more provocative questions:

- What if you no-till drilled the perennial pasture during its dormant period with a cereal crop? What would happen?; and
- Why couldn't nature assist in this process?

They sought to get underneath their current practice and explore possibilities. Colin was thinking like an ecologist, using his experience since the terrible fire of 1979 to open himself to other ways of seeing familiar things.

What is central to this story is how Colin could observe and think more widely, more systemically, and begin to imagine new possibilities. Possibilities that many traditional local farmers would neither consider nor tolerate. Colin's pasture cropping idea pushed the envelope, and brought other cherished beliefs forward for testing.

Charlie equally started with curiosity and questions. But these led him initially in a different direction than Colin. He began talking to experts in all fields of agriculture, asking many naïve questions, leading him to Jim Watts, a maverick scientist. The latter had developed a new method of breeding sheep that were easier to sheer and produced better quality wool. Charlie began using Watts's methods, quickly achieving excellent results. His first experiment encouraged Charlie to question everything he knew and, at the same time to tackle wider issues within agriculture.

8.6 Take on the establishment

In 2011, Charlie published *Breaking the Sheep's Back*. He sees the book as his personal Royal Commission into the wool industry, highlighting that the scheme set up to protect farmers was bad for the wool industry in several ways. He describes how the reserve price for wool (RPS), the centerpiece of the wool industry's sales and export strategy, was an instrument for government interference in agriculture, overprotecting growers, and inhibiting innovation and change. The scheme led to decisions being made on political grounds rather than on a commercial or ecological basis.

While the system worked well for many years, by the late 1980s, overconfidence had led to unrealistic wool prices, impacting production, and prices dropped dramatically. Finally, in 1991, the RPS was suspended, with many farmers and wool-related businesses going bankrupt. What galled Charlie was that he had warned the Australian Wool Corporation and the government of the looming crisis, but neither had taken it seriously, ignoring him.

The RPS was a perfectly aligned system for the outcomes it generated, demonstrating how established processes and structures are tough to change without a crisis to bring the underlying problems to people's attention. But, as Charlie discovered, a sole voice is usually ineffective if there is a prophetic aspect to its criticism and suggestions, highlighting the seeds of an impending crisis.

Charlie could see that the wool scheme approached what systems thinkers refer to as "the edge of chaos." This is the point Mitchell Waldrop describes in his 1993 book *Complexity*—when a system in chaos ceases to function, it is starved of variety, of new ways of doing things, and becomes too rigid. The RPS provided no flexibility for its users. As such, it contained the seeds of its downfall, helped along by the apparent benefits that flowed to its members when it was working. Charlie argued for a more differentiated market, one with more variety in sales and marketing channels.

While challenging industry sales and marketing, he also challenged the hegemony of the Wool Board and RPS more directly. He spoke out and wrote widely, including a series of articles in the *Australian Farm Journal*, criticizing the economic and political interests that the RPS served and how individual farmers were disadvantaged. The powers that be responded rapidly and strongly and placed a legal injunction on Charlie's writing. Thirty thousand copies of the journal were destroyed.

Charlie faced the pushback that comes when you provoke an entrenched and powerful system. But he persisted despite receiving threats and late-night phone calls from senior bureaucrats. He says, "I realized I'd poked a stick at a nest that no one wanted to talk about."

Charlie did not hold back. Instead, his relentless questions and observations highlighted the impact an informed insider can have when using provocative and direct language, and the role such stimulation plays in breaking open groupthink and entrenched practice.

During this period, Charlie's actions demonstrated the risks of creating high levels of heat and the potential personal costs. Without his history in the industry and his marshaling of solid evidence, it is doubtful his challenge would have had the impact it did. Of course, his campaign was aided by the collapse of the RPS in 1991 and the ensuing financial devastation across the wool industry. No one needed persuading anymore.

With the benefit of hindsight, many saw that Charlie's analysis had been accurate. It became clear that industry leaders had actively resisted and rejected advice from experts. The support Charlie received years after his critique is a helpful reminder that intervening provocatively in a system does not always yield the desired outcomes immediately, if at all. The ripples Charlie caused were strengthened by the work of others, ensuring that change is possible, however slow it may be.

Orchestrating change in a system that is resolutely blind and deaf to news of difference makes for hard work. The odds are stacked against you and can lead to extreme behavior. Sometimes, having strong beliefs in the face of tyranny, stupidity, or simple rigidity will lead reasonable people to take fatal steps, both literally and figurately. Charlie's extreme language has alienated many people. Still, he has managed to navigate his way through the storm he orchestrated, despite the vicious and personal attacks his challenges elicited from those with a vested interest in the status quo. Despite legal opposition, he continued regardless, saying, "I was determined to keep telling the truth, and the best way to fight was to write what I knew. They were all guilty of groupthink, and the hubris was stupendous."

8.7 Increase the pressure

Following his experience with the Wool Corporation, Charlie turned his attention to farming in general, including the powerful agri-businesses. He understood if he wanted to change the system, he needed to identify and activate leverage points. Charlie challenged farmers to consider how they could and should change their farming practice to protect the delicate and increasingly damaged ecosystem, appealing to environmental issues. He pushed political leaders and the National Farmers Federation to see how existing policies reinforce maladaptive activity. He provoked consumers to think about their relationship with the land and what it produces. In so doing, Charlie introduced a new frame of reference about farming the land, encouraging greater ecological literacy and consideration of sustainable living among farmers, political authorities, and the public.

Such capacity involves the ability "to read a landscape, to appraise the state of its health and how it is functioning, and thus to know how to address any issues." Here, Charlie was fostering a new language with which to view the problems farmers face, and with a new language, new behaviors and habits of mind follow. He appealed to consumers who sought green products and those grown sustainably, knowing that consumer action would pressure agri-business. As a producer of some of the finest Merino wool in Australia, Charlie's was a credible voice. He used his growing visibility to increase the pressure on the government authorities.

Charlie began to market his Merino wool both for its improved quality and its humane methods of production. First, he spoke with Italian buyers who loved the quality of wool he produced. Then, with a group of colleagues, he negotiated a lucrative deal with the Japanese company Itochu, which was committed to sustainability, animal welfare, and the notion of Sampo-yoshi—"Good for the seller, Good for the buyer and Good for society." The provocative break from longstanding traditions changed how wool could be sold overseas, which endeared Charlie and his fellow practitioners to their clients, but less so to the industry bodies that were supposed to represent them.

Here, he provoked the industry indirectly by forging an independent path with his customers, demonstrating how his ethical and sustainable farming approach appealed to a broad consumer base. Rather than provoking farmers head-on, which he had a propensity to do, he disturbed the system from the outside—in and relied on other groups to maintain pressure.

8.8 Experiment and introduce variation

While Charlie still had a sheep stud, he, too, began to trial new methods. Early on, he pushed production capacity, lowered costs, and achieved high fertility rates while avoiding the inhumane practices seen on most farms. For example, he stopped mulesing, which involves removing pieces of wool-bearing skin from the buttocks of a sheep to prevent infection by flystrike. Charlie's innovation made shearing easier and offered higher quality wool. Yet, most farmers were slow to change and were annoyed when Charlie made a case to move away from traditional practice, reframing it as an animal welfare issue.

As an early adopter and advocate for issues that were not yet ripe in the farming or general community, Charlie spoke out and challenged his colleagues. He recognized that values and beliefs change very slowly but that without pressure, nothing would change. Subsequent events, including controversy regarding the live animal trade, caused concern in the wider community, especially among urban consumers. Charlie harnessed this.

Charlie's advocacy for new humane practices shook many people. For example, a sheep classer that Charlie had long relied on was opposed to the latest methods and took away his clients. Charlie's joint work with Jim Watts highlighted the importance of having well-informed allies when you want to debunk longstanding myths and practices. Taking a moral stand about an unethical practice like mulesing is one thing, but quite another to offer a scientifically proven alternative.

Provoking change by challenging the status quo is a dangerous business. Charlie and Jim were attacked in many forums, but they persisted and didn't dilute the message about their approach's economic, ecological, and humane advantages. In some ways, Charlie cut his teeth as an advocate during this period, and his ambition expanded. But trying to change an industry whose own history and mythology has become intertwined with a nation is no trivial matter. It involved constant disequilibrium as he sought to raise awareness of the damage done by long-established methods.

After initial struggles, Colin also began experimenting and taking risks. Even though he was in his early thirties and his father remained nominally in charge of the farm, Colin started a series of trials, most of which he said: "were not based on any evidence or research, just instinct." He did this out of necessity rather than because of any ideological leanings. "We did it to rehabilitate the farm as cheaply as possible, and removing plowing and herbicides helped." Colin also started experimenting with new grazing methods, which allowed natural grasses to grow, thereby encouraging variation. "I realized we needed no-input agriculture rather than high-input," he said. "I started to search for ideas. In the beginning, I was the only one doing this."

Colin confesses that he had many doubts after he stopped using weed control and fertilizers. It seemed counterintuitive, going against generations of traditional practice, but he stubbornly persisted. For several years, his farm was unproductive, and neighboring farmers considered him crazy to continue with the regenerative approach.

However, one of the very things that the new model attempts to overturn is the short-termism of the mechanical farming paradigm. Given that he was turning his back on the old ways, Colin found himself on his own. The usual sources of advice, such as the local agricultural supply warehouse or the government agronomist, either didn't know what to advise or were openly hostile toward him. His challenge cost him relationships, and access to resources.

But remarkable transformation occurred, fueled by Colin's natural curiosity, commitment to his great-grandmother's creed of nurture, and his predisposition to try things out. Ultimately, Colin was presented with an opportunity to express his adaptive capacities, and his perseverance paid off. Today, Winona's grasslands contain a wide variety of plant species with a dramatic reduction in weeds, pests, and insect problems because of its balanced ecosystem.

8.9 Take risks

Initially, the risks taken by Charlie and Colin were personal and reputational. Their livelihoods depended on their farms, and their experiments took them into unknown territory, with others questioning their sanity as they allowed weeds to grow on their land. However, as they began to talk about and advocate fundamental change, things shifted. As soon as they started to engage with and attempt to mobilize others, as you saw with Charlie's confrontation with the Wool Board, they encountered hesitancy, resistance, and a degree of social isolation.

The new paradigm of Regenerative (or Regen) Agriculture is still not universally accepted or welcomed. Traditionalists have dismissed Charlie and Colin as "judgmental" and "way too clever." Many in the farming community feel criticized and misunderstood, given their effort to turn their farming practices around. One conventional farmer, for example, questioned the inference of the term Regenerative Agriculture in a 2020 AgTech Podcast, arguing that if he is not regenerative, then it is assumed that he is a degenerative farmer.

It is feedback that Charlie takes on board even though it is at odds with what he believes.

> *I don't try to push people directly or say you should not do this or that. The people I talk to mainly choose to listen, so they are already searching for something different. I try to walk them through what I, and others, have learned and keep it practical.*
>
> *I rarely use dramatic language when I talk to people, only when writing. I don't want to miss the opportunity to challenge people's thinking and get them to reflect on their mindset and whether this works for them.*

Nevertheless, Charlie's language is striking. At times, it can be dramatic and emotional. In trying to get people's attention, he does take things to the edge. For example, he describes traditional agriculture as "a culture of death," which involves dumping pesticides into the ground, and the aggressive use of machinery, and caging of livestock for reasons they were not "evolved for." He uses powerful metaphors to describe current practices, criticizing humankind's tendency to exercise "control over a subservient and powerless land," highlighting how "we are killing everything." Charlie intends to dismantle prevailing paradigms and mental models governing agriculture and our relationship to the land.

While he doesn't talk directly about provocation, everything Charlie explains shows he understands that for a system to shift, whether related to a person or a farm, it needs to be disturbed. Disturbance leads to mindset changes as people reconfigure what they believe and begin to act and intervene differently. But the disruption needs to create ripples across time and activities so that there is still pressure for renewal and transformation. Charlie has kept himself within the productive zone of disturbance, learning enough to ensure that his new approach to farming remains viable and worthwhile. This process took years to develop and required both external pressure and constant personal leadership. Increasingly, though, Charlie has found his attention turning outward to other farmers and agricultural institutions.

8.10 Reflections from the land

The provocation experienced and generated by Charlie and Colin, as they changed their farming practices and resurrected their land, reminds us that when dealing with adaptive issues, at whatever scale or level of complexity, the problems are found at the intersection of natural and human systems.

It is the human adaptation that must occur first. Otherwise, we will continue with what we know without such change. The change stimulus can be external, such as the drought and fires in Australia, or self-generated. No one asked or required Charlie to challenge the Wool Board or Colin to ponder whether perennials and annual crops could coexist. In these cases, they initiated the provocation, acting to challenge the status quo, and effect change.

It is a hallmark of adaptive provocation that Charlie and Colin also evolved and thrived by allowing themselves to be challenged. They based their paradigm-provoking efforts on:

- Seeing and expressing things others can't or won't notice;
- Building the conditions for change;
- They persistently asked questions and challenged the rules of the prevailing paradigm;
- Trying things out to demonstrate how the new can work; and
- Being single-minded, purposeful, and persistent despite opposition.

Their stories also provide us with some warnings about the risks of provocation. Their actions and challenges sometimes went too far, turned the heat up beyond what others could bear, and alienated them. We will examine further the risks of being provocative in Chapter 16. In the following chapters, however, we will provide more examples of provocative practice.

References

AgTech … so what? (2020). *Regen Ag Series #4, 'Greenwashing' … or Good for Business?* AgTech Podcast, 9 September 2020. https://www.agtechsowhat.com/agtechsowhatepisodes/2020/9/9/regen-ag-is-it-greenwashing-or-good-business. Retrieved 10 January 2021.

Kuhn, T. (1962). *The Structure of Scientific Revolutions.* University of Chicago Press, Chicago.

Massy, C. (2011). *Breaking the Sheep's Back.* Queensland University Press, Brisbane.

Massy, C. (2017). *Call of the Reed Warbler: A New Agriculture, A New Earth.* Queensland University Press, St. Lucia, Qld.

Meadows, D.H. (1999). *Leverage Points: Places to Intervene.* The Sustainability Institute, Hartford, CT. First published in Whole Earth, Winter, 1997.

Scharmer, O., & Kaufer, K. (2013). *Leading from the Emerging Future.* Berrett Koehler, San Francisco.

Waldrop, M.M. (1993). *Complexity: The Emerging Science at the Edge of Order and Chaos.* Simon & Schuster, New York.

9 SURVIVAL—KIBBUTZ YIZRAEL AND THE EVOLUTION OF AN IDEOLOGY

It is not the most intellectual of the species that survives; it is not the strongest that survives, but the species that survives is the one that is able best to adapt and adjust to the changing environment in which it finds itself.

Attributed to Charles Darwin, The Origin of the Species[1]

9.1 Introduction

In 1988 after years of economic struggle Kibbutz Yizrael, a small collective settlement in northern Israel was declared by the Ministry of Finance, part of the "club of 19"—a group of settlements that were considered not viable and unsavable. Like the rest of Israel, Yizrael had lived beyond its means, was deep in debt, and its strong socialist ideology restricted its capacity, economically and socially, to respond. Yizrael was on the verge of collapse. This chapter examines how this community stepped back from the precipice, transformed its economic base and reputation, and worked to create a new model of communal living. They not only rehabilitated themselves but thrived by challenging their core beliefs and practices, and through building a set of adaptive capabilities.

To avoid a collapse two members, Shimon Zelas and Peter Pezaro, had to challenge their colleagues and neighbors to let go of the deep socialist ideology that underpinned their very creation and existence, help them accept and celebrate capitalist values, and do so while keeping the central aspects of communal living alive.

9.2 A gathering storm[2]

Shimon and Peter have lived on Kibbutz Yizrael for over fifty years. They share a background in the sciences, have a penchant for using data and analysis, and love to solve problems. Both men have a passion for sport too, and built a makeshift antenna so that they can watch the New Zealand All Blacks play rugby.

After its foundation in 1948, Yizrael's survival rested on its members' commitment to the egalitarian values of kibbutz life, including equal distribution of income, collective ownership of all property, mutual assistance, and cooperation. Yizrael's life blood was agriculture and for a period the economy grew and sustained its members. But life was hardscrabble, indebted, and with no future comfort in sight. They were young and having some hardship confirmed the nobility of their cause.

DOI: 10.4324/9781003321200-14

The seeds of the crisis that hit Yizrael and other kibbutzim in Israel were sown during the early years of its existence when conditions were conducive to growth: a left-leaning government that supported the kibbutz movement, demand for agricultural products grown on these settlements, and people committed to agrarian socialist ideals. Like the proverbial frog in the jar, by the time you notice the rising temperature of the water, it is too late.

By the 1960s, however, the first cracks in the kibbutz ideal appeared. The agricultural economy proved tenuous, given the lack of water for crops and declining demand for agricultural goods. To broaden its economic base, Yizrael started a new electronics enterprise, but also took out loans from the government, growing its debt.

The settlement's culture did not lend itself to the kind of early adaptation that might have made life easier. Ideals guided all decisions, even when these decisions were not economically rational. But its collective strengths increasingly undermined their ability to make hard and rapid decisions. For example, the General Meeting (Assefah Klalit) made all decisions, a process that was profoundly democratic and maddingly slow. Members with specialist and professional expertise were not permitted to work outside the kibbutz thereby limiting economic potential as well as personal satisfaction. There was a growing disconnect between its socialist agrarian economy and the emerging global capitalist system; their complete reliance on agriculture for income was creating vulnerability. By focusing inwardly and reinforcing its ideology, the settlement was becoming insular and cut off from the mainstream.

Yizrael always had debt, but it was seen as part of their way of life, and they believed they would be supported and protected. The kibbutz felt safe while the government continued to provide cheap loans. The risks were hidden and became part of the DNA of how they did business. But the community's fragility became more apparent.

In 1977, the Likud party, headed by Menachem Begin, won the national election, starting a radical restructuring of Israeli society. The government opened the economy, relying on market forces and abandoned government subsidies, including to kibbutzim. Yizrael was exposed. Kibbutzim now could not rely on external ideological and financial support. They had to reinvent themselves or die.

9.3 An inflection point

In 1984, Israel's inflation rate reached over 400%. Because Kibbutz Yizrael's loans were linked to the rate of inflation, it was about to be drowned by debt at the very time that state support stopped. It was a perfect storm, and revealed that most members did not have the skills or experience to know what to do. Their predicament laid bare their fundamental vulnerabilities—overreliance on external support, an ideological model that restricted thinking, and rising conflict over the very values that had created and sustained them.

As the effects of the financial crisis reverberated through the Yizrael community, first Shimon, then Peter, who held the position of business manager (Merakez

Meshek) during this period, found that they had to act on behalf of the community at large, arguing that the government was not going to stand behind them. But they were reliant on systems and protocols that had been developed under different conditions. Expertise was required in an environment where experts were at best acknowledged only as advisors, not decision-makers. New talent was needed, as were new, less cumbersome decision-making processes that did not depend on the General Meeting to determine whether money could be spent on a laundry machine, a harvester for the field crops, or overseas travel to visit a sick relative.

The ideological edifice on which Yizrael was built was shaky. Shimon and Peter, together with a group of influential members, began to see if anyone would be willing the break ranks by arguing for a loosening of the collective ideology?

9.4 The first provocation: Prune dying branches

By 1984, during his second term as business manager, Shimon could see that the kibbutz faced profound economic problems. This was not a differential equation he could solve, as he did in his early career as a traffic engineer. Yizrael could not address the problem using known approaches. It became clear to Shimon and his allies that they needed to change how they operated, how they lived as a community, and, more fundamentally, how they thought about their lives together.

Shimon made a bold move and encouraged Yizrael to close Elex, its fledgling electronic factory, because it was losing money and the arrangement with external partners was not working. There was resistance from Shimon's colleagues, the engineers, and managers in the factory who had the most to lose. They were seen by some kibbutz members as heroes because of how hard they fought and the principles they upheld.

Shimon was willing to tolerate many of his neighbors losing their livelihoods and dreams. In turn, some members felt he was disloyal and argued vociferously if not viciously against him. To them he was selling out their shared past, turning away from the values that had held them together. For some it was like trading away the family.

Adaptation can be a cruel and impersonal process because losses occur unequally. Some are forced to give up more than others and experience this as deeply provocative and unfair. Despite this, for the first time on Yizrael, someone was pushing the community to confront its problems rather than pretending they would be saved by the government.

In nature, some DNA is lost and pushed out during natural selection and the fittest survive. This is an invisible process that occurs over generations. In human systems, such as a small collective settlement, one contentious decision sends seismic oscillations out across the community, impacting visible connections and relationships. The act of closing their first non-agricultural enterprise was so confronting that some felt it was no longer their community. For some, the Elex was their lifeblood, their future. Trust was broken, values and beliefs compromised, and people's toil disregarded. However, the closure was a signal, which punctuated the previous period of stability. While one problem had been solved, another had been created, and the systemic nature of the challenges Kibbutz Yizrael faced became clearer.

The decision to close the factory seeded the idea that if Yizrael was to rehabilitate itself, it needed a new and radically different attitude to talent, business expertise, financial management as well as how and where it sold its products. First, Yizrael had to stop the flow of money and talent out of the kibbutz. It had to manage its debt and deal with the fact that within weeks of the factory closure, a flood of members had left the kibbutz, hurt and shocked, that something they valued had been discarded.

9.5 We've closed the factory, now what?

Closing the electronics factory really was a provocation test for the kibbutz. Could it confront the reality it faced and survive the ordeal? Some have argued that it didn't because, over the following months and years, nearly 25% of the members left including many considered the best and brightest. It took a long time to recover from this shock. Good friends were lost, marriages and families broke apart, and for some, "the heart of our life together was ripped out. We had acted in ways we didn't think we ever could."

The factory closure, though, was just one step in stemming the tide and managing the crisis. As Shimon says, they knew they had a debt problem but didn't wake up to the severity of it until too late. Shimon and his friends could not put their heads in the sand any longer. Strict discipline and plans for survival were required.

9.6 Confronting the tsunami

Shimon moved to a new role in 1987, and when Peter took over as the business manager Yizrael had hit rock bottom. It had few sources of reliable income, despite trying several different avenues, and people were desperate. He had to help them manage the crisis first before they could address the root causes and adaptive problems.

Peter shepherded through an agreement with the government which would allow Yizrael, like other kibbutzim, to pay off its debt, increasingly funded by what was to become the kibbutz's transformational savior—Maytronics which manufactured a pool cleaning robot. Although the debt agreement, signed in 1988, helped stabilize the situation, the underlying problems remained. The issue was visible to everyone on the kibbutz, but they were not ready to face the fundamental changes that would threaten the heart of their beliefs and values about collective life, their raison d'être.

Shimon and Peter prepared themselves and others for what was to come. As accomplished sportsmen, they were trained to tackle things head on and knew that there were likely to be some bruises. They increasingly put their heads above the parapet, spoke out, asked challenging questions, and made suggestions that previously had been unthinkable. Shimon came to be seen as a troublemaker and "know-all" by some of his colleagues as he increased the level of provocation to within an inch of what was tolerable to others. He continued to ask questions, describe problems, and made proposals others were uncomfortable with. With considerable risk and increasing discomfort in their daily lives and relationships in the small, closed kibbutz community, they pushed and cajoled their peers into considering what they were prepared to lose for the prize of survival.

Shimon and Peter knew that different behavior and difficult decisions were needed to help the community develop new "adaptive muscles." Sacrificing some cherished socialist ideals had to be on the table to save the enterprise. Conflict had to be invited to enable the tough decisions that would ensure their future, albeit one very different from early ideals. The role and power of the General Meeting in kibbutz life also would have to come under scrutiny, challenging the fundamental tenet of their collective life to date. The pain endured was evident, but they persisted, even risking alienating people to break through to a new mindset. But every major decision was decided by the community, through the General Meeting, which meant Shimon and Peter had to persuade most members to support their efforts. Persistently and gradually, they succeeded.

As they did in their fruit and nut orchards, Yizrael would have to prune dead branches, root out unproductive activities, cauterize bleeding stems, and be prepared to sacrifice some of the harvest to protect the rest. The platform for the contentious change was the new Maytronics factory and the role its growth played in forcing the kibbutz to confront its shortcomings to have a viable future. Critical pivot points emerged where they had cause to hold tight to the bigger goal, shepherding through creative conflict, insisting on hard decisions to get to the point of overturning an established way of life. Each involved the incremental building of what our colleague Juan Carlos Eichholz calls in his book adaptive capacity. Having cauterized the bleeding they now began rehabilitation, learning new ways to live together, and building strength.

9.7 Confronting our own values: The Maytronics story

At the heart of Kibbutz Yizrael's recovery and current economic success is a small, reptile-like, automated swimming pool cleaner called the Dolphin. This was the product of Maytronics, the fledgling second factory. But the true miracle was the way this community navigated fundamental adjustments in their thinking and behavior. They emerged with the ability to tolerate disturbance, to challenge the conventional wisdom of kibbutz life, to experiment with new ways of living collectively and to adjust core values and practices. They developed an adaptive capacity.

In 1982, Yizrael purchased the patent to a simple automated pool cleaner as another attempt to diversify their economic base. By 1987, Maytronics was showing great promise, even though, as the new CEO, Shimon declared that he and others did not have the technical or managerial expertise to build a sustainable business. He was right. They had embarked on a risky experiment.

They needed greater technical and managerial expertise than they currently had. The challenge was whether they could withstand importing this talent to make the factory work. To do so, they had to shake up underlying cultural and attitudinal issues. The biggest barrier was themselves. There was to be a test that would make or break the case for the capacity that Shimon and Peter's earlier provocation had delivered. They had to confront their origin story and ideology.

First, they confronted the idea that to be a "proper" kibbutz, they had to do it all themselves. Shimon proposed that Maytronics should be governed by an independent Board of Directors headed by an external Chairperson, thereby bypassing control of the powerful kibbutz Work and Industry Committees. Though quite normal for growing companies, this was a deeply contentious proposal for the settlement because it placed their economic future in the hands of outsiders, inevitably threatening a loss of control.

Forty years of hard labor had built a strong sense of pride, which was now being questioned. "We've always made decisions collectively, it's who we are and now that's not good enough?" Shimon and Peter ploughed on, living, and working in an increasingly tense environment. There was no respite or opportunity to regroup.

For many years, socialist kibbutzim had insisted that all the work, even the most mundane, was undertaken by community members irrespective of their skill sets. For example, David, a sociology professor and Avraham, a writer and philosopher, picked fruit and washed dishes, rather than work in their chosen professions. To many, it felt as if these sacrifices had been for nothing. The resistance to outsourcing decision-making to a professional Board poked sharply at identity. As they grappled with a new decision-making model for the factory, Yizrael also loosened other restrictions. More members were permitted to study and more could work outside the kibbutz. The decision to encourage outside work and professionalization undoubtedly contributed to greater development of the economy and the community at large.

Finally, the kibbutz agreed to establish a Board of Directors with three kibbutz members and three external appointees. Decisions affecting the factory would no longer be made by the General Meeting or by the internal committees. "It was a radical idea at the time," Shimon explained, "a real provocation to everything we knew and understood as we had always run our own show." He continued,

> It was relief for me and those of us trying to build a viable business but a deep shock to the majority of members who all had their hands on every decision right down to whether we purchased a new tractor or we invested a $1000 to paint the social club.

For Shimon and the other drivers of change on the kibbutz, the existence of a professional board was a sign that change was possible, and that a major hurdle had been overcome. As their risky efforts paid dividends, it was also easier for Shimon and Peter to build support, as more and more of their colleagues saw the benefits of making deep adjustments. Shimon and Peter could also avoid being seen as saviors, or as nuisances, untenable roles in a small community.

9.8 Differentiating to thrive

By the early 1990s, Maytronics was providing a regular and growing income for the kibbutz, revenue that could be used to service their debt obligations but also revive civic life. However, adaptation is never a smooth or even ride. Just as you come around a bend and see the road straightening ahead, you hit another pothole created by overuse, neglect, poor materials, and a strategy of putting off until tomorrow what could have been fixed today.

The next pothole came in the form of an unexpected setback for Maytronics when a French distributor went bankrupt still owing the company five million shekels (about US$1 million). After a legal battle they received a refund of 3 million shekels. This was an opportunity to share some of the rewards directly with members, improving the quality of life after a decade of difficulty. However, when Shimon requested money from the Treasurer to invest in factory expansion, he discovered there was no money left from the payment. He was shocked but not really surprised. "The money has been used," the Treasurer informed him, "to dig other sectors of the kibbutz out of unforeseen financial difficulties." The dairy needed repairs and didn't have the money, and the poultry farm had debt to repay.

Shimon saw that this underlying problem was only becoming visible because of the kibbutz's economic progress. "The factory could make profit for us," he said, "but we would not benefit while financial control and accountability in other sectors of the kibbutz was poor and went unchecked." The old culture was holding back the new, and battle lines were suddenly visible in the tension between a new emerging model of economic co-existence, a socialist collective and a capitalist hi-tech company. He saw that Yizrael had, as Joseph Tainter described in *The Collapse of Complex Societies*, "exhausted its (original) design." They needed a new design.

Shimon felt compelled to act. Legacy short-term management practices were not sufficient for the kibbutz to adapt and grow. This time the provocation was about how their accountabilities would need to be reframed-about them as members of the collective.

He argued for a new model of financial control and accountability that would put pressure on each economic sector to become more responsible. In so doing, he mirrored the agreement the government had made with the kibbutz in the mid-1980s. Shimon proposed that each of the economic sectors operate financially independently, each becoming responsible for paying its own debt and making ends meet, without the possibility of being bailed out by the rest of the community. They had to stand on their own two feet.

Inevitably, there was an outcry, with community members fearing a loss of power and flexibility. The proposal also raised profound questions about the kibbutz socialist model. Under the original model, each person contributed to their full ability and all people received equal returns. In the same way, each sector—fruit, poultry, factory—did the same. The successful sectors helped the less productive sectors, with the profitable subsidizing the loss makers. This ethos of collective responsibility was under challenge, and the disturbance was deeply felt.

Shimon and his allies argued that the only way to ensure financial security was to strengthen the viability of the factory, using its success to invest in expansion. They knew that success would result in profits flowing back to the community. But this economic argument was very alarming to many who wanted to preserve the integrity of the kibbutz model. This felt like an existential threat not just an economic one. If weak sectors were left to fend for themselves, rather than being bailed out by successful activities, the kibbutz could not be a collective entity driven by the creed of "each according to his ability, to each according to his needs." As such, the risks and disturbance were profound.

Accepting the new model was a tipping point that would lay a foundation for Yizrael's survival. Shimon helped the community understand the issue as one of collective survival. As challenging as it was, the proposal asked questions that helped the community think about a future based on a new, reconstituted set of ideals. Despite its shortcomings, the community's General Meeting had robust protocols to foster heated debate. Shimon, Peter, and their growing allies maintained the pressure over several months and many meetings. Eventually, a new agreement was reached even though many members had reservations and feared what they were relinquishing.

As the problem was collective, so would be the shift. The rules that had guided them in decision-making and financial accountability so far had to be swept aside. With the new capability in mind, the sectors inched towards becoming more autonomous, more accountable, more open to scrutiny, and free from collective interference. Held firmly through extreme discomfort and threat, they came to understand and enact collective responsibility in a profoundly different way.

Maytronics now had its own budget, independent financial and governance systems, and its own management and board. The business could operate as a capitalist enterprise but owned by a socialist settlement. The new arrangements melded two different economic and social systems, with the benefits and shortcomings of each emerging from creative tension.

As a postscript to this story, we can see that change forged through provocative processes of collective effort and dialogue almost never run smoothly. Within a year of the decision to separate the finances of the sectors, it was discovered that there had been a reversion to the old ways. Money was still being moved between entities because the accounting systems made it easy to do so. Old behaviors were hard to change. The hard-won collective decision was being bypassed. In response, new, clearer protocols were established, firewalls built into the accounting software, and the agreements were made public. Ultimately, the major winner, Shimon declares, "was the community at large because we had money and could start to look after ourselves."

9.9 Provocation reinforces core values

Yizrael's rehabilitation continued and by the late 1990s, Maytronics was central to kibbutz life. The new systems and agreements had been normalized, establishing how the community lived and did business together. Born out of crisis and heartache, Yizrael had become a productive, increasingly viable and more harmonious community. It had shifted from an ideologically driven, inward-looking community to a pragmatic, value-driven and outward-looking entity. The old affiliation-based settlement that was founded on a sense of belonging and purpose, had adapted. Mutual responsibility, consensus-based decision-making, and caring hadn't disappeared. The previous hard decisions had allowed the community to incorporate new values such as efficiency, differentiation, and market awareness. New economic and social DNA had been introduced so that adaptation could occur.

Yizrael was determined to hold onto as much of its core as it could, and not let its increasing economic success pollute the way of life that was so important to all its members. This was the way of life that attracted people in the first place. While many other kibbutzim were privatized, shifting away from a collective ideal, Yizrael navigated a path through the storm and emerged stronger, buttressed by the ongoing commercial success of Maytronics. Of course, the story didn't end there. What was adaptive eventually becomes the status quo, and the cycle begins again. The test of success is the capacity to recognize and respond to the shoots of emerging or potential challenges.

9.10 How much change can we take?

In 2012, Haywood, the giant US pool products company, offered to buy Yizrael's 65% share in Maytronics for 345 million shekels (about US$90 million), or 40% above the market value of the company. It was an enormous amount of money for the kibbutz, given their history of debt and hardship. It would allow them to get ahead, invest in projects such as new housing.

Even though most of Maytronics Board members supported the offer, it was not an easy decision. Peter elaborated, "Many people felt unsure because we didn't know what we would do with the money. Yes, we'd have cash but that wouldn't give us a livelihood or a purpose." So, in some ways, fears of the unknown challenged people to clarify what was important to them. "We were in a better shape but were strapped for cash and this would give us oxygen."

The debate was vigorous and lengthy, raising many issues about kibbutz life and what was important to people. Did they value economic security and certainty more than supporting a growing but still fragile business that had promise but also presented risk? What would a large windfall do to the remaining socialist ideals, many of which Yizrael has carefully maintained while other privatized kibbutzim had jettisoned them?

In the end, a majority voted against the buyout offer. This surprised the Board advocates, who had assumed the members, less financially literate than themselves, would follow their advice. But as Peter observed, the members were invested in the factory in more than just economic terms. "This was our baby; we had nurtured it from modest beginnings, and it was showing some promise. We were not going to give it away. We felt committed to it and what it meant for our future."

The provocation here is a curious one because it was less about change or transformation, about breaking away from the past, than about realizing and reinforcing critical values: pride and a belief in the kibbutz's efforts and innovation. As with the original members who pioneered a new agrarian community, this decision was about holding onto the emerging form of a twenty-first-century kibbutz, pioneering a new form of collectivity in a high technology environment. This decision nudged the kibbutz toward a new model of communal settlement, one that combined the best of its socialist and egalitarian origins with the best of capitalist enterprise. Importantly, this time the push came from the community, not its leaders.

While it was an emotional decision, it was also showed a shift in the community's ideology. There was a new adaptive maturity that both honored the past and embraced the risks and innovation that would carry them into the future. A belief in that future was more persuasive than a financial windfall. "On reflection," Peter observed, "had Haywood offered to buy 50% rather than insisting on the full 100%, I think we would have taken it. But we all felt strongly that we wouldn't give away our baby that easily!" It was another tipping point.

This decision was a turning point in their provocative capacity and a sign of collective learning. Instead of Peter or Shimon challenging the community, it was the community itself that did the work. Rather than accepting the advice of the Maytronics's Board, the Extraordinary Meeting flexed its muscles and pushed hard against the tide. The capacity to challenge and provoke had shifted and could now come from anywhere.

Since the Haywood offer, Maytronics has increased in value to over 7.4 billion shekels (over US$2 billion), holding fifty percent of the world market. In 2022, the factory produced 20,000 robots in one week, double its entire output in 2000. Yizrael's increased wealth has enabled community expansion, investment in social capital through education and the arts, and a degree of comfort for its older members that had been unimageable during the 1980s.

The new socialist-capitalist model works very well. As one of Maytronics senior executives said, "In order to maintain a cooperative kibbutz system we need a very successful (capitalist) industry." The earlier triggers have given way to a new accord which finely balances two sets of values and behaviors. As with all healthy ecosystems, this has introduced more variation into life on the kibbutz. Allowing some foreign ideas into their previously strong ideology has ensured not only their survival but also their thriving and dynamism. While the decision to incorporate a capitalist entity into their socialist community was made years earlier, the Haywood decision provoked the kibbutz to reaffirm and wholeheartedly commit to Maytronics and its magic Dolphin. They have used the factory to protect their core values and their future.

9.11 Adaptation is ongoing

Yizrael has continued to grow and adapt, addressing other challenges; the community can identify issues and act early, undertaking adaptive work in anticipation of a problem. Progress was predicated on refashioning a set of loyalties and making new, flexible agreements.

By any definition, Yizrael is a success story. But it is only a success because people confronted the challenges they faced. Yizrael survived and thrived not only because of the work of Shimon and Peter, who questioned, reframed, and challenged, but also because their provocation allowed others to find their courage and respond so that new capacity could be built. Shimon and Peter identified critical windows to open, and the community jumped through. Not without pain, hardship, and loss, but they jumped through all the same. The changes annealed a transformation in kibbutz life. Existing structures, roles, and mechanisms were reorganized, redefined, or replaced. Yizrael now has more heterogenous structures that give the economy and social life greater strength and resilience against future shocks.

Yizrael now has a richer DNA and can tolerate, even embrace, foreign ideas. Capitalism now coexists with a socialist-inspired communal life. There are flat polycentric structures alongside expert-driven hierarchies that value critical thinking. Provocative strategies infuse a life of creative destruction, enabling a constant search for what is next, all part of staying fresh, continuing to learn. This is now a community in which adaptation is a way of life rather than simply a response to the latest crisis.

Notes

1 This expression was initially phrased differently but popularized by Leon Megginson (1963) in Lessons from Europe for American Business in the *Southwestern Social Science Quarterly*, *44*(1), pp. 3–13. Quote at page 4.

2 This chapter is based on direct interviews with Shimon Zelas and Peter Pezaro who are long standing friends of ours. Michael grew up with them in New Zealand before they settled in Israel.

References

Darwin. C. (2003). *The Origin of Species*. 150th Anniversary Edition. Penguin Books, USA.

Eichholz, J.C. (2014). *Adaptive Capacity: How Organizations Can Thrive in a Changing World*. LID Publishing, Greenwich, CT.

Megginson, L. (1963). Lessons from Europe for American Business. *Southwestern Social Science Quarterly*, *44*(1), pp. 3–13.

Tainter, J. (1990). *The Collapse of Complex Societies*. Cambridge University Press, Cambridge, UK.

10 SMASHING IT TO BITS—RISKY TACTICS TO CHANGE FIRST NATIONS' EDUCATION

It is important to know who you are to step out into these really wicked problems, which, as you describe are complex, and hold you in place. All of that is woven in you, and comes out as you being really sure about who you are. This allows you to step into the mess that was there with very strong principles. It comes straight from your heart.

Maxime Fern in discussion with Chris Sarra 2021

10.1 Introduction

Sometimes, someone seems perfectly suited to tackle a critical challenge, to break open the status quo. They may not know it at the time, but they have prepared for this moment. Life experiences and hard choices all served as a training ground, allowing the individual to develop the provocative capacities required for this specific challenge.

Often, they possess certain qualities and characteristics. First, they know themselves; they understand where they have come from and what drives them now. Second, they have undergone a profound personal transformation, and their response has given them more complex ways of seeing the world. Third, they can observe, comprehend, and diagnose the dynamics of the system they wish to change. Like the character of Neo in *The Matrix*, they have ideas about how to crack its code or, at least, where to begin.

This description fits Dr. Chris Sarra,[1] an Australian academic, author, teacher, senior bureaucrat, and social entrepreneur who has spent over twenty-five years discovering ways to change First Nations' education, a sector that has been resistant to it despite the overwhelming need. Now the first Aboriginal Director-General of Aboriginal and Torres Strait Islander Partnerships for the Queensland State Government, Chris has applied a model for transformation of indigenous education built on a philosophy that emphasizes a belief in the capacity of First Nations children. But to do so, like the parachutists discussed in Chapter 4, he stepped into an already distressing situation and leapt out, taking many risks and using approaches that others wouldn't use.

It is difficult to rapidly implement systemic change when the status quo is so deeply entrenched—200 years of white settlement in Australia with ingrained racism and antipathy toward First Nations Australians. Chris saw early on how everyone in the indigenous education system colluded with established beliefs about the ability of

DOI: 10.4324/9781003321200-15

Aboriginal children and what was good enough. He was determined not to. Instead, he would, in his own words, "smash it to bits!"

Chris could see that shifting people from what they knew and were familiar with was neither easy nor comfortable. It required disciplined provocative action which directed people's attention to contentious issues. If for no other reason, he needed to help them see how they had colluded with, and been captured by, the status quo. This was the foundation for opening the community's minds to alternative and better ways.

This chapter outlines Chris's journey. We examine the nature of his risky moves and how provocation becomes less contentious when you are committed to clear goals. We also discuss several essential ingredients for effective provocation: self-belief, persistence, flexibility, and love, which both increase and decrease the risk.

10.2 Self-belief as training for risk-taking

Chris Sarra finished high school in 1984. His teachers did not expect much from him, and he was advised to take an agricultural course. "Most teachers just saw us as average or below average academic achievers," Chris recalls, "and we just went along unquestioningly and maintained our place." These low expectations reinforced social and intellectual invisibility. Teachers didn't see his natural capacity because they didn't look, nor think that they should. They colluded with the assumption that indigenous children should not expect much. Throughout the 1980s and 1990s, and even more recently in some places, the educational system for indigenous children was set up to deliver poor results, underachieving children, and a reinforcement of the racism that permeated schools and broader society. Generations of people had cemented the status quo. It would take a significant provocation to unsettle it.

Chris claims that he became a teacher "quite accidentally" when his mentor Gary MacLennan encouraged him to study at a local teachers college. Chris speaks of his early academic training as constantly wondering whether he belonged in this institution, far from what he believed Aboriginal kids could do. Fortunately, though, Chris, who now holds a Ph.D. and is a university professor, received strong support from his parents and siblings. He worked hard, inspired by the example of his Italian father, and followed his mother in taking pride in his Aboriginal roots. Her advocacy on behalf of her people had taught Chris first-hand what it meant to ask hard questions and challenge the status quo.

While at college, Chris learned how teachers' expectations affect the outcomes of children's education. Even the special conditions he received as an indigenous student reflected the idea that Aboriginals needed coddling. These compensations were well-intentioned and recognized that indigenous people who began tertiary study did so despite hardship and constraints. But Chris realized that such help also implied he was less able and needed more time to complete.

His mentor challenged Chris to consider his assumptions about himself. If his mother had lit a fire in Chris's belly, then MacLennan "had come along and thrown petrol on it," changing how he viewed himself. He would no longer accept second best or "collude with the idea that Aboriginal kids couldn't do as well as others, or even better." This prompted Chris to start taking risks himself, and he insisted on the same conditions as his fellow students, putting in the extra effort to catch up and finish the program at the same time as them. By the time he graduated, Chris had started to develop a philosophy of Aboriginal identity that would later form the backbone of his educational experiments and the orienting purpose of his leadership.

Like the people Robert Kegan describes in *In Over Our Heads*, Chris transformed not just how he behaved or felt but also how he knew and saw the world. Remarkably for a young graduate he could see the system of disadvantage caused by the low expectations of Aboriginal children. Everyone was captured and imprisoned by their actions and beliefs. Chris recalls how determined he was to change this situation. "I explicitly decided to perceive myself differently to how everyone else perceived me. I began to see myself as capable alongside these others, and I started to outperform them. I chose to collude no longer." The demands of his circumstances, including the psychological pressures he felt, bumped against his worldview and capacities. To adapt, he changed the latter, responding to the provocation to challenge himself.

Chris persisted in exploring alternative approaches to education for indigenous children based on a simple but confronting premise: valuing the children's heritage and traditions. He believed that Aboriginal children should get the best education possible, not some ersatz second option. He wanted them to be Strong *and* Smart, stand tall and proud, and learn their way into better futures. So, having challenged and changed himself, he set out to challenge and change Aboriginal education. He also encouraged others to try new approaches but often he found that his appeals went unheard. He needed a larger canvas to realize his vision.

This came from left field when he was invited to become the Principal of Cherbourg State School in Queensland. It was here that Chris developed the Stronger Smarter philosophy[2] on which the Stronger Smarter Institute (initially called the Indigenous Education Leadership Institute) was founded in 2005.

10.3 Cherbourg State School: A provocative environment

When Chris arrived at Cherbourg in 1998, he knew that he had to consider two elements. First, the unique context of the school, particularly its harrowing history as a mission reserve. Second, the existing power structures in the community, especially with local elders, with whom he had to establish his own credibility. Chris was about to embark on a provocative journey full of risks and couldn't ride these waves alone. He needed sturdy relationships between himself, the teachers, and the community.

Given the situation in the school and community, he had his work cut out. Despite being the first Aboriginal Principal at the school, Chris was an outsider. He was not a mission person[3] and did not have the same history as those in this tight-knit community. A crucial part of his work as Principal would be to engage with the parents and community elders to win their trust and increase their involvement in the school, treading carefully, at least initially, because the status quo was in a delicate balance. These choices were designed to strengthen the environment in which he could make risky moves.

Some did regard him with suspicion. They saw him as no different than all the others who had come "to do good work" in Cherbourg. The community had seen over many years how ineffective the school was. The results spoke for themselves. Many had come to believe that this was the way things were: that they, as Aborigines, shouldn't expect anything else, with education viewed as a "white-fella activity."

Chris had other ideas, which were the wellspring for his audacity. He believed sincerely that all indigenous children deserved a decent education, and that the foundation of this had to be a robust Aboriginal identity. However, decades of overt and benign neglect had eroded the strength of identity among many of Cherbourg's inhabitants. Chris could see that many did not believe he could bring about any change.

With its attendant social and health problems, the present community was a product of a violent history of dispossession and neglect. Indigenous people had been forced off their homelands and relocated in 1903 to the new settlement, initially named Barambah, where many children experienced a harsh life in mission dormitories. In her foreword to Thom Blake's book *A Dumping Ground*, local resident Ruth Hegarty observes that despite decades of neglect, abuse, and institutionalized racism, the community held together—they "maintained a sense of otherness" that set them apart from the white officials and church authorities. But understandably, residents remained suspicious of educators, especially outsiders.

Chris's early impressions of the school were bleak. He recalls feeling depressed by the apathy, dejection, and squalor he found in the school. Children ran wild, climbed on the building roofs, and stole food left in the fridge by staff. They came and went from classrooms as they pleased, treating them as daycare sites rather than as places of learning. "Even more depressing," Chris recalls, "was that there was a sense of acceptance of it all." There were chronic levels of underachievement, with almost all the children "caught in the net," performing below age-group expectations in reading, writing, and numeracy. Everywhere he looked, there was a lack of pride.

As a proud Aboriginal man, Chris wanted the children and their parents to feel the same way about themselves, that they were worthy of a decent school environment. However, it was clear that he would have to confront the well-established cycles of blaming others, putting up with second best, and accepting the situation as an "Aboriginal thing." He faced a complex and deeply entrenched system of failure that he would have to overturn.

10.4 Where to begin? Challenging ourselves as a starting point

Chris faced an adaptive challenge, reflecting centuries of displacement and neglect. He began a process of provocative action, some of it relatively straightforward, all designed to improve life for children at the school. While it was a daunting task, Chris was excited at the prospect of beginning to express his Stronger and Smarter ideas. He was ready to paint and fill the canvas that was Cherbourg State School.

The starting point was encouraging self-reflection and addressing individuals' contribution, unwitting or otherwise, to the systemic issues. It was too easy to blame the community, the societal and historical context, for the children's poor academic performance. Instead, the teachers need to be challenged and questioned, while the children need to be encouraged to let go of old and unproductive stereotypes about themselves. They needed to "aspire to achieve," stretching themselves while embracing their Aboriginal identity and developing self-belief.

10.4.1 *Signal your intention*

From the start, it was essential for Chris to signal to everyone that he was different. He meant business, and he believed change was possible. Chris also was clear that the school would not collude in old ways and attitudes. He told the children, "Things are going to change here, and I'm not going to put up with bad behavior. If you play up, then there'll be consequences."

In effect, Chris encouraged the children to let go of the old ways and embrace the notion that children can be Strong and Smart. He also wanted to make it clear that he was no pushover. He would join respectfully with the locals and care about the students, but he would also challenge them. He understood that effective provocation, and the learning that can be derived from it, requires a combination of sustained challenge and evident caring and support. For him, it was a matter of integrity, of wanting what was best for the children.

On his first day at the school, Chris decided to wear a tie, signaling that he was proud to be there, mirroring what principals did in other schools. He reinforced this message at the first school parade when he declared:

> *The most important thing that you will learn from me is that you can be Aboriginal, and you can be successful. We're not mongrel dogs ... We're not second-rate citizens, and we deserve to have a nice school. We have to create that for ourselves.*

In two simple actions, Mr. Sarra, as the children started to call him, laid out his philosophy and the foundation for his approach to change: he was there not just as a headmaster but as a facilitator of change. He was Aboriginal, successful, and proud of it. He and the school were no longer waiting for others, especially white Australia, to improve things. Blame was fruitless and would cease. Responsibility was productive and about to start. Chris confronted the children, teachers, and parents with a new reality. It must have been both bewildering and disorienting to be told that the old rules no longer applied and to hear about Chris's high expectations.

His high expectations, while challenging, were also an affirmative move. Like Frank Farrelly, who constantly signaled his belief in his client's capacity, Chris expressed his confidence in the strength and ability of the children in his care. He believed in them.

Chris intended to change the mindset of all involved and to do so purposefully. He chose "strong" and "smart" as part of his overarching philosophy because he wanted the community to associate them with being Aboriginal and attending the school. He wanted the children at Cherbourg to continue their education at high school and beyond. To do so, they needed to be resilient enough to deal with predominantly white high schools, as well as clever and sufficiently prepared to study and do well academically.

For the first eighteen months of his tenure, Chris made Strong and Smart his mantra every day until the children and parents made it their own. He reinforced this message in various ways, educationally through teaching methods and socially and culturally through a school song, a uniform, and some behavioral incentives, such as recognizing regular attendance. In focusing here, he started small by bolstering belief and having a goal he hoped his next, riskier steps would be more acceptable.

10.5 Carrot and stick: Encouragement as a provocation

One of the first problems Chris confronted was unexplained, widespread absences. The worst part was that teachers and parents accepted this as normal. Rather than punishing absence, Chris confounded expectations, establishing a system of rewards for children who attended school regularly and for classes with the lowest number of absentees. Prizes included a trip to McDonald's for those who missed five days or less. Gradually, attendance numbers improved.

This was an example of encouragement as provocation. Chris challenged the conventional idea that school attendance is a compliance issue and that punishments follow non-compliance. It was more important to have the children at school engage with them, instilling pride and encouraging them to think and act more responsibly. He confronted and broke existing behavioral patterns, replacing them with something new.

His McDonalds reward strategy was one of his first big risks. Others criticized him for bribing children, trivializing education strategies, and even for giving children unhealthy food. But no one could argue with his approach if more children were in school, attending more regularly. In 1999, overall attendance rates were 60%. By 2004, they had climbed to 94%. Cherbourg now had classrooms of children beginning to learn together. Chris had created a holding environment for the real work to start, to realize the Strong and Smart vision.

In addition to pressuring the pupils to go to class, he reinforced the message to parents, attempting to persuade them of the importance of attendance. Chris hired Richard Coleman, known locally as Uncle Hooper, as a teacher's aide to link parents and school. Hooper knew everyone in the community and was known widely himself. Instead of teachers and the principal being the only authorities, Chris could rely on Uncle Hooper's intelligence and care for the children and the input of the broader community to encourage the pupils to get to school.

Not only did Chris's approach circumvent regular practice, but it also built capacity in the community. His provocation was not direct, it didn't shame anyone, yet it turned years of tradition and expectation on their head.

10.6 Don't provoke on your own: Build alliances

In addition to leveraging Mr. Hooper's connection to the community, Chris cultivated enduring relationships with two female elders who worked at the school, one as a teacher and the other as a teacher's aide. Mrs. Long and Mrs. Langton were both committed to the school but previously had not been given a voice or invited to contribute strategically. Chris saw this as a wasted opportunity because "outside of the school these women were powerful people." Chris's alliance with them helped to establish him in Cherbourg and build credibility among the parents. They could introduce him to pupils' families, tap into the hot issues, and provide advice about how to interact with the community and when to raise problems. He understood that he needed them because, on many topics, they knew more than he did.

While their access to the community was critical, the boldest aspect of Chris's relationship with Mrs. Long and Mrs. Langton was the elevated place he afforded them in the school. Chris wanted to signal that Aboriginal teachers were more than capable of guiding the school, challenging the "big white man" model of leadership that had prevailed in the past. Chris needed Strong and Smart women to help him as the principal, sharing leadership with them over time. Again, his provocation was neither loud nor confrontational, but it was profound and unsettling, overturning decades of practice.

10.7 High expectations as a risk

Chris was determined to set high standards across all aspects of school life, and he made these known to parents and teachers. It was essential to his Strong and Smart vision that everyone experience a shift in mindset. The community did not have to settle for second. They did have to believe their children were more capable than they had been. He mobilized the parents to help with attendance, keep the school grounds clean and tidy, and support his attempts to develop pride in the school. Chris also introduced Aboriginal studies into the school program. Children learned what it meant to be Aboriginal and talked about issues affecting the community, such as domestic violence and alcoholism. "I was trying to get kids to understand," Chris noted, "that these are a product of sociological and historical factors, not a result of being Aboriginal."

It wasn't plain sailing, as parents complained and criticized him. Chris especially remembers one group. "They wanted to run me out of town. But I was confident about where we were going and about what we had on offer." He sat with the parents for several hours, listened to their concerns, and acknowledged his mistakes, demonstrating flexibility. He did, however, reinforce his core message, encouraging parents to let go of their old attitudes about what their children could achieve, working together with him to offer better learning opportunities. He was clear that he would prefer them to expect too much of the children than too little. He advised them that when parents tolerated pupils' bad behavior, they were complicit in the poor educational outcomes. Chris's interventions helped parents understand how they unwittingly had become caught up in the status quo.

As he continued to engage with the wider community, Chris also kept talking to the children. "I told them I knew how strong they were, how smart they were. I told them, and I told them until they started believing it." Eventually, the children could see the results for themselves in the classroom. By 2004, Year 7 literacy levels had risen from rock bottom to 81% achieving state averages. Year 2 literacy improved by over 60% in just two years, and there were many individual stories of triumph. Chris recalls one girl phoning her mother from school, proudly and excitedly reporting that she had read a book. She had defied age-old expectations and progressed beyond what people thought she was capable of.

Chris maintained the pressure, constantly challenging children and teachers alike, keeping the school in a productive zone of disturbance and learning. He was clear and determined that the provocation was warranted even though it was often exhausting and upsetting for him and the children. At times, he took more visible risks because he wanted the children to know he was serious. For example, when he found several children swearing and throwing stones into a classroom, he intervened. In this case, he raised his voice and displayed anger to ensure he had the student's attention. Like Muhammad Ali, who we discussed in Chapter 4, he was nimble, responding to a complex and challenging situation, he used the tools at his disposal most suited to the problem.

Someone reported the incident to the education authorities, who reprimanded him. But Chris insisted he would not let the children continue to damage the school and abuse others.

> *I was not going to let them think it was OK to throw stones and tell me to get fucked. I didn't want them to think this was acceptable. They are or can be better than that.*

Chris wanted to hold them to high standards and not diminish their pride in themselves and the school. As a result, a few people accused him of being too rough with children or even abusing them. This charge challenged by one of Chris's colleagues in a 2004 ABC *Australian Story* interview, who asserted that the actual crime was condoning absenteeism and delinquency). While there may have been better ways to confront disruptive and damaging behavior, Chris believed he had to demonstrate to students that he cared so much about them and the school that he was willing to risk his reputation.

His responses in this situation were provocative in several ways. First, he startlingly confronted the pupils, making them see that their actions were not trivial or acceptable and were inconsistent with being Strong and Smart. Second, he challenged the prevailing mindset that "this is what Aboriginal kids do because of their underprivileged background." Whatever their circumstances, this did not prevent them from acting with pride. He wanted them to reject longstanding stereotypes. Third, he confronted the prevailing wisdom that educators and school leaders shouldn't raise their voices and get angry with children—even if this is a tactic to be avoided in general.

Every controversial act that Chris undertook was underpinned and informed by his Strong and Smart philosophy. He was engaged in revolutionary practice, challenging, and seeking to overturn the status quo eventually. Without his strong belief and commitment, as well as a lot of trial and error, he would not have succeeded.

10.8 Create commitment as a provocation

Among the most resonant acts of provocation that Chris deployed were those he applied to the teaching group. While parents and children increasingly were persuaded by his Strong and Smart philosophy, this was not initially the case with the school's teachers. Many teachers argued against Chris's proposals, claiming that the community's social problems made them impossible to realize. The status quo, they believed, was as good as it was going to get.

Chris noticed the minimal effort many teachers made, with some of them acting more as babysitters and entertainers than teachers. Only a handful saw their job as helping the children lift themselves out of their current situation. As their principal, Chris was motivated to change how the teachers saw the children and understood their roles. However, he was not willing to collude with attitudes that denied the possibility of change or the ability of the pupils to learn. Instead, the teachers needed an emancipatory mindset, helping students, in the words of cultural theorist Henry Giroux, "to make despair unconvincing and hope practical."

Chris worked persistently with the teachers because he understood that they were the frontline, enacting the Smart and Strong vision every day. He appealed to their professional integrity and sense of honor, to the fact that they had a duty to exercise leadership in their classrooms, regardless of what occurred in the outside world. He encouraged them to empathize, too, asking them how they would feel if it were their children, nieces, or nephews who were in the situation the children in Cherbourg. Incrementally and consistently, he built his case for change.

After eight months, he posed a critical challenge to his colleagues, declaring at a special staff meeting.

> *It is my core belief that indigenous children can perform just as well as any other child, and if you don't share this belief, then Cherbourg is no longer the place for you.*

With this tipping point, Chris asked the teachers to choose between maintaining the status quo or committing to a process of change based on his philosophy. It was a simple but powerful form of provocation, forcing the teachers to see themselves as part of the problem. Half the teaching staff left the school, replaced by people who subscribed to the Smart and Strong vision.

Provocation sometimes is like a sharp arrow that goes straight to the heart of an issue at just the right time. The extraordinary staff meeting was one such moment. Chris had been at the school long enough to have a clear idea that his diagnosis was at least reasonable. He had built a set of strong relationships with Aboriginal teachers and parents, and his credibility in the community was rising. He understood that he had created a holding environment that could withstand a more galvanizing intervention. He concluded it was worth the risk and the ire of the teacher's union and education authorities in Brisbane.

Some people, including the union, criticized him for pushing too hard and devaluing the staff. He replied in a highly provocative way by saying, "Give me something to value, and I will value it!" Chris maintained the pressure for change and stood his ground. His stance at this moment was critical, signaling that he was willing to push hard as he worked toward the vision. He accepted that there would be some enduring loss of position, status, identity, and comfort because of the changes.

The teachers who left found that the security they had derived from their old teaching practice was no longer tenable. Their previously tolerated beliefs and mindsets—reinforced by the educational authorities—had held Cherbourg's children back from realizing new possibilities. Chris's risky move had made it clear that their old ideas were redundant. In this way, the principal's challenge pushed people over the edge and created conditions where they had to choose. Some voted with their feet and, in so doing, created space and opportunity for a new generation of teachers committed to a more emancipatory view of their job.

As he expanded the children's and community's identity and sense of self, Chris expected even more from the teachers, going beyond the organization and delivery of a set curriculum. In line with Giroux's ideas, they needed to become culture workers who "help students overcome economic and social injustices and humanize themselves in the process." Students had to be treated as capable of overcoming their existing constraints and bringing a unique language of critique together with a vocabulary of possibility. Indeed, the Strong and Smart vision combines a critique of current thinking about the capability of indigenous children with a radical revision about future expectations.

Chris wanted teachers to stop colluding with old practices and expectations—to challenge absenteeism actively and regularly visit parents of pupils who failed to come to school. He wanted them to support and embody a high-expectation environment, explaining the missed opportunities and clarifying what needed to change to help the children learn. In a high-expectation climate, the teachers had to pose the same challenges and questions to themselves as they did to pupils and parents.

10.9 Adaptation is disturbing

Chris understood that he needed to break the cycle of low expectations that previously had shaped education at Cherbourg. He knew that poor educational outcomes don't occur by themselves but result from accumulated attitudes and actions. Though he doesn't use this language, he understood two core adaptive principles.

First, he had to increase the pressure and disequilibrium without knowing what people could withstand. He knew there would be pushback and that people would urge him to reduce the demands. But he was determined to hold "their feet to the fire" over a sustained period.

Second, he had to address the "lifestyle support system" that surrounded the children and parents at Cherbourg, tackling all the attitudes and behaviors that allowed for low expectations, absenteeism, vandalism, rudeness, poor classroom behavior, laziness, lack of attention, and racism on the part of the teachers.

Between 1998 and 2004, the Cherbourg school transformed itself under Chris's leadership when few believed it was possible. He introduced quality literacy and numeracy programs like those found in white schools. As attendance improved, the old truancy paradigm broke down, and children began to see how capable they were. "Children became strong and proud to be Aboriginal," Chris recalls, "and smart enough to mix it with any other child in any other school."

The positive results continued. The model Chris developed at Cherbourg was strengthened and deepened through the Stronger-Smarter Institute, established in 2005 and utilized in many schools across Australia and other countries. An indicator of success was that pride and belief in the children's capacity to achieve were no longer unusual but normalized. So, also was the fact that Stronger Smarter changed from being Chris' vision to being one shared by teachers, elders, parents, and children at Cherbourg and beyond. Reflecting on this progress, Chris observed, "It signals a belief that Aboriginal people are capable of lifting themselves given the right opportunities to do so."

10.10 Conclusion

A new order was created at Cherbourg by jolting the homeostasis. The change in dynamics caused the system to oscillate, to act in a different way that had the potential for some growth and progress. Through instinct, as well as trial and error, Chris learned how to regulate the perturbations caused by his unusual and risky tactics so that they didn't get out of hand and undermine his work. But he came to see how he needed to put pressure on different parts of the Cherbourg system regularly. He had to accept the possibility of failure and losses if he were ever to disturb the status quo, overcoming resistance to his new views and methods. Change required both provocation and sacrifice—and neither would have happened without Chris's risk-taking, commitment, steadfastness, and care for the issues and people involved.

Several lessons are evident from Chris Sarra's experience. If you are going to take risks and use unconventional approaches, it is essential to:

- Have a clear, relevant, and compelling purpose;
- To build a robust holding environment and local relationships;
- Start small, test people's tolerance;
- Affirm your belief in others' capacity;
- Be selective and focused in your provocation;
- Be a model risk-taker—show you are willing to get your own "boots dirty"; and
- Seek feedback and hold steady.

Chris Sarra and the Cherbourg State School are rare examples of the willingness to take risks in the service of something you care about deeply. Community-wide provocation and engagement are sometimes necessary to push people to examine and adjust their beliefs and attitudes. It was personally and collectively difficult, where the people involved had different experiences: some positive and some less so. The impacts and effects of change rarely are evenly distributed.

Chris's experiences at Cherbourg also illustrate that leadership is also essentially about love, about not being willing to accept outcomes for others that you wouldn't accept yourself. If you don't act, then, in effect, you are saying these people don't matter. His enduring care was a blanket he could wrap around his riskier actions, so people didn't lose sight of his intentions. Chris wouldn't and couldn't deny the humanity of the children at Cherbourg. This love was perhaps the greatest gift he could offer them.

Notes

1 This chapter is based on a combination of our own interviews with Chris Sarra, third-party interviews, articles, and ABC's 2004 Australian Story *Good Morning Mr Sarra.*

2 For an overview of the Stronger Smarter philosophy see https://strongersmarter.com.au/wp-content/uploads/2020/08/PUB_Stronger-Smarter-Approach-2017_final-3.pdf.

3 Missions, reserves, and stations were areas of land to which Aboriginal people were forcibly relocated. Missions were in the control of churches and missionaries, and had little or no government oversight.

References

ABC (2004). *Good Morning Mr Sarra*, Australian Story, 4, October 2004. Transcript Also found in Appendix of Chris Sarra's Ph.D. thesis. https://www.abc.net.au/austory/good-morning-mr-sarra-oct-2-2004/9999366. Retrieved 10 March 2021.

Blake, T. (2001). *A Dumping Ground: A History of the Cherbourg Settlement.* University of Queensland Press, St. Lucia, Qld.

Farrelly, F., & Brandsma, J.M. (1981). *Provocative Therapy.* Meta Publications.

Giroux, H. (2010). *Teachers as transformative intellectuals.* In Canestrari, A.S., & Marlowe, B.A. (eds) *Education Foundations: An Anthology of Critical Readings.* Sage Publications, Los Angeles, pp. 197–208.

Hegarty, R. (2001). *Foreword.* In Blake, T. *A Dumping Ground: A History of the Cherbourg Settlement.* University of Queensland Press, St. Lucia, Qld.

Kegan, R. (1994). *In Over Our Heads: The Mental Demands of Modern Life.* Harvard University Press, Boston, MA.

Sarra, C. (2005). *Strong and Smart: Reinforcing Aboriginal perceptions of being Aboriginal and Cherbourg State School.* PhD Thesis submitted to Murdoch University, Perth, WA. September 2005.

Sarra, C. (2014). *Beyond Victims: Dr Chris Sarra on the Challenge of Indigenous Leadership.* Speech on ABC Big Ideas with Paul Barclay, 8 September 2014. https://www.abc.net.au/radionational/programs/bigideas/beyond-victims:-the-challenge-of-indigenous-leadership/5727864. Retrieved 12 February 2021.

Stronger Smarter Institute. (2017). *Implementing the Stronger Smarter Approach.* Stronger Smarter Institute Position Paper. https://strongersmarter.com.au/wp-content/uploads/2020/08/PUB_Stronger-Smarter-Approach-2017_final-3.pdf. Retrieved 1 February 2021.

11 LIVING WITH CONTRADICTIONS—M&T BANK AND THE TRANSFORMATION BATTLE

We had to hold people in a safe place while also creating new but more unsettling spaces to innovate and grow in. And to manage the contradictions.

René Jones, CEO M&T Bank—comment during an interview

11.1 The state of things at M&T Bank[1]

In early 2016, René Jones was the Chief Financial Officer of M&T Bank, based in Buffalo, New York. After a twenty-five-year career, he began to feel frustrated and would write what he called "the state of things" notes to himself, storing them in his desk drawer while he reflected on the issues that bothered him. His discontent could be traced back to several operational and management systems that, despite his organization's success, were outdated and not functioning well.

Eventually, René shared his misgivings with senior colleagues Kevin Pearson and Rich Gold. He was both shocked and relieved to discover that they shared his concerns that the bank was resting on its laurels because of its record of growth, profitability, and community recognition. As such, it risked becoming insular and complacent, ignoring deep-seated issues. They discussed how they could remedy the situation. However, before they could escalate the matter a period of grief and change was triggered by the deaths, first, of bank President Mark Czarnecki and then of iconic founding Chairman and CEO Robert Wilmers.

Fortunately, robust succession planning had resulted in the appointments of René, Kevin, and Rich as Vice -Presidents following Czarnecki's death. Each of these executives, with their different styles and approaches, had long experience with the bank. Their joint promotions signaled that the future at M&T would involve more distributed leadership, with each of them challenging themselves and each other. While their critical partnership was forged during a period of loss and transition, the trio was ready, having long thought about the need for change. René's previous caution about speaking up flagged that the M&T culture was an area that needed to be addressed as a matter of priority.

When René succeeded Wilmers as Chair and CEO, he became responsible for what is now the eleventh largest commercial bank in the United States. This was a successful business that had enjoyed an uninterrupted run of quarterly profitability since 1976 and was one of only two banks that continued to pay dividends during

DOI: 10.4324/9781003321200-16

the Global Financial Crisis in 2008. It was a weighty legacy to inherit, encompassing a thirty-five-year period of growth and profitability.

At his first shareholders meeting, therefore, René assured people that the traditional M&T way would continue, with its emphasis on "simple community banking." His initial job, he believed, was to calm things down and comfort people during a time of grief and uncertainty. But René, Kevin, and Rich remained determined to implement twenty-first-century banking methods, such as online services, without compromising the fundamental values that had underpinned the bank's success. Kevin told us that 'success can breed stagnation and insularity, where we say to ourselves 'we've got this, we know what's best, and we don't have to worry about what's going on outside. This top team was determined to reignite a burning platform of purpose-driven banking for M&T, driving change while reinforcing continuity. They quickly realized they risked becoming yesterday's good news story unless they transformed the company.

In this chapter, we'll examine how M&T Bank was galvanized to stay fresh and innovative, teasing out the provocative strategies used to ensure relevance, outward focus, and untethering from a "glorious" past. We'll explore how bringing attention to hidden and ignored issues enables greater agility and how provoking an organization to change requires "giving the work back" to staff. Finally, we'll consider how M&T senior executives had to learn to let go and trust their people with the change and how they used the perspectives of an external coach to challenge them.

This is a story of more gentle and incremental provocation, appropriate to a pressured and complex environment. There was no business crisis to push M&T into heightened action. The organization was not on the brink of collapse. While responding to the radical discontinuity in senior personnel and recovering from grief, the key moments that focused attention on critical issues had to come from within. The motivation to change, to tackle restrictive ways of operating, had to be self-generated.

Change because you choose it requires a different kind of energy and leadership. Drawing on his "state of things" notes, René acknowledged the contradictions the organization faced rather than ignoring them, starting a process of more active and open debate about how the bank could continue to be successful.

Gradually, M&T Bank began to change. Very particular forms of less obvious and humble forms of provocation became instrumental in the adaptation that ensued. During this ongoing process, four main themes have emerged:

- Living with and working with contradictions is a form of provocation;
- Introducing new talent and capability into a successful operation can have a profound impact, with new people adding much needed variety to the organizational DNA;
- A graduated approach to audacity and challenge is required in a more cautious environment; and
- The three leaders had to learn new skills and mindsets to create and work with disturbance.

11.2 What's the problem when you are successful?

Under René's stewardship, M&T Bank has followed a steady strategic direction, integrating new thinking in several key roles and through the targeted use of technology. The bank's stated aim is:

> *To drive customer focus and understand their needs but through more contemporary and sophisticated technologies. We need to use more data instead of our old ways of throwing bodies at problems and opportunities, and we have to be nimbler and more adaptable.*

While implementing strategic objectives, René and his colleagues have learned that changing the way a successful but conservative business operates is more complicated than it looks. Their values, ways of seeing, and decision-making methods needed to change because what worked before cannot be relied on going forward. They elected to challenge the whole bank to transform itself while also provoking themselves and each other, relying on two intertwined processes.

First, they have acknowledged that the bank's strategic goals contradicted each other, creating competing commitments that generated tension and conflict. Fundamental issues are now more apparent but harder to resolve because the leaders hold different views. They ask themselves how they can move forward more experimentally and with greater velocity while honoring the need for predictability and stability. They want the baby and the bathwater.

They wish to be purpose-driven stewards of responsible banking while also being innovation-centric, introducing technology-driven products and services, and investing to future-proof the business. The findings of Accenture's (2021) research support their approach, showing that the best-performing banks combine the most intensive, purpose-driven strategies with higher levels of digital maturity.

Second, René, Kevin, and Rich have needed to clarify how to lead the bank collectively while looking after their functional responsibilities. This means working closely together, learning to manage, respect, and counteract each other's strengths and defaults, and finding a productive means to deal with their differences. They all agree on the long-term vision for the bank, but at times they disagree on the tactics to use, the pace of change, and the degree to which people can withstand the intensity and disturbance of the transformation. For example, the trio see how being more nimble, agile, and tolerant of risk, pulls against the deeply felt need for caution and prudence, which were essential to the bank's past success and will need to be part of its future. But they each have a different view on the best balance.

They will not allow M&T to become just another bank because they and their customers highly value the care and connection built over many years. As a result, there is a tacit agreement that they will each take on the role of brakeman, regulating the speed and impact of change. This was evident when they had agreed on a new senior hire, but the employment documents were still sitting unattended on one of their desks four weeks later. On the surface, the delay appeared legitimate, but closer examination suggested that one of them had reservations about the decision.

11.3 Introduce new blood

Between 2018 and 2020, René and his colleagues appointed several outsiders to critical roles, including the Chief Information Officer (CIO). The questions they asked during the search surfaced the cultural values they needed to confront because, like most significant appointments to date, each of the trio had been promoted internally. They could see the value of continuing with this tradition but also wanted to explore the alternative, seeking a wider perspective by introducing new ideas that challenged the old ways, and giving themselves an opportunity to learn from others. They also wanted to embed provocation deep within the bank's operations because that was where it was required. They needed to signal that certain things would be different from now on. As Kevin said, "We spun the chair around and went outside the bank."

Inevitably, there was internal opposition to this approach, especially among those overlooked for promotion. There is always a risk in inserting a "foreign body" into a high functioning but well-established system. As with a virus, systemic antibodies can be activated to excise and block what is alien. Some have described M&T as being unsafe to outsiders. Longstanding employees know where they stand and have learned to accept and work within the hierarchical, compliant culture. They are wary when outsiders come in and tell them how it should be. But René and his senior colleagues wanted them to be exposed to alternative methods and models.

Criticism has come from those who worried that the rapid injection of technology-based banking solutions will alienate traditional customers and from those concerned that the substantial investments in technology have resulted in an increase in the bank's operating expenses and a reduction in profitability. Because it is a low-margin business, bankers are highly susceptible to fluctuations in their balance sheets and shareholder pressure. It is difficult to persuade people that short-term losses are worthwhile because of potential long-term gains. The tension has disturbed many in the bank, but René has held his staff to the path they have embarked upon despite the risks involved, reassuring them as best he can.

Having been steeped in conservative banking traditions, René, Kevin, and Rich viscerally understood risk, stability, caution, and customer safety. Nevertheless, they remain determined that the bank be exposed to risk-taking rather than avoidance, experimentation as well as tradition, and acting with velocity instead of always being inhibited by caution.

Kevin recalls that one of the reasons behind the appointment of Mike Wisler to the new role of CIO was to "bring in the capacity to operate at scale," although he confesses that he didn't fully understand what this meant at the time. For executives used to having everything at their fingertips, hiring something they didn't fully understand was a contentious move. For some time, each hiring decision felt like a provocative test. How much uncertainty and disturbance could they each withstand until the experiment with the new DNA yielded results and the oscillations flattened out? But they choose the new CIO to be the necessary shock, to use technology as a stimulant and enabler of change, and to help M&T Bank catch up.

The recruitment pathway was provocative in two ways. First, it broke tradition and the unspoken cultural contract. There was resentment among those overlooked, a loss of promise and possibility, and a consequent diminution in loyalty, previously unquestioned.

Secondly, the three senior leaders also had to trust their judgment, manage their anxiety, and give the new people enough autonomy to do the very things that the business needed instead of doing the things the company was comfortable with. Five years down the track, they are increasingly confident that this new way is proving itself and that they, as individuals and as an executive trio, have learned and improved, benefiting from the multiplier effect of a challenge that took them and the business to the very the edge of what they could tolerate.

As the newcomers have built credibility, they have been quickly integrated into the business. Mike Wisler, for example, has been instrumental in reinforcing M&T's deep connections with the community in Buffalo by actively promoting the bank's new technology hub. He has insisted that software development and coding is done in-house instead of being outsourced, resulting in an expansion of local recruitment. In this way, he is delivering something new while remaining true to an ethos held dear by long-term employees, winning potential naysayers over as a result.

11.4 Using old methods for new purposes: Data as provocation

Gathering customer feedback is a long-established practice in banking, but M&T, like many other banks, had not used big-data methods to analyze their feedback until recently. One of M&T's recent new hires, Aarthi Murali, Head of Customer Experience, found gaps in customer experience data, and set about rectifying them. Aarthi's application of new methods exposed several suboptimal patterns that undermined M&T's purpose as a customer-oriented bank. When she presented her findings to the Executive Leadership Team (ELT), their reactions revealed how good data can provoke precisely where it is needed, highlighting how it is possible to use data methods to challenge conventional thinking.

The ELT listened to the customer stories Aarthi told to illustrate her findings. They were shocked and initially did not believe what she was telling them, preferring to think she was being selective in the examples used. The data and stories vexed the whole team. They did not recognize their own organization, and their reactions and questions revealed a certain reality that now could not be ignored.

Aarthi recounted the story of a customer who was informed he would have to pay a $30 penalty because he had overdrawn his checking account even though there were significant funds in another account. His protests were met with intransigence rather than empathy. The next day he withdrew all his funds and opened an account across the road at a different bank. Aarthi then revealed that the bank he had joined was M&T.

She used the example of another bank's poor behavior to get the executives' attention, allowing them to think that it was their own business that had treated a customer so poorly. By using a counterfactual, she built an expectation that they had a severe problem, and created pressure that something should, and could, be done about it. As René, who was part of the meeting, put it,

> *There was a chance for us to make this crazy difference right in those moments that matter to customers. We all fell off our chairs in relief it wasn't us. But we could see how what we had always assumed was working well, no longer was.*

René and his colleagues had a profound experience in these meetings. New data revealed how hard-working front-line staff were burdened by the rules and procedures which were too inflexible and outdated.

M&T's core purpose created a paradox. The more successful the company was in realizing it, the more René and his colleagues needed to adapt how their objectives were achieved. He understood that the bank needed to ensure staff were not blamed for what were systemic issues.

Aarthi showed her senior colleagues how new ways of thinking and approaching ongoing problems could help the bank grow and thrive through more sophisticated and scalable methods. The ah-ha moments they experienced as a result of her insights reinforced the critical need for ongoing culture change. René and his colleagues were determined to support new team members like Aarthi, and ensure that they could thrive in the expanding M&T ecosystem.

11.5 Permission and forgiveness

When René had drafted his "state of things" notes in 2016, one of the trends that had troubled him was how hierarchical, deferential, and risk-averse M&T had become. The company had become permission-oriented, with people rarely acting when they were unsure, waiting instead to be told to behave differently. This "play it safe and fit in" culture stifled new ideas. The values that allowed M&T to remain successful (caution, conservativism, and consistency) were starting to undermine its capacity to adapt to changing circumstances. The pond they swam in was low in oxygen, inhibiting growth. M&T needed an infusion of new beliefs about what was possible in order to sustain its long held values.

René, with the support of Kevin and Rich, began to challenge M&T's unwritten rules of permission-seeking, hoping to build a more empowered and self-determining organization. René did this in subtle and often indirect ways. There were no loud campaigns or banners declaring a culture change. Instead, he used a practical and experiential approach, provoking people gradually on the ground, in regular meetings, and during customer interactions. René created a new environment in which they could practice and develop new skills.

An example from the weekly executive team meetings is illustrative. Deviating from Bob Wilmers' insistence that everyone be physically present in Buffalo for this Tuesday meeting, René made virtual attendance an option. But, more importantly, he changed the purpose of the discussion by instituting what became known as Mission Maryland.

Despite success in Buffalo and other markets, M&T was losing ground to competitors in Baltimore. René began to use the Tuesday meetings for strategy and learning discussions where new types of questions would be asked, with pressure placed on participants to expand how they thought and contributed. René informed his colleagues, "We are only going to talk about three things: how we generate ideas, how we nurture these ideas, and what we will do next." The rhythm of the meetings changed. "We were now creating a space for more exploration and there was new pressure," he observed. "People weren't used to it."

The ELT was learning more about transforming their business as they progressed meeting by meeting. A holding environment for challenge had been created. There was steady pressure to engage in different ways, apply new Agile methods of problem-solving, and build new adaptive capacities, including the ability to live with the contradictions generated by the business. Often, the ELT members felt out of their depth, stumbling and far beyond their comfort zone. René, Kevin, and Rich held their ground, though, slowly moving the team toward more robust conversations. They kept the tension between what was known and what was new, between the safe and the uncomfortable.

Tuesday meetings took on a new meaning across the business as capacity was built. One day an ELT member complained that the sessions were only for Mission Maryland and wondered if they could discuss other markets and challenges. René's reply was clear and sent a charge through the group. They were able to raise other issues providing they focused on the three core reasons: ideas, exploration, and actions. They would be pushed and challenged in ways that would help all the participants learn. René wanted his executives to discuss how they developed different practices, but they needed to own the conversation and not seek permission.

Attendees had to turn up ready to work and experiment together, seeing things through however uncomfortable they felt. Eventually, they stopped struggling, reconciling themselves both to their confusion and to their greater freedom. They began to engage, taking ownership of the workshopped issues. Most members saw that they had been caught up in the old permission-seeking behavior, just as was the case with the front-line staff. Work still remained to be done across the wider organization, but most senior officers had shifted from the old ways and begun to take on more responsibility, becoming more tolerant of risk and uncertainty.

M&T's Tuesday meetings became an incubator into which, René, Kevin, and Rich introduced new behaviors and attitudes, inviting their colleagues to play and experiment. They didn't demand that the team buy the new ways, only that they try them out in this provisional space. Their hope was that the perturbations might continue long after their colleagues exited the ELT meetings.

René's reconfiguration of the weekly meeting illustrates how provocation comes in a variety of forms. The provocation was gentle but firm, regular but not constant, new but incorporating the known, and flexible but based on the three core reasons. He built a specific, time-bound holding environment for building new cultural practices. The meeting was no longer solely René's, but it belonged to all members of the twenty-person ELT. Finally, the nexus between risk-taking and permission seeking is at least partially severed.

11.6 Flirt with danger

Provocative change requires a delicate balance between taking what works for you into the future and discarding or modifying that which is no longer helpful. The holding on and releasing process is always contested and frequently a source of significant conflict. We have seen already how dangerous it was for the three leaders to suggest to their colleagues that they relinquish some of their previous ideals to accommodate the integration of external talent. A critical task for leaders is to learn to have these difficult conversations while looking after the relationships and the business. René and his colleagues have been attempting to navigate the competing pressures and needs that are inevitable if they are to remain vibrant and successful.

But learning these capacities, like the conversations themselves, are fraught with danger. Executives like to think they can do it all, that they have what it takes. Acknowledging that they don't know how to do something is difficult in a competitive commercial environment, mainly because their personal shortcomings become more apparent over time in front of colleagues.

M&T Bank's senior leaders realized that they had to learn to engage with each other in different and more robust ways. They each needed to learn new skills and ways of thinking, but they had to do so collectively. This was a very unsettling idea to each of them, knowing that any shortcomings or errors would be seen and felt by their colleagues. But, determined to grow and learn, they decided to engage an executive coach and leadership advisor to assist them.

Jeff Lawrence, a leadership consultant, already had a relationship with the bank, as well as a reputation for being willing to prod executives and hold them to their goals. His presence is a provocative intervention into this system designed to shift unproductive behavior patterns and develop a greater tolerance for conflict and disturbance both at a personal and an organizational level. They also asked Jeff to help them naviagate the banks contradictions and keep them accountable, whenever they drift away from a commitment.

René, Kevin, and Rich all went to Jeff to "flirt with danger." Earlier experiences confirmed that he could show how their behaviors and attitudes, developed over many years, undermined their effectiveness. René and his colleagues felt sure that Jeff would help them challenge each other, identify their limitations, and apply their learning more widely. They wanted to be challenged and learn to thrive among the tensions and uncertainties the bank faced.

11.7 Direct challenge

An example illustrates René's willingness to be provoked. A junior executive left a conversation with him, thinking he had an agreement but not realizing how it would affect one of Kevin's initiatives. Jeff reminded René that when he agrees with something, his staff take it to mean that they are authorized to act. But they may not see the whole picture. René was initially taken aback by Jeff's observation. However, he has learned to step back and take stock, using a new self-steadying phrase, "I'm working on myself." Jeff notes that René, as a relatively new CEO, forgot that his actions, even simple conversations, became significant events for subordinates, and, sometimes, he overlooked the potential downstream consequences of his utterances. As disturbing as they were, Jeff's insights showed René, as they did his colleagues, the ways their actions were sometimes strategies for avoiding the contradictions that existed and hindered their change goals.

René also reports that after several years of coaching, as day-to-day work captures him, he hears Jeff's words in his mind. For example, Jeff has repeatedly said, "there is no such thing as a dysfunctional system, just one that is perfectly aligned to get the current outcomes." Now, when caught in a familiar but unhelpful pattern of exchange with a colleague, René tries to behave differently—he uses this aphorism to get above problems and re-enter the fray with a different response.

Such moment-by-moment provocations led these senior bankers to improve their change efforts. René now says to others that "every time somebody says something to me about my actions, I will take it on the chin, I will go first because I am working on myself. And I invite you to come along." He uses the power of humility, an important element in helping others accept the personal impact of change. As a coach, Jeff holds René and his two colleagues to something more demanding, more revealing than usual. The challenge to these three executives mirrors the challenges the bank faces in keeping to its mission.

Strikingly, the trio keeps coming back for more—to test the limits of their thinking and capacity. And then, they go back into the fast-moving bank environment to see how far they can go before the constraints of that system push back and restore equilibrium. They reflect, learn, and then apply what Kevin calls the 1% rule—small changes that will compound and pay dividends tomorrow. He said, "Instead of looking for the big bang and trying to change things 20 degrees, let us find twenty, one-degree moves."

11.8 Testing relationships

Jeff's work has helped the executives recognize their strengths, shortcomings, and defaults. They now understand the cyclical nature of their interactions, where each member plays a different role at any point in time. Three notable roles appear—that of the optimist who does not or cannot see the barriers to change and wants to thrust forward; a realist who sees things as they are and is concerned about the pace and impact of change; and the enabler, who works hard to build consensus and enlist people. Each man can play any one of these roles, even though they each have a favorite (a default).

The ferment generated by the interaction of the three roles provides sufficient impetus to progress change. Sometimes forward, sometimes not; sometimes checking for "landmines" that might destroy something valuable and other times constructing a bridge, into something new, by experimenting and building prototypes. But the trio reflects and highlights what is playing out across this growing business. They are collectively creating just enough pressure to test the bank's old DNA and enough reassurance that they will consider staff's needs for familiarity and certainty. Jeff has taught them to accommodate the polarities that exist. For example, they no longer rush to reassure people the minute there is some criticism or concern. Instead, they hold steady and at times continue to challenge even more.

The dynamic between René, Kevin, and Rich reflects a healthy and flexible relationship built on trust, respect, and personal insight gained through shared experience and coaching. With increasing awareness and courage, they can choose to test or calm each other and their colleagues. With growing confidence, they can toggle between invoking fear-inducing momentum or providing familiar and reassuring comfort; they have learned more surely when to confront and when to support. Together they are creating a self-regulating provocation ecosystem that drip feeds just enough stimulus and pressure for the organization to learn, try things out and embed new practices without blowing up the old ways, which are at the heart of who they are—a conservative, prudent bank. Their interactions and preferences have benefits that could not be provided by any one of them alone.

As their coach, Jeff recognizes the fluid dynamic and the contradictions that need managing. He acknowledges how attached they are to their defaults and, therefore, has chosen an incrementally challenging approach, encouraging them to value and play with their differences. For example, Jeff has asked them to push harder for the planned changes while also cautioning about taking too many risks. The daily balance of comfort and discomfort the three leaders are prepared to experience, even seek out, is integral to their growing provocative capacity. Increasingly all three will surprise each other by taking up a less comfortable role.

11.9 Indirect challenge

Jeff has also worked with the three leaders on their strategy execution to break away from their traditional roles and try new and contentious approaches. He pushes them to "mix it up" by using both soft and firm techniques, standard methods together with new ones. For example, he proposed that Kevin be less direct when trying to solve a criticism that the regulator made about record keeping and documentation shortcomings in the banking practice. Rather than chastising the officer in charge ("George") or counseling him to ensure that the requisite processes were in place, Kevin experimented with a bank-wide working group to review the problem, applying the recently implemented Agile methodology.

Kevin framed the project as an opportunity to learn the method rather than a problem-solving exercise and encouraged George's team to contribute without being held responsible or blamed. He provoked indirectly because the Agile methodology required the very thing that had been lacking—paying disciplined attention to detail and record-keeping. The process forced them to produce deliverables on a regimented schedule and create a public body of best practice methods without confronting George. Instead, George had to accept the working group's findings or acknowledge that he didn't understand the requirements and needed help. The challenge to George and his team was indirect. New data, evidence of the advantages of accurate records, was made available, making future action more likely because it became impossible to refute the benefits. The evidence pressured the defective practices rather than the individuals involved (those some wanted to blame).

Kevin changed his behavior by trying this different approach and he learned that spreading responsibility and engaging many viewpoints offered a model that he could use elsewhere. Jeff helped him learn that he didn't have to push and insist, which had in the past been a favored tactic.

These examples show how Jeff has helped the executives to progressively change their behavior and meet the bank's challenges. Deliberate, often almost invisible, changes over time inexorably moved the bank so that it not only kept pace with the changing world it serves but is increasingly becoming fit for its purpose. Jeff's provocation has also gradually weened these accomplished leaders off their past and assisted them to feel more certain about navigating M&T's future.

11.10 50 Shades of provocation

M&T Bank offers five critical lessons in the use of provocation.

First, the role unexpected, disturbing events, in this case, death and loss, can play in creating conditions conducive to change. The grief and confusion caused by the deaths of the senior leaders pushed René and his colleagues (and all of M&T) into taking stock. Losing an iconic figure left a big hole and exposed the patterns of dependency that had grown, as well how M&T's culture needed reinvigorating.

Second, without one or two individuals who are willing to stand up and identify what needs changing, even the dramatic discontinuity caused by the death of a CEO won't be enough to catalyze necessary change. The challenge for René and his colleagues was how to productively provoke the bank just at the edge of what it could take, at a time when, at least initially, what was required was reassurance and stability. They did this by reaffirming the legacy of Bob Wilmers, and the values that had made M&T so successful, but they spoke of how these values needed enriching so that the business could thrive in a changed environment. By adding to what existed rather than denying it, they established a basis to expand out and challenge critical aspects of the business.

Third, they nudged, prodded, and confronted their people and M&T's operating models but only at a pace and intensity that the conservative, and initially shell shocked, business could withstand. The 1% change principle was part of their DNA. They used it repeatedly and in many different parts of the company—from recruitment to record-keeping—recognizing it was better to have multiple small changes that, like a good bank deposit, would lead to compound growth. Provocation will not be effective if the intensity does not match the system's learning capacity during the disturbance. Therefore, in more cautious environments, or where the issues are less ripe, a strategy of small, incremental galvanizing moves can create significant momentum. As Kevin said, "We only turned the dial by one degree on each occasion, but three years later, that modest move has taken us in a completely different direction."

Fourth, René, Kevin, and Rich, together with their critical new hires, stimulated the business with a wide variety of interventions—from more extensive, systemic actions such as those used in introducing new technologies or analytic approaches, to those that targeted very particular operational elements of the bank, such as gathering customer experience data. In addition, they provoked by challenging their meeting practice, record keeping, and use of new talent, unsettling longstanding beliefs and attitudes.

Finally, M&T Bank, under its new leadership, has danced close to the edge of its adaptive capacity because René has made what is possibly the most provocative request to his staff—to live and work in the middle of a set of competing pressures and commitments. He has asked them to accept greater uncertainty, risk, and experimentation while also asking them to continue to be stable and prudent risk managers.

By using a wide range of novel and confronting approaches, gentle and incremental steps, together with accepting the tensions of contradictory approaches, René and his team have created "Fifty Shades of Disturbance." M&T Bank is building the provocative capacity to be more flexible, change-oriented, and to capture the productive energy from introducing variations in approaches and capability. The transformation of M&T Bank and its people is not finished. While pleased with the progress, the three senior protagonists are clear they have a long way to go. They remain a group of colleagues who are "working on themselves as well as on the business."

Note

1 This chapter is based on our interviews with René Jones (Chair and CEO, M&T Bank), Kevin Pearson (Vice-Chairman, M&T Bank), and Jeff Lawrence (Organizational Agility Advisors).

Reference

Accenture (2021). *Purpose: Driving Powerful Transformation for Banks*, Report 5 May 2021. https://www.accenture.com/us-en/insights/banking/purpose-driven-banking-powerful-digital-transformation. Retrieved 1 August 2021.

12 CONFOUNDING EXPECTATIONS—HOW A PUBLIC SECTOR BUSINESS BEHAVED LIKE A START-UP

The situation needed us to foster innovation, but I understood it would mean challenging current thinking and tradition.

Dr. David Gruen, Australian Statistician during interview

12.1 Introduction

Innovation and change can come from unexpected places and people, often in response to unforeseen events and opportunities. This truism is evident from studying nature, and in successful companies. Evolutionary biologists have shown that it is possible to speed up change in communities of animals by creating an artificial shock. For example, in their book *Perspective*, Andrew Hendry and Michael Kinnison examine unusual events punctuating the typical evolutionary trajectory, demonstrating that a species, such as the guppies they studied, does not always rely on longstanding processes to evolve. Random events or shocks are the sources of adaptation. A sudden change in the environmental conditions can lead to a rapid transformation, changing fundamental features. By stripping away certain disabling conditions, it is possible to activate more enabling characteristics.

Businesses around the world have had to make rapid adjustments to the shock of the Covid-19 pandemic. According to a 2021 McKinsey research paper, 75% of businesses believe the crisis could create opportunity for innovation and growth. But only a quarter reported that capturing new growth was a priority. Most businesses hunkered down, protecting their core business. The gap between believing in opportunity and seizing it is wide. Yet this global shock—characterized by uncertainty and dislocation—is the kind of disturbance from which new ways of operating can emerge. This unexpected event is a provocation on a wide scale, causing the barriers that once took years to overcome to become easier to surmount, and, in some cases, destroying them entirely.

In community and organizational life, however, unpredictable events cannot be relied on to provoke change. Adaptation requires leadership to initiate relevant change or to harness the energy of an exogenous shock, such as a sudden increase in oil prices, a bank collapse, or a pandemic. The questions organizations around the world need to address during periods of shock are: How do we create the conditions that strip out old habits and practices that will hold us back during change? And how do we innovate? These are provocative questions at the heart of adaptation,

DOI: 10.4324/9781003321200-17

prompting us to consider what to conserve, what to discard, what to create, what to adopt. For the public sector, this is also confronting, demanding a reassessment of procedure, transparency, and risk.

Yet, we have seen dramatic examples of innovation in services provided by governments as they have responded to Covid-19. This chapter examines one example, that of the Australian Bureau of Statistics (ABS), and how it shook off the damaging experience following the 2016 E-Census and confounded expectations. This is a story of the resurrection of reputation and self-belief, illustrating how a small, conservative, civil service agency—a guppy in a large pond—responded to changes in the surrounding environment, using the conditions created by an external crisis to strip away its well-rehearsed routines and procedures and transform itself, providing essential information at a crucial time to the Australian government and public. It outlines how, for a short period, a rule-based, risk-averse bureaucracy behaved like a start-up.

Like Bob Dylan who once declared that his job was to confound expectations, the ABS did so by translating creative ideas into practical action and surprising their users in the process. Also notable were the unexpected attitudes and actions of Dr. David Gruen, the new Australian Statistician, who provoked the organization to act differently.

12.2 You can learn from experience

David Gruen[1] has been thinking about how to respond to societal shocks for over thirty years. He is an eminent economist who has worked in various public sector roles, most recently as the Australian Statistician and head of the ABS, succeeding David Kalisch, who had begun the culture change journey. David Gruen remembers feeling unsettled in 2008 as a senior executive in the Australian Treasury when the financial crisis exploded, impacting economies around the world. He and his colleagues were not unprepared as they had planned for different scenarios in anticipation of such an unpredictable challenge. However, David was frustrated that they didn't have good quality current data to inform critical decisions. He remembers how quickly they moved, making decisions that at the time were enormous in scale and impact. In some ways, they were sailing blind, relying on their deep expertise and the collective intelligence of Treasury employees at the time.

When the first signs of the coronavirus pandemic appeared in early 2020, David "had the feeling that something big was coming and we would need good quality data, quickly." Now on the other side of the data production equation, he knew what his public sector colleagues would require. David was determined to create the conditions to foster this but understood it would mean overturning decades of statistical practice and tradition at the ABS.

The ABS prided itself on its professionalism, accuracy, thoroughness, and predictability. Yet, it also was known for its insularity, disconnection from stakeholders, and protectiveness regarding both its expertise and practices. They built their reputation on surveys with high design integrity, but these took a long time to implement and distribute results. But in recent years, the ABS had suffered not only from the fallout from the problems with the 2016 Census but from reduced budgets, which had limited its capacity to keep up with technological advances. Morale and self-belief had dropped in the face of public criticism.

Under the previous CEO, the business had embarked on a transformation process, updating, and integrating its systems. This new infrastructure created sophisticated statistical automation, which reduced labor-intensive manual tasks, brought together various datasets, and enabled new statistical products. These included the quick delivery of new survey instruments and outputs and the ability to rapidly get from the field to publication. It provided the Bureau with an enhanced technical capability to respond to future challenges.

12.3 Build it, and they will come

On February 28th, 2020, David Gruen met with several of his colleagues. News of the spread of Covid-19 from Wuhan to Italy and beyond was beginning to concern Australian authorities. Given his prior experience, David believed his organization could provide much-needed data but would have to reconfigure how they did business. David told his staff:

> *We need to respond quickly, flexibly, and be less concerned about quality. What is important is gathering data that will be useful to the government, our colleagues in other agencies, and the public at large. What can we do?*

His question was simple but provocative because it targeted several assumptions about how the ABS did business: slowly, carefully, and to the highest standards. It led to a series of rapid experiments in gathering and disseminating data, turning decades of practice on their head. The ability to provide real-time data transformed the public perception of the ABS. Having been referred to as "reckless and incompetent" in the past, it was now being lauded as "our secret weapon."

What now mattered was the degree to which the ABS would allow past practices and professional values to hinder novel responses—because new was what was required. David did not want his public sector colleagues to base critical decisions on old data when the circumstances were changing so rapidly that yesterday's information was already outdated. Even though no one had asked for it, David knew that what was needed was immediate information that was updated regularly and could be adjusted as new needs emerged. This form of data would require speed, agility, exceptional design work, and an acceptance that traditional design and sampling parameters could not be met. Most labor force surveys,[2] for example, require face-to-face interviews and follow up, but Covid-19 restrictions made this form of collection impossible. Other less accurate methods would have to do, with ABS staff sacrificing their professional standards.

In the wake of the problems with the eCensus, there was latent energy within the organization. People were ready to strip away the shackles of the past and show the world what the ABS was capable of. No one outside the Bureau doubted their expertise, but many had doubted its ability to pivot, to take risks and innovate during heightened uncertainty. The organization, despite any misgivings, was about to display its adaptive capacity and ability to respond to uncertainty and provocative conditions.

At that first meeting, several executives and specialist officers surprised their boss and continued to do so throughout the following months. It was as if the unprecedented circumstances combined with the clarity of David's initial question about what the ABS could do unleashed a wave of creativity that had been lacking given the organization's traditionally risk-averse culture.

12.4 Let's do it: Ready, fire, aim

While there was clarity regarding what was required, there was uncertainty about how people would respond. Innovation and novelty were not only permitted, but they were actively encouraged. The old systems were too slow and labor-intensive for current needs. The ABS had to become more agile, risk-tolerant, and experimental, acting, learning, and iterating even as they delivered what their stakeholders required. As with tech companies like Google, they had to use a ready, fire, aim philosophy in their approach, introducing new features, while constantly testing and refining them until they had a viable service.

The ABS had to treat its response as an alive entity, regularly learning, growing, and adapting to feedback from its environment. This stood in contrast to its usual approach, which involved a lengthy design and testing process, sophisticated data collection, and a finished product that was intended to remain in place. The pandemic circumstances provoked David and his colleagues to think differently about how the ABS delivered its services.

When one executive tentatively proposed running a small business survey David immediately told them to proceed. The business team then designed the survey, collected data by telephone, and published the results, all within three weeks. The ABS had never done anything like this before, but they quickly iterated the process, rerunning the survey with some minor tweaks. David commented, "I didn't know if we could do it, but we got an incredibly positive reaction, and so we continued."

"We learned some things quickly," David explained. "For example, by doing telephone interviews instead of face-to-face, we learned how people responded to our questions and so we adjusted the sampling and tolerated reduced accuracy." They gave up accuracy in favor of speed. "We now had the infrastructure for fixing up surveys that weren't accurate and smart people who loved to do so." They used technology and people but in novel ways. The ABS was challenging itself and rising to the provocative occasion. This initiative went way beyond what people expected of them. The surprise nature of the new offering created an energy especially within the organization but also alerted data users that more was possible. An old barrier has been, at least temporarily, breached.

12.5 We'd like some of that!

A hallmark of innovation, provoked by opportunity and circumstance, is the replication effect. A successful and novel experiment becomes what is sometimes called a "strange attractor."[3] That is where a new event unsettles existing practice and triggers a cascade where novelty flourishes. A strange attractor informs and alters what others do, drawing them in. At the ABS, the household survey team saw what had been achieved by the business team and told David that they would like to do something similar, running new household surveys.[4] This team repurposed an existing platform and immediately provided a snapshot of changing economic and social situations for Australian households and how they were responding to the pandemic. The new rapid survey added and modified questions as different government agencies clamored for information, including questions about mental wellbeing and use of public transport. All the invaluable insights were immediately made available.

David described what unfolded between March and June 2020 as an experimental sprint driving the ABS to change. They started small, trying a new survey every few weeks, and modifying the next iteration according to the responses and the needs. As the Australian government raced to curb the spread of the new virus, the ABS adjusted its surveys to provide the most relevant data. Small provocations built momentum in a pattern of ongoing adaptive tests that helped the business expand its innovation path.

12.6 Maximizing agility, minimizing constraint

Public sector organizations are, legitimately, governed by procedural and financial rules, all designed to ensure probity and transparency. But such practices are intended for stable times when routines are both possible and required. However, in 2020, the ABS found themselves in unprecedented times, and the governing rules, including those around budgets, were a significant restraint, such as when a team leader would request funding to a new survey. Several executives raised questions about the budget and whether the ABS should ask for additional funds. David's view was that they should not, given the time it would take, and the bureaucratic steps involved. Instead, they should simply press ahead, delivering what was required. David argued that the costs were manageable and that the ABS could continue to be responsive. In his head, he was having a conversation with the Finance Minister, informing him, "I'm sorry, I've run over my budget by $1 million. Here's what I've produced. What do you think?"

The ABS believed that its innovative and unexpected stance was quickly proving itself, and so instead of asking permission, they acted. Usually, this is a risky approach for a public agency, but the results spoke for themselves. In June 2020, the ABS went to the government with a funding proposal that effectively argued that if the government was content with what the bureau was doing now, then it needed to provide an appropriate budget for the year ahead. The government, stretching its tolerance of the unusual in these turbulent times, agreed to the proposal. David's instinct to experiment and demonstrate public value had proved itself, and, with the new budget, innovation expanded and became more ambitious, venturing into new areas.

12.7 Iterate and scale

The next phase of the ABS's innovation proved to be the most provocative even though it built on existing technologies. As the business was learning to harness its adaptive capacity it created several novel incubators to prototype new ideas. As Google did with many of its products, the prototypes, David explains, were initially "done on a shoestring, by a bunch of smart kids on computers." What initially took ten hours could now be done in twenty minutes. David was clear that they had the technology and expertise but were trialing new ways on small budgets.

In this way, the ABS took a page out of Google's innovation protocols. They accelerated their innovations by using production systems to scale the operation of new rapid surveys and data analysis, seeking exponential improvement by adopting the 10X approach. A 10X goal forces you to rethink an idea entirely. It pushes you beyond existing models and forces you to reimagine how to address them.

The ABS would allow users to try out, to "taste," their new products and services, learn what they did and did not like about them, then refine them. This was far from the pursuit of perfection that had informed the old ways. Having discovered the public appetite for rapid-fire, useable data, the ABS wanted to provide more complex and challenging information.

Nevertheless, setting such challenging goals is disorienting, and David was aware that some in the ABS were uneasy with what was being asked, especially the implication that some dearly held values, such as precision and certainty, might be compromised. The risks and losses inherent in his innovation pathway were becoming apparent.

12.7.1 Cross-border excursions

The first big idea came unexpectedly when an executive advocated access to the Australian Tax Office's (ATO) enormous employment and wages dataset through the Single Touch Payroll (STP) system.[5] This system provided immediate information on employment and wages. Its data also reflected current conditions, while the ABS's own Labor Force Survey, based on 50,000 interviews per month, was expensive to run and took over five weeks to publish. David gave the go ahead to approach the ATO.

The ABS was able to rapidly organize access to the STP file and it proved to be a masterstroke. Using big-data technologies, a new team began processing and analyzing the employment and wages data, publishing it only seventeen days after the end of each reporting period. David enthusiastically describes this outcome: "It is just extraordinary. It is such a huge thing. That's about connecting with the sources of data that traditionally used to take months to process."

The new data provided insights into the workforce and the impact of the government's stimulus and support package that hitherto was unavailable. The latest results had an immediate effect. Another benefit was to have a significant stakeholder, the ATO, engaged and collaborating in new and productive ways. With David's encouragement, the ABS went into places they hadn't ventured before, using the continually changing external conditions as a prompt, a stimulus, and provocation to their partners to find new ways to co-operate.

Peter Martin, a well-known Australian economics journalist, had been a strong critic of the ABS in the past. But he wrote in a 2021 opinion piece that the ABS made "an inspired decision to obtain and publish the near real-time payroll data." The Bureau was winning friends and influencing people in multiple ways and at a time that mattered.

The changes made were revolutionary for the ABS and those who made use of statistics. The provocation, in this case, was less visible but nonetheless occurred in three ways. First, by providing authorization and ground cover, David created a holding environment for the unusual request made to a sister agency. The ABS had been in discussions with the ATO to get access to this STP data for some time. What was new was that, with the outbreak of Covid-19, there was enormous value in obtaining the STP data immediately, rather than at the end of an extended period of consultation. David explains:

> *What was very new was the speed—the ATO recognized the importance of moving quickly and we got access to the STP data in double-quick time—the first data transfer was at the beginning of April 2020, and transfers have been weekly from the ATO since then.*

Second, the change shifted the relationship between the ABS and the ATO. They were now collaborators and partners. In the past, the ABS relied on the ATO's largesse, but the turmoil of the pandemic required a different response, and old patterns were broken and replaced with something more productive and appropriate.

Third, the ABS took a ready, fire, aim approach, not quite knowing if the application of its considerable expertise to this problem was sufficient. David elaborates:

> *If we didn't have the expertise to solve this problem and moved too quickly, we could have been totally wrong. Users would criticize us if our new approach and the speed of releases resulted in inaccurate data.*

There was virtue in speed but not at the expense of reasonable accuracy. In this way, the ABS pushed itself to the edge of and beyond its past experience and practice, finding a new way to produce critical data sets. The risks created ambiguity at a time when there was enormous uncertainty in the external environment. But David held steady with his quiet but provocative stance, and the launch of the new labor force and wages data was a success.

12.8 Why stop now?

As 2020 unfolded, David maintained pressure on his organization to take every opportunity possible. He wrote letters to the CEOs of all four major banks requesting access to their transaction data, which would provide insights into consumer spending and saving. When they agreed, the ABS was able to process hundreds of millions of transactions, providing another source of up-to-date information. Similarly, they secured agreements with supermarkets to broaden the use of scanner data, while also analyzing electricity consumption from digital smart meters thereby estimating the degree to which people were staying at home.

These ventures took the ABS into unknown territory but allowed it to repurpose its technology and apply statistical expertise to new sources of data. This was trailblazing innovation, making use of existing resources to solve new problems that the ABS had never tackled before. By partnering with banks, businesses, and other public agencies, it was possible to generate millions of datapoints that could be used for the public good. The time was ripe to leverage these opportunities as many companies wanted to be part of Team Australia during the pandemic, with some hopeful of resurrecting their reputations after previous corporate failures.

12.9 Confronting the past

The new ventures weren't all plain sailing. In deploying its existing skills and resources, the ABS confronted a set of longstanding internal constraints and began to tackle them head-on. For example, the retail trade team suggested publishing preliminary data rather than waiting the standard five-to-six weeks. But they were hesitant, concerned that to do so would mean having a smaller sample size (80%), which would make the results less accurate. Despite their reservations, the group were encouraged to release data early.

What they discovered challenged their long-held beliefs, with the preliminary results for retail turnover closely aligned with the final results, in effect shortening the time to produce the data by two weeks. If there had been a big difference between the preliminary and final output, the ABS would have been open to the criticism for providing the data too soon and causing confusion. Under David's guidance, though, the retail trade team had tolerated that risk and added value. Again, the ABS had discarded old practices to positive effect, as David explains.

> *As a result, we got nothing but praise for this innovation, and the retail trade team was able to share in that praise. Our users completely understood the revisions we published, and they found the faster publication very useful, especially in the context of huge movements in retail trade and other economic indicators.*

The ABS has continued to release this preliminary data together with an explanation of the sample size and the potential for reduction inaccuracy.

Even the simplest of changes can be provocative, as this example illustrates. David challenged the core beliefs of his professional staff. Even though they were willing, the traditions of precision and accuracy held them back. They needed a push, a nudge, as well as evidence that nothing untoward would happen. Fortunately, the results and subsequent review demonstrated that the perceived risks were not as significant as many believed. Instead, there was further evidence that accuracy could be sacrificed for speed to the benefit of stakeholders and without any reputational loss. Indeed, making the process of statistical compilation more transparent had other benefits. It created a dialogue and relationship with the many invisible users, who were now trusted with an inside perspective.

12.10 Act like a start-up

The changes and innovations that the ABS implemented offer insights into how a public sector agency can act like an innovative start-up. Like the famous cellist Pablo Casals who said better to make a good copy than a bad original, the ABS played from the start-up guidebook, experimenting, testing, and iterating until it was clear what worked. Unlike the businesses reported by McKinsey that hunkered down, the ABS did the opposite. Driven by David Gruen's inquiring mind and sense of possibility, the ABS pivoted rapidly, while protecting its work force and selecting which core activities to maintain.

The ABS adapted in five notable ways:

- Changing the operating model: The ABS realized quickly that it couldn't rely on traditional interview methods, so it used multiple forms of digital engagement, treating the adjustment as a virtue, allowing staff to undertake both routine and novel activity. They used behavioral insights, seeing how people behave in unpredictable ways and how it is necessary to test methods with users before implementing them.
- Providing new offerings: As with the museums that created and streamed digital content to keep their customers engaged, the ABS developed several new streams of survey activity. They developed rapid turnaround surveys based on smaller samples and released preliminary data. The users were very happy.
- Responding to changes in user needs and behavior: The ABS anticipated the needs of government and other users for relevant and constantly updated data. When senior politicians and bureaucrats began to give daily briefings during 2020 and 2021, the information used was often drawn from the ABS's rapid response surveys, enabling the government to keep up-to-date with an emergent and evolving situation. Staying on top of the facts is essential for maintaining calm and confidence during a crisis.
- Forging new relationships: Rather than retreating into "Fortress ABS," the agency became a networker, broker, and collaborator, building relationships with new partners, such as the banks, and revitalizing existing connections,

such as those with supermarkets and the Australian Tax Office. The latter example allowed one of the most innovative statistical products seen in decades to be produced and laid the foundation for ongoing productivity gains and efficiencies, with the new production processes saving significant labor.

- Venturing into competitor spaces: Strictly speaking, as the national statistical agency, the ABS doesn't have competitors. But there are a range of businesses that collate and distribute data that, until recently, the ABS did not or could not access. For instance, in addition to the examples already provided, the ABS reconfigured the way it utilized state government databases of doctor-certified deaths to provide provisional mortality data. Instead of waiting for the annual release of coroners' data, the ABS, yet again, was willing to sacrifice accuracy for speed, thereby reducing publishing lag and uncovering a range of informative new results.

12.11 Sustaining change

The adaptation in the ABS since early 2020 has infused what had been a somewhat bruised organization with renewed vigor and self-belief. David Gruen has played a critical role in mobilizing the organization to respond in so many new ways, but it is equally clear that he hasn't done this on his own. There has been widespread enthusiasm for the collective experiment, for testing the boundaries of what is possible and what needs to remain the same. David has brought fresh eyes to his organization, taking on the twin roles of provocateur and encourager-in-chief. He also acknowledges the legacy of his predecessor David Kalisch, who did the hard yards in beginning culture change.

David doesn't try to make people feel uncomfortable, so his provocation is gentle. Sometimes you don't see it coming. He will ask his staff seemingly innocent questions, such as, "Why don't we do that?" or "Should we try doing it this way?" These questions serve to untie knots in the ABS's adaptive capacity. They invite the exploration of possibility. David shows his people how to build a provocative mindset, taking risks, being nimble, exploring options, and acting counter to the established culture. He has encouraged the power of pull, of the "build it and they will come" approach, freeing his team to experiment and innovate. Provocation often orients people to their current reality and helps them identify what is precious and should be carried forward and what should be discarded. Pushing people into thinking about possibilities is contentious, even when undertaken gently.

The uncertainty generated throughout 2020 and beyond means the ABS had to discover what its users wanted and what mattered to them. This then reshaped behaviors and work patterns at the ABS. What was critical was the way the organization monitored the environment and tried to interpret what it meant for its vital work. The ABS took advantage of the huge need for reliable information and responded, acting like a start-up when it had to. In this way, the bureau staff defined critical problems for consumers of statistics and tried to solve them, making themselves relevant and indispensable.

The ABS has added "some new strings to its bow," in David's words, rather undergoing wholesale organizational transformation. However, in tackling some of the old ways of doing things, especially the proclivity for accuracy and thoroughness, the ABS has revealed that their critical work can be done very differently without "the sky falling in" or extensive sacrifice in terms of performance. To release information quickly brings additional value to users—something that wasn't there before.

The case study described doesn't provide a complete picture of how difficult it has been for the statisticians to change their practices. The very things that made the ABS successful in the past were found to be restricting their responses to user needs during a time of crisis. By confounding expectations, the organization has adapted to new waters like the guppies mentioned earlier, changing how the ABS thinks and acts. David has provoked his organization into deviating from its tried-and-true course, introduced greater variation into how they think and act, and has fostered an experimental mindset that has yielded dividends. Now more staff are willing to try things, demonstrating their adaptive capacity. There should be no going back.

The ABS's challenge now is to sustain the new adaptive capacities and to ensure that others can take on the role of provocateur-in-chief, stirring things up when necessary. There is a need to institutionalize disturbance in the ABS, ensuring that post Covid-19, there continues to be small shocks to prevailing wisdom and procedure. Like Honda, they need to keep "kicking the ladder out." This will help the organization avoid the risks of inertia, staying flexible enough to respond to emerging needs. An evolutionary capacity to constantly test the organizational DNA, to challenge orthodoxies, will ensure that all aspects of the ABS's business model stay relevant and fit for purpose.

To use a computing analogy, the ABS has hacked some of its coding, some of the software relating to mindsets and behaviors. It has started to rebuild the hardware supporting processes and human infrastructure that will help hold the changes in place. But giving both the software- and hardwarededicated attention is demanding and provocative work. It is easy to slip back into legacy systems and thinking. The ABS still has some cultural incompatibility problems, and for the innovations of 2020 to stick and grow, the business will need to continue to challenge itself. For now, though, the ABS has broken the stranglehold that caution, and risk aversion had on its collective psyche, giving itself a new perspective and lease of life.

ABS staff discovered that most of the barriers to change were internal, in people's thinking. "Many of our limits are self-imposed in terms of what can be done or tolerated," David observed. "Long-delayed changes were deployed in weeks versus months or even years." It is possible, then, to test limiting ideas, to experiment and iterate, while still producing reliable and usable statistics—the lifeblood of the organization.

Notes

1 This chapter is based on a combination of our own interviews with Dr. David Gruen, ABS documents, as well as earlier contact we had when David was an executive in the Department of Treasury and the Department of Prime Minister and Cabinet. We also

acknowledge Mr. David Kalisch, the previous Statistican, for his work and contribution. The chapter is also informed by our earlier study of the ABS's expereince during the 2016 E-Census- see Johnstone and Fern 2017.

2 ABS (2021). Households within selected dwellings are interviewed each month for eight months, with one-eighth of the sample being replaced each month. Information is obtained either by trained interviewers or through self-completion online. Generally, the first interview is completed face-to-face and subsequent interviews conducted by phone. All respondents in the sample are also offered the option of completing the survey online. https://www.abs.gov.au/methodologies/labour-force-australia-methodology/mar-2021.

3 Borrowed from mathematics and chaos theory, for example, Ruelle and Takens (1971).

4 ABS (2021).

5 The majority of businesses in Australia now use the Single Touch Payroll (STP) to report salaries, wages, and tax paid to the Australian Tax Office. STP streamlines the payroll reporting process while also ensuring that employers are compliant and paying superannuation and employee tax obligations on time.

References

ABS (2020). *Innovation in a Time of Crisis: The Australian Bureau of Statistics Response to COVID-19.* 29 May 2020. https://www.abs.gov.au/websitedbs/d3310114.nsf/home/innovation+in+a+time+of+crisis. Retrieved 30 April 2021.

ABS (2021). *Household Impacts of COVID-19 Survey.* 16 March 2020. https://www.abs.gov.au/statistics/people/people-and-communities/household-impacts-covid-19-survey/latest-release. Retrieved 7 July 2021.

Casals, P. (2010). Quoted by terry king, page 250. In Piatigorsky, G. (ed) *The Life and Career of the Virtuoso Cellist.* McFarland & Co, Jefferson, NC.

Google (2015). *Creating a Culture of Innovation: Eight Ideas that Work at Google, Google Workspace,* https://workspace.google.com/intl/en_in/learn-more/creating_a_culture_of_innovation.html. Retrieved 10 May 2020.

Hendry, A., & Kinnison, M. (2017). *Perspective: The pace of modern life: Measuring rates of contemporary microevolution.* Evolution: International Journal of Organic Evolution, Wiley Online, 31 May 2017. https://onlinelibrary.wiley.com/doi/abs/10.1111/j.1558-5646.1999.tb04550.x. Retrieved 1 May 2021.

Johnstone, M.A., & Fern, M. (2017). *Holding on and Letting Go – An Australian Story of Organisational Learning in the Bureau of Statistics.* Unpublished Working Paper, Vantage Point Consulting, Canberra, Australia.

Martin, P. (2021). *How the ABS Came Our Secret Weapon.* Peter Martin Economics, Online Newsletter, 10 March 2021. https://www.petermartin.com.au/2021/03/you-cant-fix-economy-if-you-cant-see-it.html. Retrieved 10 April 2021.

McKinsey (2020). *Innovation in a Crisis: Why It Is More Critical Than Ever.* Research Paper, McKinsey & Company, 17 June 2020. https://www.mckinsey.com/business-functions/strategy-and-corporate-finance/our-insights/innovation-in-a-crisis-why-it-is-more-critical-than-ever. Retrieved 18 May 2021.

Ruelle, D., & Takens, F. (1971). On the nature of turbulence. *Communications in Mathematical Physics, 20*(3), pp. 167–192. Open Access. https://projecteuclid.org/journals/communications-in-mathematical-physics/volume-20/issue-3/On-the-nature-of-turbulence/cmp/1103857186.full. Retrieved 11 September 2021.

13 ORCHESTRATING CONFLICT: LARGE-SCALE REFORM

Leadership is the activity of getting people to open their eyes to the reality they are a part of ... and is adaptive when it allows a group to respond to changing conditions and conflicts. And conflicts—if handled appropriately—are resources for sensing and addressing the underlying problems in a group.

Alma Blount, The Art of Teaching Leadership

13.1 Provocation and conflict

Conflict, by its nature, disturbs those involved when there is a threat to fundamental values and no clear path to resolution. Conflict is uncomfortable. People and groups naturally prefer to keep the expression of their differences in check to prevent escalation and the fear of unmanageable consequences. But without an opportunity to focus on the problem and how you solve it, tensions rise, risking either avoidance of the crisis or unskilled confrontation. The point at which people face either of these reactions indicates the potential for a provocative intervention. Such tensions are also usually an expression of an underlying dynamic that helps keep the system in balance.

You can observe these patterns in personal and small-scale conflicts. For example, it is easier to see the shape of disagreement and the leverage points for resolution within a team or a single organization. On a larger scale, however, the complexity of social and environmental issues makes it harder to see that the same rules apply. Several principles enable us to see beyond the apparent chaos:

- Adaptive problems require the status quo to be challenged. As such, they are inherently conflictual;
- Different groups have competing values, loyalties, traditions, identities, and needs. Inevitably, they have diverse ideas about how to solve problems;
- Once equilibrium is disturbed by conflict, it becomes clear not only that deep intervention is required but where the key leverage points are; and
- Intervention in any system changes and disturbs the existing distribution of critical resources, impacting varying degrees on power, control, autonomy, access, and recognition. This leads those affected to worry about what matters most to them and consider what they might lose. This is where the real work of adaptation begins.

DOI: 10.4324/9781003321200-18

To this end, the contentious issues of the conservation and distribution of limited water resources show how the tasks of adaptation remain constant, despite apparently unmanageable complexity. Worldwide, policy conflict and protest have centered on the use of natural resources and environmental management. In Żurawlów, Poland, for example, farmers have occupied land in protest against hydraulic fracking. Meanwhile, dissent has flared up over water rights in the Nile basin and along the Mekong River. In the United States, on the other hand, there have been a series of demonstrations regarding wastewater discharges into rivers. History is rich with examples of such conflicts that have escalated and become truly damaging.

No matter the size and complexity of the system under consideration, people in their subgroups or factions will have to alter their expectations when change occurs. To ensure their needs are meet, they will begin to exert pressure, and as they do, previously hidden tensions become visible. As pressure is applied, the conflict then emerges. As a leader, your role is to harness this energy, disturb the system, and orient participants to their work.

The task that follows, at all levels of action, has several objectives:

- Understand the nature of the conflict;
- Help the players describe and name the truth they face, acknowledging their different perspectives;
- Create conditions where long-term work, negotiations, and refashioning of behavior can occur;
- Help those affected recognize and confront self-interest; and
- Assist people to use any learning or insight that supports the implementation of change.

Recent and ongoing water reform in Australia illustrates how provocative policy and legislation can be deployed to confront a slow burning, wicked problem. In this case, the government created a structure to hold tensions and conflicts so that long-established practices could shift toward more equitable and sustainable water usage.

When governments intervene, they usually do so because there is some political, economic, or social imperative to act. Indeed, transformational public policy is often introduced in response to a crisis, an opportunity, or signals that the market, the broader context, has become unbalanced. Water policy in Australia is one such case.

Overuse of riverine resources and conflict between agricultural use and environmental demands and between different rural sectors led policymakers to act. The system was out of balance. Tensions were increasing, disputes were escalating, and only the Federal Government had the power to intervene. Reform harnessed the inevitable conflict and created processes to manage the implications of its impact.

The example of water reform highlights three aspects of provocative action on a large, national scale:

interests rather than help the system learn, adapt, and grow. Governments intervene when a sector needs help to recalibrate, to be pushed into a more virtuous, self-regulating cycle.

This case study helps us understand how system-wide change will be disturbing even when carefully crafted and well-implemented.

13.3 Whole system disruption in Australia

The eastern half of the ancient, fragile, and drought-prone Australian continent is kept alive by several great river catchments notably the Murray, the Darling, and the Murrumbidgee. Until recently, the established water use system enabled landowners along the rivers to expand their properties, drawing more water from the increasingly distressed waterways.

David Parker is the former Deputy Secretary of the Department of Environment and Water, responsible for water reform. He explained, "You run up against a collapse situation where there is a constraint, which is poorly conceived or understood. More and more land was developed, past the point of the ability of the river to deliver."

Policy experiments were crafted, over many years, in response to water scarcity, environmental degradation, and the unregulated use of a public good. The reforms redrafted water management laws, redefined water rights, and created new government institutions and a market that is admired and loathed in equal measure. The Federal Government established a national *Water Act 2007*, a National Water Commission (2004–2014), and the Murray-Darling Basin Implementation Plan of 2012.

These instruments provided regulatory and advisory mechanisms that enabled the government to divert water for environmental purposes and develop new water markets. They changed the management of the river systems, the fluvial agricultural landscape, and the political relationships between the states, the Federal Government, and a range of rural lobby groups. Alongside these technical attempts to mediate the problem, the new policy confronted longstanding traditions and expectations, creating a widespread disturbance, which continues to this day.

13.4 Describe the truth, change the basic rules

Like other significant transformations, water policy has pushed a wide range of players to change their habits, routines, and beliefs. The blueprint broke open well-established agricultural and commercial practices that were no longer sustainable or in the national interest. The biggest shift came from disputing the assumption that water usage was an individual right. "Rather than people being allowed to irrigate whatever land they had," David summarized, "you are allocated water that you could use, sell, and buy. Over time, water was turned into an economic input. The policy created a new commodity and market."

In the first 100 years of the Australian colony, land and water rights were inseparable, based on the old English riparian doctrine, which gave landowners the entitlement to use water on their land. In 2004, land ownership and water rights were separated to improve water distribution efficiency and address what until recently had an unthinkable idea: that farmers should not have an automatic right to take water and use it as they wished.

The conflict and struggles between different groups that followed water reforms remind us of the origins of the word rivalry. This powerful noun, which the Cambridge Online Dictionary defines as "a competition for the same objective or superiority in the same field," has its origins in the Latin word *rivus*, meaning stream or river, with the root meaning of "to run or flow." In both Latin and French, *rivulis* means "one who uses the same stream" or "one on the opposite side of the stream." These etymological sources have influenced economic thinking where both goods and producers of goods can be rivalrous. For example, water is seen as rivalrous if its consumption by one farmer limits the consumption by another.

As in the case of water reform, public policy will always be contentious if it questions individual rights, especially if these rights have been in place for decades and they conflict with the public good. In this sense, the reforms became a tipping point for many people, for access to water and individual freedom to choose are bedrock values in democratic nations. To challenge personal freedoms and demand change is highly provocative. In addition to resolving existing struggles, the reforms created new ones.

New policy started from a simple first principle: Irrigators were removing too much water from the rivers. With a new framework, the Federal Government created the initial shock and then introduced a set of processes and institutional settings within which changes could occur on the ground. As governments regulated how much water farmers could use, historical rights were challenged and, in some cases, overturned. It became apparent to those who relied on river water for irrigation that the policy revoked their assumed right to unlimited water—the policy provoked by changing a fundamental rule that guided the water system's operation. The unimaginable had been identified and legislated.

13.5 Confront self-interest

The battle over individual rights and self-determination versus collective regulation by the state ignited debate along the Murray-Darling Basin and beyond. There were rivalries between farmers and the Federal Government, dairy farmers and cotton farmers, irrigators and environmentalists, and different jurisdictions of government. The conflicts arose because the reform agenda attempted to refashion Australia's relationships with water, fundamentally altering people's way of life. Policy provokes, stimulates, and focuses both those affected and those orchestrating the adaptive work.

New political and scientific disagreements also emerged. There were competing narratives between, for example, dairy farmers and cotton producers, who saw the problems and solutions differently, revealing the classic adaptive challenge. Water reform in Australia placed many people "on the opposite side of the stream," highlighting how any significant policy intervention disturbs the status quo.

The reforms ensured a creep toward more equitable access to water resources by confronting entrenched beliefs and values, most notably self-interest.

13.6 Changing mindsets

Water reform has had a broad impact, ranging from changes in farming practice to different cropping regimes, with hundreds of millions of dollars invested in water infrastructure. While many dispute the efficacy of the reforms, there is no doubt that the new policies have changed ways of thinking and behavior, especially concerning water usage.

The creation of a water market that allows users to sell and buy their water rights is significant. If provocation is an intervention that destabilizes and nudges a system in a productive direction toward a common good, then these reforms have been among the most provocative seen. Farmers who were irrigators also became traders of water as a commodity. As their mindset shifted, so did their economic behavior and farming practices.

The fundamental rules and drivers of this industry were changed.

Even conservative irrigators, who strongly resisted, began to use the new trading systems, and rely on them for their livelihood. The connection between water rights and the water market created incentives that activated irrigators' self-interest. At the same time, farmers realized that many of their fears were unfounded, and many saw they now had more diverse means to protect their livelihood. Environmentalists supported these initiatives because they could see how they provided much-needed water for ecosystem repair.

Ten years after its inception, the water rights market is now valued at almost A$3 billion, creating a new industry of brokers, water exchanges, and other intermediaries. Thus, not only did the reform process disrupt what had previously existed, but it built a new set of institutions, markets, and relationships.

In contrast, some rural stakeholders say the reforms are the worst thing that has happened to them. David Parker elaborates: "Previously, all farmers were in the same boat and were slowly 'going broke together.' Now there is a competitive edge to water ownership, with winners and losers." Winners acknowledge that the reforms have increased their land values and their water allocations. Overall, they have improved the efficiency of the irrigation industries. Farmers can now make a lot of money selling their water rights, and many have changed how they engage with each other and their land. But some have lost out, in terms of both businesses and traditions.

It takes time for reform to demonstrate its benefits, and those that emerge may have an uneven impact on those affected. Little wonder that the ripples from the initial policy disturbance are widespread and continuous.

13.7 Provocation resolves and creates conflicts

The task for government and bureaucrats, following the initial reforms, was to respond to and manage conflict and opposition. They needed to understand the nature of the resistance, creating conditions that fostered acceptance and refashioned behavior. The reactions from those affected were both predictable and, at times, uncontrollable and played out over many years.

This is a reminder that provocation is a multi-phase process. Part of the work is to respond to and orchestrate the heat and disturbance generated by the initial actions. Government officials understand this. People like David Parker spend a lot of time in meetings listening to people's heated reactions. In the case of the water reforms, farming and commodity lobby groups worked hard to delay change, procrastinating and politicizing. Many felt betrayed by the politicians who had supported the legislation. They expressed their fear and anger, making the situation more volatile.

In October 2010, for example, a crowd of about 5,000 people crammed into the sports club in Griffith, New South Wales, to hear executives from the Murray-Darling Basin Authority respond to their questions. This area grows 30% of Australia's grapes and 90% of its rice, and farmers were facing cuts of up to 45% of their current water allocation. Many were fearful both for their livelihoods, and the future of their communities. The crowds had deep concerns about implementing the Water Act, bank foreclosures, job losses, curbed productivity, and the demise of towns in the region. People were furious, heckling and jeering those who spoke, resisting persuasion, and cheering a group of young men who burned copies of the Draft Plan.

Like a breached dam wall, the pent-up anger was an expression of disbelief that all they had built could be threatened, highlighting how a provocative action is hard to control once launched. But outrage and disbelief are to be expected with any system-wide change. Change will deeply unsettle people. Their strong reactions are an indication that the intervention has hit a sensitive pressure point. In this instance, strong opposition signaled that the basic rules had changed, and people did not like it. Then, the task was to hold steady and understand that the disequilibrium was a natural part of the adaptation process and was not yet over. Shepherding adaptation became a matter of responding to legitimate criticism and not being diverted by a personal or political attack.

The disequilibrium continued. The following year, another very hostile meeting took place in Griffith. Again, no amount of rational argument or data seemed to help. The fact that compensation was available for any losses did not seem to matter to irrigators, and most were indifferent to any environmental gains. All people could see was a loss. David Parker, present as an advisor, recalls the meeting: "Emotions continued to be very high. Water was being taken away, and farmers simply didn't like it. They were losing something they had been used to, and many believed was a right." From this perspective, it made sense that they were worried.

13.8 A new status quo: Gains and losses

The protests and political opposition to the reforms highlight the complexities of provocative action, perhaps more so because it occurred in the public domain. People were reluctant to give up their routines, habits, and practices only to replace them with something new and unfamiliar. The threat to identity, loyalties, and sense of place remained real, though not necessarily objectively accurate. When people feel threatened, they are prone to strong reactions and susceptible to supporting politicians who promise to reverse the change.

It takes time for old traditions to change. Irrigators had gained a lot from the old system of water usage. There were tangible gains, such as revenue, and intangible benefits, such as autonomy, and for generations, they had the freedom to farm the way they wanted. However, agriculture is a very conservative industry, as we saw in Chapter 10. Sometimes it takes a severe shock and holding steady with all that follows to provoke and orchestrate change.

Over time, the need for reform and the benefits it could generate has become more evident. The new framework provided more explicit guidelines and more certainty. Overall, they address the underlying causes of the problem, including the ecological and environmental implications of water overuse.

Despite a recent drought, early signs of progress have included the survival of irrigated farming in the Murray-Darling Basin. The feared catastrophe did not eventuate, and the value of production remains the same because farmers distribute water around as needed. When there is not enough water for rice, the rice growers sell their water to generate income rather than struggling to grow a crop with insufficient irrigation. Some dairy farmers did go out of business, but many adapted, producing as much milk as before but with less water consumption. Generally, they are showing increased resilience and flexibility and no longer adhere to the traditions that no longer serve them. Overall, the reforms have been effective, prompting other countries to follow Australia's lead. But, for all they are admired from afar, many locals hate the changes despite the environmental and economic benefits. As David summarized, "Several generations of people have needed to shift the dial in ways that got better outcomes for the environment, and that's obvious, but also shifted the economic foundation of the irrigation industry and the use of water."

13.9 Provocative change is rarely smooth

The process of adapting to a major reform with all its attendant changes is turbulent. Provocation creates disturbance until new ways are proposed and explored, the unknown becomes more familiar, and a new equilibrium is created. Reform and adaptation rarely run smoothly, usually happening in fits and starts. Moments of heat and tension are followed by times of calm and collaboration. While public servants and their political masters have come to accept these truths, it is rarely straightforward. Reform requires a firm holding of the long-term aspirations and goals.

The irrigators and other farmers affected by recent reforms needed support to make the required technical, economic, and psychological transitions. Many had to adjust their ideas regarding autonomy, independence, and loyalty. They had to give up some of the privileges the old arrangements provided and share responsibility for the social and environmental consequences. Failure to adjust would have left them in the past, which was no longer viable. It would also have meant that they could not benefit from the new water regime.

The changes also overturned existing relationships and alliances, sometimes pitting old allies, such as farmers and miners, against each other. For example, new conservative political parties such as the Shooters, Fishers, and Farmers Party have enticed disgruntled rural voters away from the established parties. The provocation has also forged new and seemingly unnatural alliances, as evidenced by discussions between farmers and environmentalists aligned over efforts to protect productive land and water systems from fracking or coal mining.

When bold actions change the structures and relationships, it is necessary to know how to regulate the disturbance that follows and understand that the reverberations will continue for some time, often in unpredictable ways. A disturbance may be an indication of policy success rather than failure.

Public servants like David Parker believe that further water reform is still necessary and possible, but it will involve "deliberate incrementalism." Big-Bang, one-off transformation is not the correct approach. By its nature, an adaptation of human activity grounded in the natural world, such as a river system, is long-term and evolutionary, and there rarely is a "first-best" solution.

13.10 Reflections from public sector provocation

This case study provides several lessons. First, government intervention is almost always provocative because it indicates market forces or self-organization have broken down. The reforms outlined catalyzed movement in a system that was not changing fast enough to resolve its internal contradictions. A contentious policy created temporary upheaval, followed by ongoing disruption, that helped resolve an underlying crisis. It forced compliance, even temporarily, fractured existing relationships, and overturned long-term economic and social practices.

Second, because large-scale change occurs across a network of relationships, any shift in structural arrangements will affect that network. For example, creating a new water market, with its audit and regulatory structures, pushed irrigators to decide whether to join in or oppose it, thereby realigning relationships. Formal structures disrupt existing dynamics and stimulate pattern change. But regulatory mechanisms are a form of control, and human beings are hardwired to circumvent rules that do not suit them. When you provoke people and reinforce any change through formal mechanisms, such as legislation, you should expect a degree of non-compliance. Like water, people will find cracks in the new system.

Third, legislation was provocative because it changed the rules, overturning a century of land and water rights. It targeted particular aspects of how the old system functioned. But it also acted as an irritant, pushing different agricultural sectors and irrigation companies to engage with each other and public servants, thereby beginning a dialogue that gave airtime to differing perspectives and forged new approaches. Like an oyster farmer who inserts a grain of sand into a fresh oyster knowing that the organism will absorb the irritant and, in doing so, may eventually produce a pearl, government policy acted as an irritant to the long-suffering water system. Thus, legislation, institutions, and markets helped establish new relationships between the factions, enticed new players into the water and irrigation business, saw inefficient producers fall by the wayside, and allowed the vast inland water ecosystems to rebuild.

Fourth, a provocative actor cannot do the work of adaptation on their own. At best, their actions serve as a catalyst, creating conditions for those involved to develop new attitudes and behaviors that will help the system correct itself and thrive. The government became a powerful enabling force, backed by legislative reforms and new regulatory frameworks. Its policies pushed farmers, irrigators, funders, bankers, and investors into new ways of working together. As policy designers and implementors, public servants became "positive friends." They were allies on the side of reform goals, protecting those harmed by change and encouraging everyone to be actively involved and engaged. The government continued to use all the tools at its disposal to maintain invigorating pressure, including incentives, sanctions, social pressure, and regulatory control.

Finally, the bigger the provocation and the subsequent changes, the more it is necessary to be realistic about what can be predicted and controlled. Legislators and policy designers like David Parker learned that while the regulatory and legal tools can shape behavior through control, the longer-term goal is to govern the new system through cooperation and self-management. As the ground-breaking 1998 research by Elinor Ostrom shows, when certain conditions around incentives, trust, and graduated sanctions are in place, people are capable of sustainably managing their shared resources. While some way off this ideal, water reforms in Australia have rebalanced the equation, and the system is moving toward a more productive state.

The reform agenda aimed to reduce the conflicts, fix market distortions, change the behavior of many people, and bring the system back into balance. However, to do so, policy designers had to craft legislation and tools that pushed those involved to examine their own behavior and contribution to the problem. In addition, they required a wide range of long-standing activities to be modified, creating new arrangements that benefited some players while disadvantaging others, leading to new conflicts.

The ultimate test of any reform, catalyzed by initial policy—and annealed in the heat of reaction, discussion, and conflict—is creating the greatest public good with the smallest amount of damage. The policy intervention helps achieve outcomes that go beyond the internal conflicts of the original problem. The interactions between people and the natural ecosystem become more productive.

Public policy can stimulate and start a process, with the government as the instigator, but it cannot control the ensuing reverberations. This complex and ongoing story of the adaptation of a fundamental resource illustrates the necessity of a shock to begin and shape the process of change. The reactions generated by the first tranche of policy action become the second wave of provocation that requires ongoing attention. When a complex system is challenged, the perturbations continue for a long time.

The next steps in this vital process in Australia are currently being considered.

References

Blount, A. (2018). *Alma Blount and the Art of Teaching Leadership*. Sanford School of Public Policy Online. Duke University. 27 September 2018. https://sanford.duke.edu/story/alma-blount-and-art-teaching-leadership/. Retrieved 22 July 2021.

Cambridge Dictionary (2020). *Online Dictionary*. https://dictionary.cambridge.org/dictionary/english/rivalry. Retrieved 10 August 2019.

Hardin, G. (1968). The tragedy of the commons: The population problem has no technical solution; it requires a fundamental extension in morality. *Science, 162*(3859), pp. 1243–1248. https://www.science.org/lookup/doi/10.1126/science.162.3859.1243. Retrieved 1 September 2021.

Meadows, D.H. (2009). *Thinking in System*. Earthscan Publishing, London, UK.

Ostrom, E. (1998). A behavioral approach to the rational choice theory of collective action presidential address, american political science association, 1997. *American Political Science Review, 92*(1), pp. 1–22.

Ostrom, E. (2009). A general framework for analyzing sustainability of social-ecological systems. *Science, 325*(24), pp. 419–422.

14 PUTTING YOUR HEAD ABOVE THE PARAPET—TAKING RISKS AND SPEAKING OUT

It's tough to be sitting at the top of the newsroom. You're never going to make everyone happy. You're probably not going to make many people happy. Leadership is tough.

William D. Cohan, quoting John Montorio,
Editor at Large, Huffington Post 2016

14.1 Introduction

On April 6, 2007, Arianna Huffington, the founder of the eponymous news outlet, collapsed from sleep deprivation and exhaustion, fell, and broke her cheekbone. She subsequently described this moment as the best thing that had ever happened to her. Usually, the burnout of a high-flying executive would only make page three of a national paper. But Arianna Huffington was not a typical executive. Her prominence built on the back of her self-named news outlet is illustrative of the challenges faced by those who break the mold, stand up and put their head above the parapet in the service of making change.

Huffington gained global prominence in 2005 when she fought to build a beachhead in the male and corporate-dominated media world. Her desire to transform the digital media business and create her self-titled political news and blog site drove her, and she used her name and increasing visibility to build her brand. AOL bought the *Huff Post*, and *Forbes Magazine* named her one of the most influential women in business.

However, her drive and success came at a considerable personal cost. In addition to collapsing, she became the target for sustained scrutiny and criticism. For example, in 2016, William Cohan wrote a series of critiques in *Vanity Fair* eliciting comments on her shortcomings ranging from her uneasy relationships with editors to her using the news outlet to promote herself. She was described as seeing herself as a cross between Oprah Winfrey and Jesus. The point here isn't the truthfulness of the criticism but rather how a woman in a man's world or any trailblazer who stands out because they challenged some aspect of the status quo makes themselves a target. She had challenged the prevailing model of online journalism and the model of how an owner and co-founder of a business should behave. She was relentless in using herself as a brand, thereby breaking the mold, challenging others.

But when you break the mold, as Ms. Huffington found, you make yourself a target. And when the arrows fly in your direction, they become a distraction to the

DOI: 10.4324/9781003321200-19

main game and risk undermining your change efforts. And becoming a target destabilizes your less visible efforts to make progress on what matters to you.

This chapter explores several people who stuck their heads above the parapet and provoked others in the service of an orienting purpose: their thinking, the tactics used, the choices made, and examines the challenges of doing so from a prominent position.

14.2 Provoke from the margins

Nyadol Nyuon[1] is an Australian lawyer and social justice advocate of South Sudanese heritage. She has gained prominence for her outspoken views on race, social cohesion, and attitudes towards refugees and immigrants. But it wasn't always like this, and Nyadol is very conscious of the implications of her rapid rise to prominence—for herself, her family, and community, and for the issues she cares about.

Nyadol had a harsh childhood, spent between Ethiopia, South Sudan, and various Kenyan refugee camps. She came to Australia in 2005, studied, practiced commercial law at a prestigious law firm in Melbourne, advocates for South Sudanese youth, is a passionate speaker, and writes on race and the immigrant experience.

Optimistic and driven by a desire to help those less fortunate than herself, Nyadol is equally driven to be authentic, find her own path, and not be governed by her family's history and legacy. Like many refugees, Nyadol has had to refashion a life in the in-between, carving out a pathway that delicately honors her South Sudanese heritage and community while drawing on all that Australia has offered her. We will discuss this in more detail in the next chapter. But finding her direction has meant she has defied convention, pushing the boundaries of who and what she is supposed to be. Nyadol now needs to stand alone in the life she has built while being connected to people in all worlds, from the privileged professionals she works alongside to those experiencing a more tenuous life in the various communities and places she navigated while growing up.

14.3 Challenge hidden assumptions

Nyadol has not shied away from naming the elephants in the room concerning Australia's attitude to race, which is inevitably contentious. For example, when she appeared on the ABC's *The Drum* on January 2nd, 2018, she was asked if young South Sudanese thugs were a significant issue in Melbourne. Her reply was revealing because she did not take the bait, but she did provoke the host by stating,

> *Race is not the only commonality between these boys. Many of them come from single-parent homes where unemployment and poor housing are common, as is a struggle in school. These are issues common to wider segments of the Australian community. The over-emphasis on race misses the point. These are young Australians who need help.*

By reframing South Sudanese youth's experience as an Australian issue, something that other disadvantaged members of the community face, she threw a pebble in the pond of racism and revealed the murky undercurrents. Her language was clear and calm. She challenged the unstated assumptions about young immigrants and people of color. Without saying so directly, she named the racism inherent in the question posed, as well as in the social media frenzy that had swept Melbourne in the days before the broadcast.

Nyadol says that she never sets out to upset people. Instead, she purposefully attempts to tone down her commentary, widening the discussion to take a more systemic view. "I don't need to be provocative," she says, "I just have to show up, to be present and speak; that is provocative enough for many people."

14.3.1 Presence as provocation

Nyadol speaks from deep personal experience, that of hardship and overcoming obstacles. That she is Black is her truth and not a quality she wishes to minimize. Nevertheless, she will challenge those who use skin color as a differentiator to justify their prejudices. "When you make our South Sudanese origin the issue, you act as if we are other people," she declares, "the young people in the street are young Australians."

The fact that Nyadol's mere presence in public forums is provocative is a source of profound insight. It undermines the argument that we must raise our voices or show our anger to gain attention. There is nothing wrong, of course, with using such approaches on occasion to reinforce your message. However, Nyadol's observation helps us understand the dilemma that she and all change agents face. If she performs the role of the angry, loud, black woman, Nyadol realizes that she will only reinforce racist stereotypes, which will be counterproductive. Sometimes, just turning up is enough. At other times, Nyadol can reframe, bringing attention to the broader context or providing additional data.

14.3.2 On being different

Chaim Potok writes about the contradictions immigrants endure in his 1981 article, "Culture Confrontation in Urban America," saying:

> *An encounter with soaring alien ideas often sets us soaring toward new ideas, or we enter into a process of selective affinity, finding in the alien thought systems elements with which we feel the need to fuse.*

But if you are an immigrant, like Nyadol, you begin life on the periphery. Any attempt to integrate elements of the dominant culture feels awkward and clumsy, often resulting in difficult moments, including rejection either for getting it wrong or for the crime of misappropriation. It also shows how far you have to travel from the periphery and invisibility to the center with its visibility. The personal adjustments required are enormous and no one can prepare you if you engage in a provocative life.

Sometimes just being in public space where few people like her appear, or are expected, she doesn't need to do much to be seen as provocative. In fact, often, she would say things others panelist have said, but it is her who gets trolled.

14.3.3 Provocation sought me out

Becoming a sought-after commentator and advocate for immigrants is part of the path Nyadol has chosen. Although, at times, she thinks it has chosen her. Her prominence as a South Sudanese woman who has carved out an independent career and become an advocate without any formal endorsement from her community has come at a personal cost. In fact, Nyadol's desire to be authentic has pitted her against her people, even her own family. She describes how her choices—to live independently while at university, leave home as an unmarried woman, and leave her marriage—have all shocked her community. These choices are culturally inappropriate and confront expectations regarding how a woman is supposed to be to behave.

Nyadol describes, for example, how her relatives in South Sudan phoned her and insisted that she not leave her husband because of the shame it would bring. Her personal choices challenge centuries-old customs. These are customs that she respects but has chosen to either modify for herself or reject.

14.3.4 Hard choices

At times, Nyadol has paid a high price for her choices, including being verbally abused on social media, often by those who see her as "setting a bad example." "Like my parents who fought for what they believed in," she observes, "I too am fighting for my beliefs. I fight for justice, fairness, and the right to become the person I want to be." Yet, Nyadol recognizes that she cannot be what she is supposed to be. As such, she continues to throw pebbles into the pond.

But, in becoming successful and a role model to some, Nyadol has provoked strong reactions and concerns from others about how she is giving up on significant customary ways. Some community members have attacked her emerging identity and tried to bring her down a notch. Chris Sarra, whose work we discussed in Chapter 10, speaks of his success as being "a crab in a bucket." The minute you try to climb out, others will nip your heels and pull you back down. Thus, by the internal standards of her community, for some, Nyadol is both a threat and a failure. For others a success.

14.3.5 Visibility as provocation

Having a visible public identity has offered Nyadol opportunities to advocate for the things she cares about. But she has grown up in public and recognizes that she doesn't know everything she needs to know and still has more growing up to do. Nyadol struggles with grace and with learning to let go when someone is attacking her. She constantly questions how she feels and wonders about what she is expected to say.

Nyadol understands the paradox of her emerging public persona. On the one hand, she is sought after because she is articulate and has something valuable to say. On the other hand, she is relatively young, an African woman who has only been in Australia for seventeen years and has had to do her growing, sense-making, and mistake-making in the public eye. That is a hard ask for anyone and helps explain why she can sometimes misjudge the timing or intensity of her comments.

She has discovered that even a brief, calm, and factual observation can unsettle white Australians. She is beginning to learn that she can't do it all and must pick her battles. "I didn't seek to build a platform," Nyadol confesses, "and I have a very awkward relationship with it." She describes having to conserve her energy and reframe her message, ensuring that she does not appear too radical. One way she downplays her provocative effect is by taking advantage of openings that others have created. She often waits for a white Australian to raise something, then provides an angle on it. This way, it's "not so controversial because a white person said it first."

Nyadol knows how to be "the grateful migrant" who has benefited from everything that Australia has offered. But, unfortunately, she has found her gratitude is never enough for some people who want her to be quiet rather than speak out. They effectively try to silence her because if she were truly grateful, she would accept what is and wouldn't point out the inconsistencies in how we relate to race and immigrants.

Increasingly, Nyadol knows how to draw on her early hardship and sense of injustice to argue a case passionately. Her tactics provide their own provocation, which is particularly pronounced when she highlights the inconsistencies. She describes how she risks being seen as ungrateful when she critiques Australian policies and attitudes and finds this a heavy burden.

14.4 Public officials as activists: Taking a stand

Speaking out for what you believe in is a hallmark of leadership. But it is easier to speak out (for or against something) from outside of formal power structures because the sanctions are more limited, especially in democratic systems. Indeed, protest movements, and the agitators in them, are built around speaking truth to power. The speaker expresses their personal truth, risking their position because they see it as their duty to improve the lives of others. You saw in Chapter 8 the power of subversion and speaking out.

Nyadol Nyuon's frankness was apparent when we spoke. She was notably open and revealing in our conversation even though we were strangers to her. When we commented on her vulnerability and openness, she replied, "I don't do interviews or speeches where I think I can't be honest. It's a waste of my time. And so, for me to pretend otherwise, living in the mainstream feels incoherent to me."

However, speaking out provides a different challenge when you occupy a senior position within a business or a public servant who works for a government.

Dr. Ken Henry, previously Secretary of the Department of Treasury, discovered this as he navigated the fine line between being an expert advisor to his government masters and speaking out to galvanize movement on critical policy matters. As we suggest, a feature of provocation is that it helps create energy and momentum on stalled or stuck issues.

Traditionally policymakers are apolitical and work to serve the government of the day—they provide specialist advice to support the government's vision and plan. Public servants who step out of this paradigm often lose their jobs or are sidelined by reputational damage or payback. However, several senior Australian public servants have reframed their role over the past twenty years, testing it as a strategic enabler of reform and stimulant to public policy. This form of activism, raising your head above the parapet in a political environment, is provocative and risky.

14.4.1 Walking a tight-rope

Dr. Ken Henry found this to be true as he increasingly spoke out on policy matters as Secretary (CEO) of the Department of Treasury from 2001–2011. He was motivated by a belief that policy reform had to improve the well-being of Australians, cognizant that reforms involve trade-offs and will create a disturbance. Ken believed that he had a unique opportunity as the head of the Australian Treasury, a powerful central government agency, to seed ideas and stretch the imagination of both government and community regarding social and economic changes. He disturbed established thinking and challenged the conventional relationship between government and public servants when he spoke out.

Over 2006–2007, Ken delivered several speeches on indigenous disadvantage, including to the Cape York Institute and the Melbourne Institute. None of these speeches were based on existing government policy. Indeed, the Liberal government was ambivalent about reform in the indigenous domain. But Ken saw it as his job to foster debate on this critical issue and increase public awareness of the need for change.

At the Melbourne conference, Ken reminded the affluent audience that Australia's prosperity masked severe deprivation. We had to correct historical mistakes. He feared the required solutions would be provocative to many. Ken was aware that his statements were controversial but continued, "We will never make progress in any area unless we are prepared to deal honestly and analytically with the underlying causes of the problems we face." He cautioned against creating more welfare dependency, arguing that such reliance had contributed to undermining indigenous development.

Ken described indigenous disadvantage as "a dull glow on the periphery, capturing our attention only fleetingly, usually when presented to us as salacious." First, he provoked by suggesting that it suits most Australians not to know or see what is happening on the ground in indigenous communities. Next, he highlighted what he saw as a critical but underfunded element of Australian social and economic policy, drawing mainstream attention. Finally, Ken concluded by suggesting that indigenous disadvantage diminishes all of Australia, not only in the fractured communities in which it is most apparent. "Its persistence has not been for want of policy action. Yet it has to be admitted that decades of policy action have failed."

His provocation was apparent. Dr. Henry pointed to a gap in Australian values between the belief in equality (a fair go for everyone) and the reality in many indigenous communities. While he didn't say so directly, he reminded Australians that their laws and values needed to change to make their country fairer. For a public servant, this speech was unconventional because he spoke out strongly and passionately about flaws in public policy. Some saw it as a criticism of the current government's approach to Aboriginal affairs, even though he didn't directly comment on this. However, this was an activist speech because he drew attention to an element of reality in Australian life that required improvement.

The work of leadership includes pushing the community and government to reexamine their assumptions, values, and priorities so that new ideas become action. Ken didn't see himself as an activist in the traditional protest sense. Still, his speeches were provocative acts because he used his considerable authority and professional status to shine a light on an issue that otherwise was marginal. Ken chose to put some of his credibility at risk because he believed that the country avoided indigenous Australians' challenges. He saw a need to wake people up and face this challenge more directly. He intended to disturb current thinking and encourage people and the government to do more by appearing in public.

Ken spoke out because he saw his department's role to influence and shape future economic directions. He believes that, in providing policy advice, public servants are seeking to influence not only government ministers but the broader community, which needs to be prepared for the implementation of any policy.

14.4.2 Becoming a target

Ken wasn't the only bureaucrat to use his seniority and credibility as a resource to stimulate and provoke, but he was prominent, and both government and the media chastised him.

During the global financial crisis in 2007–2008, Ken and his deputies spoke regularly in public, explaining the rationale for the radical fiscal interventions recommended. Many saw them as spokespeople for the government, and some critics saw Ken as a supporter of government policy rather than just an advisor. The stimulus package proposed was complicated, unprecedented, and rapidly implemented, with a significant impact on everyday lives. As such, it made sense, as architects and advisors of this policy, to communicate the reasons and implications to the public, but this put Ken and his colleagues in a new, more vulnerable position.

The provocation during the global financial crisis was not to the policy itself, even though the fiscal stimulus challenged past practice, but rather to protocol and what type of role senior public servants fulfilled. Many commentators argue that Ken never recovered his neutrality after taking these risks. Indeed, he became the subject of a campaign of ridicule because he personally supported a range of environmental and conservation issues. His personal convictions were used against him, and his integrity was attacked. The job requires frank and fearless advisors when dealing with government ministers, but behaving this way in public, even at a minister's request, was deemed by some to be the transgression of a clear boundary.

14.5 Contradict your masters

It takes courage for senior public servants to speak out to correct a wrong or ensure that their independence and apolitical role are protected. Two weeks before the 2013 Australian Federal Election, Martin Parkinson and David Tune, respectively Secretaries of the Department of Treasury and Finance at the time, spoke out because they believed the government had misrepresented policy work that their two departments had undertaken. The government had released the policy costings prepared before calling the election, claiming they were official Treasury/Finance costings of Opposition policies.

Protocol during the prelection "caretaker"[2] period would lead senior executives like David or Martin to refuse to cost an Opposition policy unless their Minister gave them explicit written legal direction. But the government's announcement gave the impression that they, the Secretaries of two central government departments, had concluded there was a serious fiscal hole in the Opposition's policies.

Martin and David were confronted with a double bind. If they left the misrepresentation uncorrected, they would be implicitly interfering in the election by allowing the impression to exist that there were costing flaws in the Opposition's policies. Moreover, they could have exposed both departments to the accusation that they had behaved politically by not correcting the facts.

On the other hand, if they commented publicly, correcting the government's impression, they knew they could be criticized for interfering in an election campaign.

Martin commented clearly:

> *This was quite a dilemma, but we decided that the truth—and the integrity of the two institutions—could only be defended, and the Australian public served by correcting the misrepresentation.*

Breaking with protocol, the two men released a joint media statement saying that before the election announcement, neither department costed Opposition policies. In so doing, they torpedoed the government's claims. They categorically denied that their organizations had examined the opposition's policies and any modeling used for costing government policies before the election could not credibly be applied to opposition policies.

Both Martin and David knew this was risky, even personally costly. Still, they did it because they believed they had a duty to the public not to allow their actions to be used for political advantage on the basis of a misrepresentation.

In this case, two highly respected public officials were willing to contradict elected politicians because they felt compromised and backed into a corner. Their stand was provocative because it defied convention and sent a message that politicians could not use them for political purposes. Had they remained silent, they would have risked compromising the roles of public servants and their relationship with the government.

Martin and David saw this as a choice they had to make even though it threatened their excellent relationship with the then current government. Their provocative stance cost them when the Labor Party lost the election, with cooler and more distant relationships than before. Some saw the two Secretaries as instrumental in taking the incoming Liberal Government's side in this costings dispute.

Like Ken Henry, Martin and David are astute people who had fined-tuned their political radars over many years. They learned to regulate the pressure in their relationships with politicians and usually knew how to read the tea leaves. So, when they chose to insert themselves into a sensitive issue where the government did not want them to venture, where the government and opposition clashed, they understood the provocative nature of what they were doing. If they stumbled and fell, they knew they had to climb back onto the tightrope.

14.6 Lessons beyond the parapet

Nyadol Nyuon and the three senior public executives discussed faced very different circumstances. For Ken and Nyadol, it was about immigrant and indigenous disadvantage, while for David and Martin, it was to correct the record and maintain their integrity. All four spoke out, using their prominence to provoke others in the service of something that mattered to them. And they had several things in common: they:

- Used their personal credibility to build a platform;
- Made forceful clear statements which identified a problem dilemma or adaptive gap;
- Made choices about when to challenge, about what, and how;
- Discovered that provocation isn't always effective and had to retreat, so they weren't derailed altogether;
- Weren't always successful in their risk mitigation strategies;
- While they were open about their motives, they didn't always reveal their tactics;
- Sometimes misread the impact of their actions on those they represented; and
- Learned to absorb criticism and personal attack.

In our conversations, they were clear on their purpose at the time, though they could see, with the benefit of hindsight, how not all their actions hit the mark or how they may have pushed too hard or at a less than opportune time.

In Nyadol's and Ken's case, they also realized that when you stand on a parapet speaking on behalf of something you care about, you take on a representative role—you are, in effect, speaking for others. But not all of them agree with you or think that you are the right advocate. Often, you have not been chosen by those you advocate for. It also became clear to Nyadol that sometimes in provoking the community at large, she could risk damaging the standing of her underrepresented community in other people's eyes. In these cases, in the eyes of some white Australians.

By standing up and speaking out on some injustice, you are in effect suggesting that others are culpable or play a role in the status quo continuing. The 2020 research by Joshua Kalla and David Brockman shows, for example, that describing others as racist increases rather than decreases racist attitudes. As Nyadol says, she has learned that directly challenging others is often counterproductive, and she tries to build an argument and push people by using their own statements.

On the other hand, Ken stuck his neck out because his government was not doing enough, and his speeches were an attempt to speed something up. His target was the government, and he was trying to ripen the issue by heating it up in the community. From his past policy failures, Ken had learned that one of the best ways to get a laggard group to catch up, especially a powerful group like a government, was to get others to put pressure on them. So, he carefully selected the locations and audiences for his provocative speeches to challenge other influential people who, in turn, might influence the government.

In Chapter 16, we explore in more depth seven significant risks of provocative action, and how to avoid or mitigate them. The experience of Ken, Nyadol, Martin, and David teaches us that you need to be fully aware of those who will come after you and not let their criticism of you or your ideas derail your efforts.

Notes

1 This chapter is based on our own interviews with Ms. Nyadol Nyuon OAM, together with reviews of her public interviews, speeches, and writing, while we also had conversations with Dr. Parkinson and Mr. Tune. The section on Dr. Henry is based on our observations of him while working in Treasury and from informal conversations we had with him during this time.

2 The caretaker period begins when the Parliament is dissolved and continues until the election result is clear or until a new government is appointed. There are a series of caretaker conventions including the public service avoiding supporting policies of any political party or interfering in the election in any way.

References

ABC (2018). *Nyadol Nyuon Commentary on The Drum*. ABC TV, 2 January 2018. https://www.abc.net.au/news/2018-01-02/the-drum-tuesday-january-2/9299748. Retrieved 10 December 2020.

ABC (2019). *One Plus One: Nyadol Nyuon*. Online Broadcast ABC News, 17 June 2019 https://www.abc.net.au/news/programs/one-plus-one/2019-06-27/one-plus-one:-nyadol-nyuon/11258150?nw=0. Retrieved 15 December 2020.

Cohan, W.D. (2016). *The Inside Story of Why Arianna Huffington Left the Huffington Post*. Vanity Fair, 8 September 2016. https://www.vanityfair.com/news/2016/09/why-arianna-huffington-left-the-huffington-post. Retrieved 8 July 2020.

Henry, K. (2006). *Managing Prosperity. Address to the 2006 Economic and Social Outlook Conference, Melbourne*, 2 November 2006. Australian Government Treasury. https://treasury.gov.au/publication/economic-roundup-spring-2006/managing-prosperity. Retrieved 11 September 2021.

Henry, K. (2007). *Treasury Chief Attacks Welfare, Koori History*, 27 June 2007. http://www.kooriweb.org/foley/resources/pearson/ct27jun2007.html. Retrieved 11 September 2021.

Kalla, J.L., & Brockman, D.E. (2020). *Which narrative strategies durably reduce prejudice? Evidence from field and survey experiments supporting the efficacy of perspective-getting.* Open Science Framework Preprint, 28 December 2020. https://osf.io/z2awt. Retrieved 8 July 2021.

Potok, C. (1981). *Culture confrontation in Urban America: A writer's beginnings.* In Jaye, M.C., & Watts, A.C. (eds) *Literature and the Urban Experience: Essays on the City and Literature.* Manchester University Press, pp. 161–168.

15 TESTING YOUR VALUES—LIFE TRANSITIONS AS PERSONAL PROVOCATION

"Zwischenmensch," a between-person.

Reverso Dictionary

15.1 Introduction

In Plato's *Allegory of the Cave*,[1] a group of people live in a cave. It is their only known world, their life. Their fire casts shadows onto the cave wall, which they believe unquestioningly represents their gods. One day, a woman from the group ventures outside the cave and sees the sunlight, the trees, and the grass. She realizes that what is in the cave, especially the shadows, is not real. The explorer faces a dilemma: to go back inside and inform their compatriots or continue their journey. She returns, blindfolded because her eyes were blinded by the sunlight, attempting to describe what she has seen. When her compatriots see the blindfold, they conclude that if they leave the cave too, they will be harmed. So, the status quo continues.

You can interpret this allegory in different ways, focusing on the power of belief, or the risks of challenging the status quo, or the opportunities to make a change. The story reminds us just how challenging it is to navigate these transitions. New knowledge or perspectives can motivate us to change, to inform other people so they too "can see the light." But the knowledge gained when leaving the cave is alarming. Those who access it are caught in the "in-between." The threshold of the cave is a liminal space between the known and the unknown, the inside and the outside, what was and what could be. Plato understood the risk of shedding light on old knowledge, deeply held values, and limited mindsets. So, he encouraged people to carefully consider journeying beyond the cave and what was required to do so.

Transitions always require you to make hard choices, reexamine your values, and learn new ways. The new routes will be challenging to start with because they unsettle everything that you knew before. In this way, the process of human adaptation is deeply conservative, as well as alarming. As Ron Heifetz and Marty Linsky remind us in *Leadership on the Line*, "when you ask people to do adaptive work, you are asking a lot. You may be asking them to choose between multiple values, each of which is important to the way they understand themselves."

This chapter explores life transitions as a provocation. We discuss the personal events that force you to confront a change, where an unexpected experience leads you to question who you are and what you believe. For example, death, divorce,

DOI: 10.4324/9781003321200-20

redundancy, illness, and emigration are all opportunities for action, crossing the bridge before you, even though you may not have all the resources you need.

We explore life transitions using the concept of liminality as a lens—the in-between space that shapes and structures two different things, a form of demarcation that is neither object. The word liminal comes from the Latin word *limen*, meaning threshold. As Plato's allegory shows, change happens between the cave and the outside world, at the boundaries of things. Life transitions are liminal experiences with these same characteristics and force you, as an individual, to pay attention to hidden or unattended patterns in your life. The chapter focuses on the provocation of unexpected events and how you can use the provocation of life changes for growth and learning.

15.2 Transitions

All those we spoke to for this book conveyed that they had experienced a transformative turning point. These became vital moments that disturbed their equilibrium over time and threw their values and beliefs up in the air. In human systems, a moment[2] develops when there is some pressure or demand, a provocative force that requires you to adapt or consider doing so. When something you believe in is profoundly tested, and you reprioritize what is important. But there is equal pressure to stay the same. Without more detailed elaboration of human change theories[3], we can conclude that you, like all of us, will experience transitional moments, whether you want them or not. Transitions involve inner transformations related to your sense of self, identity, and resolution of psychological tensions, such as between autonomy and connectedness or dependence and independence.

These passages are disorienting because they inevitably involve renegotiating what is essential to you and refashioning your values, beliefs, and loyalties. Life transitions involve testing your faith (in yourself, as well as in higher-order beliefs), enduring hardship, and building the capacity to grow and develop. Changes also lead you to question how you can maneuver when you feel provoked by a collision between two or more ways.

The *Milinda Pañha* is an ancient Buddhist text that records a dialogue between the sage Nāgasena, and the Indo-Greek king Menander I of Bactria. In one exchange, drawing on the simile of a chariot, Nāgasena explains that just as the chariot is comprised of constituent parts, such as wheels, an axle, and a seat, the self is an assembly of perceptions, values, emotions, and roles. A major life transition undermines any sense of self you may have. The collection of parts that form your being is affected, often permanently. The parts then need to be either tidied up or replaced. But you remain unsure whether the substitute part, the emergent way of thinking or being, is right for you. You remain uncertain whether the stimulus has resulted in a valuable transformation or if you are still the same person. Only experience over time reveals this.

The stories and examples in the following sections explore how you can productively use provocation in your own life for growth and fulfillment. But in doing so, our subjects inevitably bumped up against the strength of their beliefs and values and needed to consider just how useful they continue to be.

15.3 Did you jump, or were you pushed?

Most people we meet in our work don't see themselves as provocateurs or even risk-takers. Yet, on closer examination, we find that many have made bold decisions in their lives, have changed careers involving significant shifts, or have put themselves through a process of deep learning.

For some people, like our friend and colleague Geoff Mendal, a redundancy set him on a new path. He used the experience forged over the early months of the Covid-19 pandemic to complete training as a leadership coach and now has embarked on an unexpected career. But he didn't let go quickly. His chariot, his identity as an engineer, was annealed over thirty-five years. He says, "I could feel the claw marks on my identity and values as I held on for dear life, only slowly releasing my grip on myself."

For others, like Jillian, it was a mid-life crisis that led to transformation. A civil servant with adult children, left by her husband of thirty years, Jillian found herself alone at fifty-five for the first time in her adult life. It was a frightening experience, and she was not prepared. All the foundations on which she had built a life were crumbling, and she "had no tools available for reconstruction." She reflects, "Up until now, I knew things, I knew who I was personally and professionally, I knew how to use my different roles, and I got satisfaction from them all. But now I feel uncertain."

Such a disturbance is not uncommon. Fortunately, most people use it as a catalyst for change. Some explore new-age philosophies for inspiration. Others travel. In contrast, others develop new careers or new forms of expression. But, like Jillian, most come to understand that the provocation they experience arises from the stagnation, from what they have taken for granted in their lives to date.

Pulling yourself and your values apart is a profound shock, or it can be the product of slowly dawning insights. So many personal provocations happen when people don't see things coming, or when they have their blinkers on and are somehow out of touch with reality. The unexpected nature of the catalyzing experience is what is most confronting to people. It becomes a turning point or a provocative moment, akin to the doorway Alice saw on the tree that let her escape the Mad Hatter's Tea Party. The entrance became a transition moment and allowed Alice to find a new pathway.

> *"At any rate, I'll never go there again!" said Alice as she picked her way through the wood.*
>
> *"It's the stupidest tea-party I ever was at in all my life!"*
>
> *Just as she said this, she noticed that one of the trees had a door leading right into it.*

> *"That's very curious!" she thought. "But everything's curious today. I think I may as well go in at once." And in she went.*
>
> *Lewis Carroll, Alice's Adventures in Wonderland.*

Having an Alice in Wonderland moment can be both liberating and terrifying. It is what those who make big moves in their lives experience, especially those who choose to jump rather than those who are pushed. There are many examples of people who jump. They include coming out as gay or transgender, leaving a well-established and lucrative career for something else, or moving to live in another country with a different culture and language.

15.4 Sarah: I jumped to find a connection

Sarah Mali[4] is an English-born Israeli citizen, and passionate leadership educator, who we meet in Chapter 6. Sarah chose to live in Israel, drawn by the ancient Jewish tradition of "return to the homeland." She spent a good part of her early life thinking about such a transition—but thinking about it and doing so are two very different things.

Sarah describes her early life, which prompted her to cut the umbilical cord and jump.

> *Not alone but lonely because I felt the odd one out. I was a fiery, liberal, orthodox Jew, and there was pressure on me, from family and the wider community, to comply, to be someone else. I wanted a place where my connections to others were more organic and natural, where being passionate and open was all around me and engulfed me.*

Sarah didn't have to create a new identity in Israel. On the contrary, being there helped her realize more fully her Jewishness. Nevertheless, it required her to undertake a meaningful renegotiation between her English identity and her emerging Israeli identity. She became Chaim Potok's Zwischenmensch, an in-between person. Sarah describes this transition as both complex and straightforward.

> *Complex because, in some way, I replaced one type of difference with another. Although I feel at home in Israel's culture, I am still an immigrant even after a long time here. Now I am part of it but still a little separate because of the language. While I am a fluent Hebrew speaker, I express myself in simpler, less complicated ways. But it can be somewhat painful because you are left wondering, do people get me here? Even so, a part of me resists writing and reading in Hebrew because I so value my facility to explore complex ideas in English and believe that's who I am. To not do that means I am not myself, so I keep speaking in English.*

In some ways, Sarah still holds onto the umbilical cord she cut twenty years ago. Yet, she immediately found it easy to be in Israel, appreciating the local values of connection, passion, warmth, and complexity. She could feel it "in the water." Traveling on the bus one day, an elderly lady reached over and adjusted Sarah's misshapen collar. Then, with a gentle tap on the back, she commented, "Now you look good." When a stranger had her back, Sarah realized how at home and at ease she felt.

Finding your place in a new environment is tricky, and Sarah's story helps you understand that it is rarely linear or straightforward. Like Alice, you can rush through an open but unfamiliar doorway and not know where it will lead you. Sarah thought she understood doorways, but her life in England had colored all the entrances and exits she knew. Israel provided new portals into Jewish life, but the frames she passed through were different.

For people like Sarah, the provocation comes from surprising places, such as her experience on the bus or realizing others didn't understand her. Her departure from England was disorienting because it upended other people's expectations of who she was and how she should behave. Leaving was a public violation of the status quo.

Sarah's arrival in Israel was confronting because of the personal adjustments required, including the long process of building an Israeli identity recognizable to others. She recalls, "I was surprised by my expectation of myself. I was surprised by my limitations, of the pressures of negotiating and renegotiating who I was and how I could belong." Many moments were disconcerting and led Sarah to question her original choice, repeatedly asking herself, "What does it now mean to be a Jew in this environment?"

As with all adaptations, the ongoing provocative qualities of her choices and new life unfolded with time. It is only with the benefit of hindsight that, like Sarah, you will be able to see what changes have affected you and understand how the distance of either time or space has contributed positively.

15.5 Diana: Pushed into a life of disturbance[5]

Unlike Sarah, who was pulled by the aspiration to realize something bigger than herself, Diana Renner was pushed in dramatic circumstances. Diana was almost sixteen when her mother told her that she would be leaving her Romanian homeland permanently rather than going on vacation as she had previously believed, escaping the restrictions and humiliations of Ceausescu's Communist regime. She was instructed to keep the plans secret, telling no one, including her grandmother.

Diana likened the news and its effect on her to an earthquake. She felt profoundly unsettled but had to maintain a good front, carrying on as if everything were normal as she went to school and spent time with her friends. Yet, she was caught in an unnatural state, burdened by the heavy secret, which provoked her to her core. Diana felt the turmoil as her whole world shook. She wondered how she could farewell the people and places she cared for without saying goodbye and giving away her family's plans.

Diana felt pushed to ask herself unanswerable questions. But they were questions she has held onto and draws upon today in her own life and with her clients. They are provocative questions because they lead Diana, as they might you, to unexpected places. She wondered, for example, "How can you look at everything for the last time and notice all the things that you have stopped seeing?" Places of inquiry, exploration, and questioning of what is, what will be.

A few weeks after her mother had confided in her, Diana's father woke her up at night, urging her to move silently and not ask any questions. She was bundled into the family's car, along with a few possessions, as if the family was going on holiday. Within a week, Austrian authorities had placed them in a refugee processing center near Salzburg, which would be their home for the next year before their relocation to Australia. This sudden departure from her home in Romania and the different transitions that followed have been central to Diana's personal story. She has carried with her the perturbations of living in the in-between: of being present but absent, visible but unseen, of learning other languages without necessarily speaking them aloud, and of the unfamiliar becoming familiar.

Diana continues to process and integrate the lessons and wounds of this provocation, a shock that continues to reverberate more than thirty years later. Her early experience is one of exile, of a journey, taken one step, one day, at a time, but which can only be understood retrospectively—a life requiring her to make sense of displacement, belonging, and transformation.

Even though Australia has long been home, the escape from the demands of an authoritarian state and her parent's explanation of why they left is now core to Diana's identity. Like many other migrant children, her early years in Australia were simultaneously demanding and easy. Easy, in the sense of relief, life could be lived without serious threat, going without, or waiting hours in long queues. Yet, for many years as an immigrant teenager in Melbourne, Diana confronted the provocation of kindness and the complications of not quite fitting in.

Diana remembers her early experiences of speaking English. She could hear herself speak but didn't recognize herself, finding herself a stranger. At school, a group of girls was kind and inviting, treating her as if she belonged. But she still felt out of place, thinking of herself as other. It was unsettling to feel grateful and welcomed yet needing something else that couldn't be given and probably wasn't available because it had been left behind.

These experiences remind us that provocation comes in many forms. Some are more evident, others more subtle and unseen. Leaving Romania shrouded in secrecy and fear is an obvious example, but the purpose of the challenge was not one Diana chose. Living in limbo as a displaced person left her temporarily feeling self-conscious and fragmented, generating confusion about identity and place. Building a new life in Australia became like living in a shadowland of ambiguity and unknowing. Until that is, in an indistinguishable moment, Diana became part of the place when the balance shifted.

Diana is the product of multiple forms of provocation from which the lessons learned, the changes made, and the personal adaptations may not be immediately evident. But like layers of color on a finely crafted painting, she has discovered them over time. Over time, she, her values, and her view of the world have evolved.

While Diana didn't set out to realize a personal aspiration or transform herself, she was carried along by the waves of disturbance until she could navigate them herself. She found agency and meaning in surfing the provocation and now can use her history more knowingly, with insight and volition. Her early identity was fractured, but she used the experience to build a presence and way of being in the world. Some pieces of her past, her chariot, are visible, valued, and ground her in the life she built from the debris left behind in Romania and Austria.

Diana is no longer subject to the shock of exile but can treat it as something of value and has made her who she is. She does not seek provocation and disturbance in her life but, paradoxically, plays with boundaries in her professional life as a consultant and leadership educator. Her experience has given her an edge, and now she uses it rather than being used by it.

15.6 Living in the "in-between"

Nyadol Nyuon[6] lives between several cultures: her South Sudanese heritage, her life in Kenyan refugee camps, and her new home, Australia. But she also lives between her hard-earned liberal university education, with ideals of access, equality, and freedom, and the underlying streaks of racism and xenophobia that exist in Australia, as they do elsewhere. You saw in the previous chapter how Nyadol speaks out to confront Australian attitudes and how she defied convention in her community. Her experience shows you how disturbing it is to live in a nether land and how challenging it is to one's sense of self and identity. To make such a transition, refugees like Nyadol and her family must sacrifice a great deal.

In describing the reality of immigrant life, Nyadol points to immigrants' vulnerability- they are not seen as socially valuable. They must build a new identity, even though this means changing the code of conduct and challenging their existing cultural algorithm. In effect, young migrants ask their elders to renegotiate family values and loyalties at a time when the elders themselves cling to these values for stability in the face of the new environment's demands. Young refugees are caught between two cultures: one is offended because the old ways are under siege, while the mainstream Australian culture struggles to reconcile itself to people whose skin color and heritage are different from their own.

15.7 Leaving solid ground

Transitions involve a movement from one form of living, sensing, and acting to another, a passage. They entail leaving the solid ground of the familiar and stepping onto a swing bridge in the effort to arrive somewhere else. That destination is an aspiration but usually can't be relied upon. As the driver of a New York bus once told us, "Tomorrow is not promised!"

Whether they are pushed to move or choose to jump, taking the first steps themselves, immigrants and refugees end up having similar experiences once they have arrived in their new host country. They live in a nether land for some time, which Herminia Ibarra and Otilia Obodaru describe in their 2016 article as "a state of betwixt and between," a liminal zone. Liminality has several features common to the migrant experience as well as other personal and life transitions. Recent migrants describe being in a state of suspension, with few guidelines to help adapt, where strong feelings of confusion and uncertainty prevail, and where you feel peripheral to the mainstream. There is little or no certainty. Understandably, therefore, immigrants turn inwards to their own kind for a source of stability. Paradoxically, at a time when the desire to integrate is pushing them out into the mainstream, they feel compelled to seek out those who represent where they came.

15.8 Confront core beliefs

Nyadol has questioned and challenged her community's customary practices and beliefs, often regarding women's behavior. She was outspoken about the dowry tradition that continues in her new country, saying:

> *My past informed the kind of a woman I identify as and provided additional reasons for the opposition to the dowry practice. Whatever my Nuers roots compelled me to be, I was no longer only Nuer.*

But she also recognized the implications of rejecting the tradition when she said:

> *It would have been extremely selfish. I would have embarrassed my mother and denied her an opportunity to celebrate my wedding in the manner she understood. Whatever the Australian in me stood for, I had to accept I was not only Australian.*

Here, you can see how someone like Nyadol is caught between two worlds and how moving in either direction would disturb many. She understands how the tensions and contradictions of her community's values inevitably create provocative moments.

Many young South Sudanese find themselves living in a cultural war zone. They know what it is like to be identified as part of Melbourne's young black community and the risks of such identification. Their community criticizes them for breaking cultural taboos and practices, and the mainstream attacks them for being a threat. They are genuinely betwixt and between. They are seen as too white by their own people and too black by some of the mainstream. Their very presence is provocative in either community. There's no place ever to hide, to be anonymous, free from others' gaze, notice, and judgment. Black immigrant youth remind their community of the losses to customs that must be given up. To mainstream Australian society, they remind us how rigid our attitudes are to the new, to the unfamiliar.

15.9 Identity

Provocation is a means to challenge a system to reflect and learn. It entails stimulus, reaction, and response and centers on the process created by their interaction. This was Nyadol's experience. Each transition involved a shock and a reaction, an upheaval to the everyday routine, to what she knew. It is no wonder that, as with Sarah and Diana, her identity was at stake. People who undergo such a process are left questioning who they are and what will become of them.

Identity is a broad field of study which we can't cover adequately here.[7] However, for our purposes, we can define identity as the attributes that help you describe yourself, determine which groups you belong to and who you are to others. In this way, the idea of identity is both an internal and an external phenomenon. Nevertheless, your sense of identity is in a constant state of flux, constantly under pressure, with a spatial and temporal component to them.

Nyadol remembers arriving in Australia and handing her newly minted Australian passport to the immigration official who looked up and said, "welcome home." It was the first time she had any sense of an emerging new identity. But she describes how she began to look over her shoulder in later years each time she spoke at anti-racism rallies because she felt afraid. She was not seen as Australian by some and began to question herself. She said, "I am afraid to mention these moments because you don't bite the hand that feeds you." In so doing, she reflects on the conditional acceptance of refugees and the instability of her new identity.

15.10 Self-belief as a provocative value

Nyadol has chosen a life with overlapping identities, with her race primary among them. She was also a lawyer for an establishment firm and, is now the Executive Director of a legal education centre, despite some reservations from her community, she is a mentor to young South Sudanese women. Her insistence on being her own person and her drive for authenticity is a powerful form of persona, one that is readily apparent.

The choices that Nyadol has made and the provocative effect it has had on people in her community have led to her being labeled in numerous ways, having an unsought identity bestowed upon her. For some, particularly men, she is simply "that woman," the South Sudanese mother who did the unthinkable and left her husband. Others in her family still act as if she is married. They pretend by holding onto important values because Nyadol is culturally "protected by marriage," even though she is no longer married. She exists, therefore, in a contested space, receiving cultural acceptance in some contexts and no community protection at all in others.

To abandon strong community norms, becoming a different kind of woman than was expected of her has created a dilemma for Nyadol's community. On the one hand, she shows what is possible for young South Sudanese women. She is very successful by many measures and has overcome significant hurdles. She is a role model, someone to be emulated and has been recognised with national honors. But, in doing so, she has provoked strong reactions and concerns from others about how she is giving up on significant customary ways.

Self-belief provides Nyadol with a foundation, providing ballast in the face of criticism. "A lot of my core identity," she says, "is a fighter, is pushing back, is metaphorically throwing back a punch." Nyadol is fighting for what she believes: the right to live her life her way, independent and free of past constraints. Her identity has been forged through hardship and poverty, through memories as a child living in refugee camps and being told what she couldn't do or think. She describes her early experience as "her reverse privilege" because it has given her strength and perseverance, or what Arnold Mindell terms "psychological rank," – the strength and self-belief that emerges when you have developed internal resources and abilities to allow you to face challenges with higher levels of ease. She says of her experiences, "There was no time to really viscerally feel sorry for yourself because you've never seen the alternative. And it's because it's always been unfair."

15.11 Provoking loyalties

Many people we met describe how they feel torn between different parts of their life experiences. They have split loyalties. They are caught between their mixed heritage or their country of origin and where they now live. Such experiences can be both unsettling and transformative. It is disconcerting to feel like Diana did, dislocated and feeling that you do not belong either where you find yourself or where you once were. So too for people who return home and inform family or friends that they no longer wish to adhere to the old customs because they interfere with their new life, hold them back, preventing them from crossing the bridge of acceptance. They tend to provoke a strong reaction. Their pronouncement is seen as a violation of trust by those who expect them to behave in specific, cherished ways. Nyadol has also felt this.

Given that your identity is often hidden, distorted, even oppressed, there is a need to remove the remnants of the old to reveal your authentic and emancipatory self. This was true of Chris Sarra's work with Aboriginal children at the Cherbourg State School in Australia. But your view of your essential self (whatever that is) is disturbing and, at times, traumatic. Yet, despite the maladaptiveness of the old identity, it is the one you have, the one you are used to, oddly providing a degree of protection. So, the question becomes how you help people move their view of themselves to something more enabling and liberating but not damaging them in the process.

15.12 Concluding remarks

We have come to understand that one way to build a life with meaning is to test and challenge aspects of that life continually. Just as direct provocation is intended to push boundaries and ask questions about the status quo, refashioning the values, roles, and loyalties that make an identity is also contentious. In this sense, it is self-disruption. Challenging your makeup and personal coding helps you grow and stay alive. But it is also indirectly provocative to those around you because it asks them to accept a different way of living, a third way that blends cultural and familial identities.

Notes

1 From Hamilton, E. & Cairns. (1963) *Plato: The Allegory of the Cave.*
2 We discuss the origins of the concept of a "moment" in Chapter 1.

3 For example, Erik Erikson's (1950) *Childhood and Society*, or Sheehy, G. (1974) *Passages: Predictable crisis of adult life.*
4 Sarah is a long-time colleague and friend, and this section is based on recent conversations with her.
5 This section is based on conversations with our friend and colleague Diana Renner. Many of the experiences she relayed to us will be expanded in her next book on *Exile.*
6 This section is based on our interviews with Ms. Nyadol Nyuon, OAM, together with reviews of her public interviews, speeches, and writing. Including her ABC interview in 2019.
7 For example, Richard Jenkins ed. (2004) *Social Identity*, or Scheibe, K. (1995). Self-Studies: *The Psychology of Self and Identity.*

References

ABC (2018). *Nyadol Nyuon Commentary on The Drum.* ABC TV, 2 January 2018. https://www.abc.net.au/news/2018-01-02/the-drum-tuesday-january-2/9299748. Retrieved 10 December 2020.

ABC (2019). *One Plus One: Nyadol Nyuon.* Online Broadcast ABC News, 17 June 2019 https://www.abc.net.au/news/programs/one-plus-one/2019-06-27/one-plus-one:-nyadol-nyuon/11258150?nw=0. Retrieved 15 December 2020.

Carroll, L. (2010). *Alice's Adventures in Wonderland.* Penguin Press, London. First published 1865.

Erikson, E.H. (1950). *Childhood and Society.* New York: Norton.

Hamilton, E., & Cairns. (1963). *Plato: The Allegory of the Cave.* Republic VII, from *The Collected Dialogues of Plato*, translated by P. Shorey. Random House. https://yale.learningu.org/download/ca778ca3-7e93-4fa6-a03f-471e6f15028f/H2664_Allegory%20of%20the%20Cave%20.pdf. Retrieved 10 June 2021.

Heifetz, R., & Linsky, M. (2002). *Leadership on the Line.* Harvard University Press. Cambridge, MA.

Ibarra, H., & Obodaru, O. (2016). *Betwixt and Between Identities: Liminal Experience in Contemporary Careers.* INSEAD Working Paper No. 2016/79/OBH. 9 November 2016. https://ssrn.com/abstract=2866988 or 10.2139/ssrn.2866988. Retrieved 17 May 2021.

Jenkins, R. Editor (2004). *Social Identity.* 2nd edition, Routledge, London. (Professor Sociology at University of Sheffield, UK.)

Mindell, A. (2002). *The Deep Democracy of Open Forums.* Hampton Roads Publishing, Newburyport, MA, USA.

Pesala, B. ed (1991). *The Debate of King Milinda.* Motilal Banarsidass Publishing, Delhi.

Reverso Dictionary. Translation, https://context.reverso.net/translation/german-english/zwischen+Mensch. Retrieved 7 April 2022.

Scheibe, K.E. (1995). *Self Studies: The Psychology of Self and Identity.* Praeger, Westport, CT.

Sheehy, G. (1974). *Passages: Predictable Crisis of Adult Life.* Random House Books, New York, NY.

PART 5

RISKS AND LESSONS OF PROVOCATION

> *It's never easy to know when to push the boundaries or when to pull back. But you can spend a lot of time doing nothing, which is a great way to keep things as they are. Sooner or later, you have to step forward.*
>
> Comment by workshop participant 2019

Having explored the value of provocation and provided numerous examples, we also want to outline some of the key risks involved and offer some cautions and guidelines. We do this with an overview of what we can learn from the case studies provided because we want you to expand your practice and repertoire and do so with greater awareness and steadiness. Thus, we are encouraging you to step out onto the provocative edge with greater capacity and skill but also with the wisdom that comes from learning from those who "have got their boots dirty."

The final three chapters examine:

- The risks of provocation;
- Strategies for cultivating provocation; and
- Seven critical lessons in the use of provocation.

We will finish in the Epilogue with some final reflections, including describing where we have found inspiration.

DOI: 10.4324/9781003321200-21

16 RISKS OF PROVOCATION

Being subject to public attacks is one of the costs of leadership, and, while it is often hurtful on a personal level, this is not a reason to avoid leading when required.

Chris Sarra, comment during our interview

16.1 Introduction

As independent consultants, we have learned how hard it is as outsiders to help a business respond to the challenges they face, such as those of recent clients described as conservative, too bureaucratic, and not customer focused. Like many, this organization had some deeply entrenched habits and behaviors that restrained needed changes. To be useful, we had to assist them in identifying and challenging some cherished aspects of the status quo.

However, this is a hard sell. Imagine informing a client that hiring you will entail addressing difficult issues, being pushed into uncomfortable territory, and experiencing a sustained period of upheaval before their objective can be achieved. Most executives would balk at such a suggestion, and we have missed out on our fair share of contracts as a result.

There you have the paradox of change. When people, like our clients, say they want to change, they mean what they say. But they also mean they can't take any risks or disturb people. Therefore, there is always the risk that we will not succeed, especially when we challenge their organizational way of life. Despite the calls for change, what is usually paramount is minimizing distress and discomfort. Clients seek to protect the status quo even as they talk to us about transforming it.

Provoking people and orchestrating adaptive change is hard work and there are many risks in creating and harnessing disturbance for constructive purposes. Having outlined why provocation is important, explained what it is, and provided numerous examples, we also want to outline some of the risks involved and offer some cautions and guidelines to mitigate them.

16.2 Provocation is not neutral: You have a point of view

Many of our examples demonstrate that those who challenge the status quo often have firmly held beliefs. They are frequently insiders, and are driven by a commitment to

DOI: 10.4324/9781003321200-22

help their group or community adapt and be fit for purpose. You wouldn't stick your neck out if you didn't care about the issue and the people involved.

If you are an outsider, the demands are different, and you will care about other things.

However, when you care so much, you can become blinded by your point of view, driven to push forward. Charlie Massy (Chapter 8) says he was surprised by how many people resisted his ideas. Sometimes he forgot that others didn't see things as he did. When he challenged farmers about their practices, they felt judged and saw Charlie as a zealot who didn't understand them.

When Charlie battled the wool industry establishment, he was far from neutral. He was angry, and passionate. Some would say one-eyed. Such energy can be alienating for the very people you need onboard and can result in progress slowing down. The risks generated by his provocation became apparent when he was issued with legal writs and required to defend himself.

Similarly, Chris Sarra (Chapter 10) never hid his point of view. It was a deeply held desire to elevate Aboriginal children's lives and "to smash to bits" the prevailing low expectations he encountered at Cherbourg State School. Initially, however, there were risks that Chris's vision would be treated as the latest fad. After all, despite being indigenous, he was "just another outsider bought in to tell us how to live our lives." Having a clear perspective carries risks and Chris, like Charlie, had to demonstrate that he could deliver results as well as challenge others.

There is always the possibility, too, that your vision, which points to a solution, a pathway forward, doesn't work or even does damage. The more you are convinced of or committed to an idea and the provocative acts that follow, the more you need to hold contradictory views. You might be right and should continue, but there is a chance you are wrong, at least in some way, and should desist. But conviction is also problematic. As one of our clients said after being challenged in a team meeting, "If I believe something, it is a possession. I take pride in it, even if it is wrong. So, I tend to defend it and not listen to those who question it."

While René Jones from M&T Bank was deeply committed to his vision, he realized that he had to let go at times, admit his mistakes, and rely on the capabilities of his executives, as well as the array of specialists he hired. René couldn't risk his authority by pushing issues too quickly. He mitigated the risk by sharing leadership with his two senior colleagues, and, as we demonstrated in Chapter 12, they held each other in check. René, Kevin, and Rich had to create opportunities for others to be active and increase the chances of intuition, fascination, and novelty. Adaptive change requires new ideas, innovative solutions, experimentation, and learning among those most affected. So ultimately, you should reinforce the notion that knowledge, expertise, and power are not phenomena people possess in their heads but are what people create together.

16.3 You become the issue

A second significant risk of provocative action is that you overstep the mark, create a firestorm, and hurt people. This can come about because you have pushed too hard and too fast, expected too much from others, or misjudged the group's sensitivities. We saw this in Chapter 1 when Michael told a group that one of their members was like "the virus the group needed to adapt." Michael became the issue, accused of rudeness and insensitivity, going too far, and needing to adjust his style.

Attacking you personally is a well-known method to neutralize your message because others' criticism becomes the focus rather than the issue you bring to their attention. You provoke people to direct their attention to problems they face and how they are part of the problem. But if your action is too intense or simply off the mark, you risk diverting people's attention.

You saw in Chapter 15, for example, how Nyadol Nyuon's mere presence, let alone her views on race and the immigrant experience, often become the issue. Nyadol is frequently attacked for "not being grateful for what Australia offers her," implying that the questions she raises are not relevant.

In fact, as a rule of thumb, when you are attacked personally, you can assume you have touched a raw nerve. Generally, you become the issue when people don't like your message. So, the question becomes how to keep the focus on the issue at hand? In Nyadol's case, she typically tries to direct the audience's attention back to the subject in question by reminding them that what she is addressing relates to Australians in general and not just to refugee youth.

Taking a provocative stance does single you out, makes you more visible, and often leads others to criticize your prominence. This is a double-edged sword. While social change often needs a figurehead around which others can coalesce, being seen as "the one in front" is risky. Other kibbutz members saw Shimon Zelas (Chapter 9) as both a champion and an arrogant pain in the neck. Some tried to silence him through personal attacks; others ignored him because he was alienating, while others sat up, listened, and asked questions about what they could do to make a necessary change. As a colleague once told us, "If you act like Jesus Christ, you risk ending up like him."

Chris Sarra understands how his position on indigenous issues has, at times, singled him out as being too big for his boots. Some have even accused him of being a "coconut"—brown on the outside, white inside—embodying the white institutions that oppress Aboriginal people. He realized that when you challenge the status quo and refuse to collude with low expectations, it is inevitable that people will come after you.

Despite their protestations to the contrary, those who criticize you tend to be addicted to the status quo and gain from it. Therefore, it is natural for them to attack you if you ask them to give up an old lifestyle and threaten how they think about things. As Chris describes it, if you succeed, others will try to drag you back down.

16.4 You are removed from the game

When you are an external consultant or facilitator to an organization, there are dangers when you provoke because your ability to act and be useful is tied to how those in charge see you. If you annoy people, they can cancel your contract any time, and then you are no use to anyone. Jeff Lawrence, who we met in Chapter 11, discovered this during an early meeting with M&T Bank's Executive Committee and its longstanding CEO.

Jeff noticed the Committee's cavalier reaction to commentary from the US Securities and Exchange Commission in response to the bank's regulatory lapses. So, he wrote a memo to the CEO suggesting that partnering with the SEC would help repair trust and be a more productive strategy. The CEO was unhappy about the comments and a heated discussion ensued. Jeff's internal sponsors wondered if he would be allowed back into these meetings as senior authorities in the bank, as in most organizations, were not accustomed to being challenged. His intervention was very provocative, almost offensive to the recipients, and it took several months for the disequilibrium to settle. By then, the executives, the CEO included, could see the proposal's merit and considered a different relationship with the regulator. But it was a close call.

While worrying for his sponsors and Jeff's business, this trigger moment also signaled to Jeff that he needed to be more considerate with his suggestions, illustrating that even wise advice can push people over the edge. What seems sensible to you can be too disturbing. It also demonstrates the power of having an external advisor who can identify a team's shortcomings and the dangers of doing so.

Jeff's example reminds us that a core task of leadership is to keep the issue, the real work, in the forefront and not let other things distract you. When you become the target, others can avoid the actual work. Therefore, you must learn to manage the risk before you are canceled.

16.5 Risk of loss

Disturbing the status quo is risky because those most affected fear the losses involved. Too often loss is an overlooked by-product of change. For example, on Kibbutz Yizrael (Chapter 9), the losses were tangible, such as losing a job and status when the first factory was closed. There were also intangible losses for kibbutz members, as they were required to adjust core beliefs and principles, ideas that had governed what being a collective settlement meant. Asking people to give up their raison d'être is never easy. Sometimes provocation will prompt people to fight for what they believe in. At Yizrael, their struggles over the losses determined the settlement's future adaptive capacity.

In Chris Sarra's case, he increased pressure on the teachers at Cherbourg. His provocation required them to choose whether to commit to the new school vision or leave, illustrating how a transformation may be beneficial for most people but also can hurt others. Before his arrival, some teachers had benefited from the status quo, deriving social recognition from what they perceived as a hardship posting. Despite the poor outcomes, they believed they were dedicated and "doing well under difficult conditions." Chris's change program presented them with both tangible and psychological losses, as they were asked to subscribe to something they didn't believe in and make changes that they were unconvinced they could make. Herein lies another paradox of provocative moments.

The teachers who left Cherbourg had to give up what they had—status, satisfaction, self-belief, and power. But they also had to accept their psychological limitations and accept the idea that they were incapable of change. To come to terms with your own incapacity or resolve to make critical changes is potentially disorienting. Tacitly, these teachers already had given up hope and would lose even more if they agreed to renegotiate their beliefs. Chris was in effect asking the teachers to take this hit, adamant that the pupils would no longer suffer because of systemic failings.

Losses of personal well-being and status are inevitable during adaptation. If some people can't adapt, they become casualties. As the school principal, Chris knew he couldn't afford to protect all the teachers any longer. Protection kept the old system and its injustices in place. Like any leader, Chris was on the side of progress because he was deeply committed to helping indigenous children have better lives. Accepting that loss is painful is fundamental to effective leadership. Chris had to signal his commitment by holding steady despite the ripples of agitation he generated and the criticism from unions and education authorities, which suffered their own losses with the teachers' departure.

16.6 Going too far: Minimizing your impact

Taking provocative action over a sustained period is arduous work for which you need thick skin and sensitive fingers. By this, we mean that you need to hold firm, not cave in, and not take everything personally. At the same time, you must have a finely tuned radar, collecting information about how others are feeling. The disequilibrium you initiate will have ripples across the whole system, with a momentum you can't control or fully comprehend. Therefore, learning to be sensitive to the impact of your interventions is critical. Your noble intentions may not be experienced as so noble by others.

Shimon Zelas (Chapter 9) found this out more recently when he suggested his community establish an inheritance fund—something like a pension fund. Shimon noticed a flaw in the kibbutz system and felt he needed to act. Many members wanted to help their children who had left the kibbutz and lived elsewhere, but they had no savings to use for this purpose. While Yizrael was wealthy, there were few ways for a member to receive any money. This struck Shimon as nonsensical but in the absence of any fund, he left the kibbutz for a period to earn and save money to help his daughters.

In so doing, he upset his friends and colleagues. His singlemindedness was highly provocative. Some saw him as selfish, deviating from the kibbutz's rules. Others attacked him for being elitist. As they saw it, he was privileged and could earn well outside the kibbutz while others were less able. Shimon put his reputation and relationships at risk, but, ultimately, his actions helped secure change. Today, Yizrael has an inheritance fund that gives members substantial amounts to use however they choose, including gifts to children.

But did Shimon go too far? He appeared to put his family interests ahead of the community's and, temporarily, lost respect. Nevertheless, Shimon did what he thought was necessary, remaining committed and consistent with his beliefs. As he found, you need to weigh up the cost of your actions in such scenarios because there will be personal consequences when you provoke and stir things up. No matter how noble your intentions, you can suffer if you can't anticipate how others might feel.

Conflict rarely occurs because of disagreement on high order purpose. For example, few would argue against world peace or the need to protect children, but we may disagree on how to get there. Your behavior, what you do to achieve your goals, is what counts. If your action significantly changes someone's livelihood or identity, you need to know about it, acknowledge it, and recognize the loss you are asking them to sustain. Arguing that the ends justify the means will win over no one in support of your ideas.

16.7 Risks of strong pushback

Our case studies have shown that provocation will generate powerful reactions. If the need is unclear and the change logic doesn't suit others, you will feel their reactions. People will become indignant and outraged as you ask hard questions, like Nyadol Nyuon, or offer insightful observations about collusion, like Chris Sarra. David Parker (Chapter 13), for example, witnessed farmers' violent reactions and book burnings in response to water reforms and noted how "they were losing a whole way of life." What was disturbing about these incidents was the polarization that occurred and the attack on those who were testing prevailing beliefs. Without people speaking out, the status quo will never change. History shows this. Challenging the deeply held beliefs and values of your own people is a risky business.

Look at what is happening, for example, to Beth Allison Barr (discussed in Chapter 8) who is challenging the grip longstanding ideas have on Christian women. Barr is criticized for abandoning her church and leading women astray. Ownership issues have crippled the debate over who determines how Christian women live. Who are the legitimate custodians of what is proper and correct? Who decides how historical facts should be interpreted and used? Who distinguishes between fact and fiction? Often, there is more indignation than problem-solving.

Barr has become a lightning rod for existing polarized views and highlights the difficulty of having a sustained conversation about controversial issues. Attacking her is easy but listening to her and absorbing what she has to say is even harder if her words challenge the way you see the world. Unfortunately, those who raise hard questions are often attacked for letting down their side and misusing the facts. Often, they are labeled in some way and subjected to personal attacks.

Trying to make a difference in your business or for your immediate community is a worthy endeavor. Still, the pushback felt when you put the broader traditions under the microscope can be challenging. If you provoke others, you should prepare for pushback. For some, to attack is far easier than to listen. It is much harder to consider challenging ideas and assess their merits than to simply reject them.

16.8 There is already too much stress

The past few years have had a significant impact on all our lives. While different in detail, our experience in Australia is like other parts of the world. Following devastating bushfires, widespread floods, the murder of a woman and her two children by her husband, the results of Royal Commissions on child abuse and neglect in aged care, we all had to make significant adjustments to the Covid-19 pandemic. In the United States, the government's heartland was under siege in January 2021, while the country was still reeling from protests following the killing of George Floyd. And now in 2022 the terrible invasion and destruction in Ukraine. At times, it feels as if we can't bear it anymore.

In the global context of increased volatility and stress, you should question whether people can tolerate any more disturbance. Even though the problem you face is worthy, it is riskier to provoke others during such times. There is also an ethical question to consider. If you know that the broader context already unsettles those involved, is it right to provoke them further? Generally, we know that there is a limit to what people can withstand. They will feel overloaded and be less able to think and learn. Under these conditions, any additional provocation is a risk to you, as the provocateur, and to the issue.

Charlie Massy found out that other farmers have a limit. After years of devastating drought, which bought them and their families to their knees, the last thing they needed was a passionate advocate for change, pointing out the shortcomings of their longstanding farming practice. Many farmers were overwhelmed, and the idea of beginning a radical transformation of their established methods was one step too far. Some told Charlie that while regenerative farming showed promise, it was not for them. Such comments highlight how necessary it is to assess the prevailing level of disequilibrium level before providing any additional provocation. Any challenging intervention that pushes people beyond their tolerance level will usually be wasted because the recipients cannot fully absorb the ideas.

Nevertheless, there are high distress situations when provocative action is both helpful and necessary. For example, René Jones and his two colleagues faced an extremely stressful situation following the death of M&T Bank's revered CEO. The grief, uncertainty, and confusion led many to hunker down—the staff, stakeholders, and customers needed reassuring.

René's first task as the new CEO was to calm things down. However, by also acknowledging that change was needed, he temporarily increased the pressure on his people. By focusing on the bank's shortcomings, he in effect said, "We have become complacent, and we need to change the way we think about ourselves and our work." In a situation where his staff were already shaken up, René unexpectedly provoked them by acknowledging the disorientation felt, honoring the past, and challenging the present, all for a better future.

By focusing on cultural issues such as deference to authority and emphasizing a technology shift, he brought less visible problems to the fore, enabling his staff to understand where there were flaws in the business. He simultaneously calmed things down during a crisis and stirred them up by identifying the adaptive issues.

16.9 Risks to yourself

Our colleague Marty Linsky often says, "To lead is to live dangerously." He reminds us that questioning the status quo can lead to distress and opposition. No one will thank you, at least initially, if you unsettle their lives, push them to make complex adjustments, and give up what was comfortable. If people could anticipate and act on what was required, it wouldn't be necessary to provoke them to make progress. But human nature is not constructed this way. Most adaptive problems are difficult because those involved don't know how to solve them without the demanding process of changing attitudes, values, and behaviors.

Consequently, making change is fraught with hazards. First, there are tactical risks, such as determining when and how to intervene or how much pressure to apply. There are also strategic risks related to the impact of your actions on other people and their responses to you. Then there are the more personal risks of provocation, of which three stand out.

First, there is a real danger of personal attack and abuse. As we have seen in the case of Nyadol Nyuon in Chapter 14, some individuals become so enraged that they take the law into their own hands. People stalked Nyadol and trolled her online, and at times, she has been afraid in public. Such personal attacks are real, and we will have to consider how much we can manage. There are psychological and professional risks to challenging people, even in the professional leadership programs such as we deliver. But these don't compare to physical attack and, in rare cases, assassination, as happened with Martin Luther King in 1968 or Itzhak Rabin in November 1995.

Reflecting on the perils he has faced, Chris Sarra observed, "Leadership means putting the needs of others ahead of your own comfort." If that results in personal criticism, Chris was willing to accept it. However, he fully understands the individual costs of exercising leadership:

> *I know that when one pulls back the curtain and says publicly what is often only spoken of behind closed doors, people get angry and defensive, particularly those who recognize their own behaviors. I accept that some people will get angry.*

Second, there are risks that you can let the power of provocative situations go to your head, becoming besotted by your own prowess. There are occasions when, fueled by the euphoria of the moment, you overstep the mark. For example, once, when we worked at Google in Mountain View, we found that the interjections of one participant who constantly interrupted other people were distracting the group. However, our attempts to curtail his actions by regularly referring to him as the "King of Interruption" backfired when he took offense and left the session. We misused provocation to a detrimental effect.

Early in his career, Michael worked as a counselor at a local university, and heard complaints that his boss had used inappropriate sexual language with female clients. He voiced his concerns to the university but they rejected the claims, accusing Michael of maliciously attacking his boss. Instead of addressing the fundamental issue, with the benefit of hindsight, Michael, naïvely, was motivated by a sense of moral righteousness, which obscured the risks of raising such a contentious issue in a bureaucracy, and unsettling the status quo.

The third risk relates to how you can start believing in your own rhetoric and power. It is easy to see yourself as the provocateur when you put yourself forward in support of something you strongly believe in. You can think your provocative action is who you are, confusing the role you have chosen to adopt in this situation with your own identity. Over the years, we have encountered numerous change agents and facilitators who have ended up believing their own stories, conflating what they did in a challenging moment or complicated conversation with who they are now.

We have a colleague who learned to provoke people after participating in a Harvard program. He thought his work was to "throw bombs into the middle of a group, to shake them up." He was criticized for creating chaos, and felt undermined as a person. He had forgotten that provocation is a skill, something you sometimes do because it is the best approach to starting a conversation. He had taken on this skill as if it were a statement about who he was, about his worthiness. In the process, he had lost sight of what he was trying to learn and why it was worthwhile to do so. So, remember you are not your role.

Ken Henry understood that who he was and what he did as a senior public servant were linked (Chapter 14). He saw his public speeches as an expression of his humanity because he believed in the well-being of all Australians. But he also knew that other people could confuse his different roles. When he spoke out in public, others confused him as the public servant with the private person who was a committed conservationist with a preference for privacy. When commentators trivialized his conservation work, they were trying to undermine his professional credibility.

For anyone in a position of authority, be it in a business, a school, or community, your capacity to maintain that role, and the power that goes with it, is contingent on you meeting people's expectations—those related to delivering on your commitments and those connected to the social contract. When you push people too far, you risk disappointing them and undermining your credibility—the currency of leadership. If you push people beyond their limit, they will begin to question your judgment, ethics, and capacity. Indeed, there are many examples of people in powerful roles who lost their jobs because those around them lost faith. Ken Henry didn't lose his job because he challenged the status quo, but he was held at a distance for some time because his political masters questioned his neutrality as a public servant.

There is a delicate balance between the leadership act of provoking others because it is needed and reassuring people that you are not a risk to them or someone who should be avoided. A well-informed change agent who shouts at the moon is no use to anyone. Therefore, as a provocateur, you should understand what is at stake for others, which role you are drawing on, and how those critical of your goals may attack you using any means available.

As Ken's example suggests, there is value in creating a personal holding environment so that you can maintain the strength and perspective required to exercise leadership. Self-care, listening to trusted confidants, and keeping interests outside your field of work can help you separate the self from the role, question your motives, and maintain your judgment. Doing so is not only good for you but others too. They can be more assured that you won't lose sight of why you provoke and that you are there in the service of others.

~~~

This chapter attempts to put a brake on your zeal and desire to challenge the status quo and provoke others. We alert you to some of the risks of provocation, especially of getting carried away and overstepping. People who challenge others fail because they allow their passion to get in the way of being realistic and because they misjudge others' capacity to tolerate the necessary disturbance. Furthermore, it becomes clear that when you provoke with a clear purpose, you are not neutral; you have a strong opinion and value set. Inevitably, this will put you on a collision course with those with different and equally strong views or needs.

Reference

Barr, B.A. (2021). *The Making of Biblical Womanhood: How the Subjugation of Women Became Biblical Truth*. Brazos Press, Ada, MI.
~~~

17 CULTIVATING PROVOCATION—HELPING PEOPLE LIVE WITH DISTURBANCE

Smooth seas do not make skillful sailors. Sometimes the waters will not be still, and it is there, that we learn most.

African Proverb

17.1 Introduction

People frequently ask us how they can learn to live with disturbance in their lives. Optimistically, they want to cope with and draw upon the provocative moments they experience rather than withdraw or be overwhelmed by them. It is a valuable question, but it is difficult to answer for three reasons.

First, disturbance comes in many forms, including those we have discussed in this book. These include external challenges such as those Charlie Massy and Colin Seis faced or the crisis that impacted Kibbutz Yisrael. But individuals, teams, and organizations can also choose to challenge themselves to make fundamental changes. Here, the provocation is self-generated but in response to some stimulus. We saw this with Nyadol Nyuon, Chris Sarra, David Gruen, and René Jones.

Second, there is a difference between disturbance created by purposeful provocation and the perturbations that surprise us during our lives-those arising from increased levels of volatility, uncertainty and personal crucibles. In the latter case, the disturbance can be more diffuse, less recognizable, more intricate, and complicated to harness.

Third, everyone is built and wired differently. It is almost impossible to provide a one-size-fits-all approach. People's responses to a provocative moment will vary, as will how they learn to live with disequilibrium—a critical adaptive capacity. Everyone faces adaptation and the provocation inherent in it with varied past experiences, abilities, and capacity. We all arrive at the edge with different levels of skill and will. The provocative frontier is different for each of us.

This chapter discusses what we have learned to help people benefit from the many provocative moments they will experience during their lives. We will highlight the importance of building processes and structures in your work as you help people navigate the waves and undercurrents of provocative change. First, we will explore the idea of a *provisional self* and how it enables learning and adaptation. We will then provide a scaffolding that helps people develop their capacity to engage with provocation rather than avoid it. Several methods, such as practice and imitation, are

DOI: 10.4324/9781003321200-23

examined in more depth. What follows is intended to help you expand your ability to utilize the tough moments.

17.2 Building a space for change

The death of a loved one, migration to another country, changing closely held beliefs, or introducing innovative practices are major transitions for learning and change. Everyday routines disappear, and you must seek out new ones. These moments are provocative, testing your principles, belief systems, and core values. They create a liminal space within which the previously unconsidered and invisible is rendered visible.

When we ask people how they navigated significant change and transition, most cannot identify what allowed them to respond productively to the challenge or how they did it. But, with the benefit of hindsight, they became a learner, explorer, navigator of the unknown, and traverser of life's swing bridges. The time enabled them to experiment awkwardly while they worked their way into some new competence. As a result, they built what we call a *provisional self*.

Having a provisional self takes you from the known towards a hazy and novel unknown. Even clear goals or hopes cannot be guaranteed. Therefore, it is a big step to ask people to have faith that what is proposed will help them, mainly because the disturbance is ongoing rather than occurring in a one-off moment.

We have seen how the farmers on irrigated land on the Murray Darling in Australia became used to using water when and how they wanted. Then, suddenly, the laws controlling water usage changed, and they had to adjust their operation and their notion of free agency. Adaptation, disorientation, and liminality go together, but this is not an easy sell. To make the provocative journey more manageable, you need to provide people with guide rails, pointers, and stepping-stones.

Charlie Massy is convinced that he would have never changed anything without an external push, a personal provocation. But to do so, it was necessary to have a platform to leap out from. He needed a set of conditions, a series of spaces, that made his transition manageable and achievable. These conditions are a provisional self—a form of personal or shared holding environment.

17.2.1 A provisional self

A partner in a professional services firm was trying to get her colleagues to recognize the risks that existed for her company despite positive business indicators. It was hard for her to get her colleagues to discuss the pressures on legacy business, such as compliance work, that online, cloud-based tools, and artificial intelligence bring to bear. Or to have partners consider that some of their longstanding values and attitudes were no longer as relevant. So, she established two practice groups: one explored several future scenarios the firm could face, while the second asked a range of stakeholders, "What's the one big thing we are missing?" Each group provided an airlock within which they could practice, discover, and learn without any formal accountability. She called the groups "The Rough and Readies" to indicate they were not responsible for solutions only practice and that they would disappear after their two months of exploration. They were provisional.

In so doing, she created an agreement with others, a scaffolding to encourage learning. As a result, it was safe for others to question their firm's practices and experiment with new ways—a provisional identity.

Whether for you as an individual or for your team or organization, a provisional self provides permission to try and fail and briefly let yourself off the hook while learning your way into greater competence. A provisional self provides legitimacy to move beyond your past and lay down some new code, reprogramming your way into a modified future. You will remember how Charlie Massy, for example, temporarily felt immobilized because he couldn't speak with the new understandings he had developed. Equally, he did not want to use the old language. It was disabling. He was caught in an in-between zone. Or how CEO René Jones (Chapter 11) regularly said, "I'm working in myself," as an indicator that he too was challenging himself to learn new approaches.

As with a corporate start-up or a period of organizational transformation, the provisional self is subject to risk-taking, trial and error, and the creation of a prototype—a revised condition. This is a temporary period characterized by individual or group entrepreneurship, as well as ambiguity. It provokes, persuades, and convinces that innovation is worthwhile. As the economist Joseph Schumpeter suggested in his book *Capitalism, Socialism and Democracy*, as a learner and entrepreneur, you are "able to act beyond the range of familiar beacons and see your primary task as breaking up the old and creating new traditions." The provisional self begins to see and create things that prove to be transformational even though they were not apparent at the time.

Chris Sarra risked everything as he experimented with new ways of engaging his students until everyone believed in the new ways. Similarly, David Gruen (Chapter 12) pushed his designers to create quick surveys, but they had to develop new professional identities concurrently as they adjusted to doing things very differently.

17.2.2 Disciplined attention

What distinguishes people or communities who grow through provocation? Our experience suggests that their willingness to pay disciplined attention to the reality they face and to their learning makes the most difference. A crisis, some direct feedback, or a challenging encounter provokes the disorienting dilemma, which exposes them to the frontiers of their experience and meaning-making. Practice becomes a pathway between their legacy identity and their provisional self, where repeated application embeds new attitudes and beliefs. But we have also seen how most people and groups need a supportive and robust container in which to practice.

We facilitated an executive team retreat during which one participant said, "I am not used to feeling this disoriented, and I don't know which part of myself to draw on." It became apparent that the team's competence, capability, and behaviors were under scrutiny, making it temporarily harder for them to test their learning edge. We repeatedly used the notion of a provisional self to explore what it would mean for

Principles for Developing a Provisional Self
• A reason or motivation for change combined with some genuinely felt experience. • The learners confront the limitations of their current knowledge and mental models, which pressures people's view of themselves-they are or think they are, seen as foolish and inexpert. • Practice and experimentation combined with gaining perspective and being mindful are essential. • Practice needs to be embedded in relationships that matter. • An environment that both supports and challenges any new practice.

Table 17.1 Principles guiding the use of a provisional self

the team to be learners and become more flexible, using a broader range of roles and resources in their work. The idea took hold and allowed them to look at themselves more expansively while stretching into new ways of working and being. Colin Seis, the regenerative farmer we encountered in Chapter 8, notes that he needed to change how he saw himself. He was no longer a farmer, a member of the industrial agriculture club, but now was a nurturer and custodian of the land (Table 17.1).

These principles highlight that the process of provocation is not only about making a piercing comment or asking a question that tests people. Provocation also helps initiate a longer-term focus during which you build structures for ongoing learning. Perhaps they can help you learn more from experience.

17.3 A scaffold for learning provokes action

The concept of the provisional self gives many people a means, a scaffold, by which they can see themselves in transition between one way of operating and another more flexible way. The provisional self gives you a rope to grasp as you lurch across a new swing bridge. It becomes an interstitial zone where you can play, test, and experiment with different, more original, and stretching ways of functioning. One leadership educator from a recent Masterclass said, "This language gave us a way in. It enabled me to create a new identity, a probationer with a learner's permit with which to practice."

17.3.1 Practice

Practice allows for the incremental acquisition of competence. Elite athletes, for example, have potential and some natural physical assets, but like dancers, actors, and musicians, they practice as hard as they perform. A provisional self helps you recognize it is necessary to try things multiple times in similar and different ways, with the same people and in new situations. Because the line between performance and practice is often hard to discern, the provisional self learns how to practice while it performs.

René Jones and his colleagues at M&T Bank (Chapter 11) show how practicing a new routine in their weekly executive meetings can simultaneously help and provoke. René insisted on three simple rules to guide their work, so what behavior was required was clear. But it was very challenging for those involved to change their ways. René insisted his team kept practicing the new ways of doing business together, despite complaints and push back. It took six months before he and his colleagues could see the benefits and how stuck they had been. This example highlights the importance of structured practice to generate change and just how hard (provocative) it is to get experienced people to do anything new.

Nyadol Nyuon (Chapter 14) shows us what practice looks like in real-time as she grew up in public on TV and had to learn and make mistakes in the public eye. She also describes her time at law school as transformative. "Law school was radical in the way it changed my thinking about myself," she says, "because it was interesting to be surrounded by people who took so much for granted. I had to do a lot of personal self-raising as a person and really developed a sense of my own self-leadership."

Nyadol shows you that several strategies are involved in reshaping personal identity, including observation, imitation, practice, or experimentation. The provisional self evolves, one step at a time toward what is a possible but not yet fully realized identity. It entails disengagement from a legacy identity grounded in your everyday routine while exploring new roles, actions, and practices. Equally, Chris Sara's story exemplifies this trial of the possible and how he practiced and experimented his way into a new identity, constantly provoking himself and being provoked while at Teachers College.

Imagine yourself in a situation where you have no experience, resources, or personal privilege, but those around you do. How would this feel? In what ways would you feel challenged and provoked? Identity is forged in the heat of a transformative experience, in the invisible flames of personal and situational upheaval. Chris and Nyadol illustrate how much hard work and practice are required to emerge with yourself intact, functioning authentically with a new identity.

When her family relocated to Australia, Diana Renner (Chapter 15) had to practice her way into becoming Australian to fit in. "Even now," she says, "I frequently feel on the outside, looking in." Diana has practiced sufficiently but somehow carries the carapace of her provisional self with her wherever she goes. Like the secret she held onto when leaving Romania, Diana has a continuous provisional identity, living betwixt and between, becoming comfortable with ambiguity. Her well-developed capacity to tolerate and seek out uncertainty has taken a lot of practice and can make others, who do not have such experience, perturbed. Diana's life-long provisional self is both a resource and, at times, a constraint.

17.3.2 Imitation

Imitation is used in a variety of personal or professional development settings. For example, the master cellist Pablo Casals was asked if students could develop their own unique learning styles. "No!" he exclaimed while drawing a line on a wall. "The student must act as an apprentice. The master draws a line, and the student retraces it." For Casals, imitation was seen as a legitimate and necessary part of learning a complex craft and a means to create a provisional self -a stepping-stone from student to a competent musician. Indeed, as noted earlier, Casals was also reported to have said, "A good imitation is better than a bad original."

The ability to copy, model, and practice is at the heart of developing new skills and expanding your repertoire, including living with, or initiating, provocation. But adults feel inhibited when copying others or being seen doing so. Helping those affected by change overcome such inhibitions is a key to developing a provisional self—the best trial version of who and what they want to become. Once you appreciate that you can act that way, you can change how you see yourself.

Colin Seis was confronted with an ecological disaster on his farm, one compounded by a devastating bushfire. He knew he couldn't continue with farming as usual but didn't know what he would do. However, he followed his instincts and started to imitate what his land did naturally. He copied the natural rhythms of land regeneration, and, without interference, his property came back to life. He watched, interpreted, and learned, but he stood back. Inaction is very difficult for a practical, action-oriented farmer, but it offers a living example of the superiority of an excellent imitation.

When teaching leadership educators to use his provocative methods, Ron Heifetz once said, "First, do it my way and then develop your style." Michael had the experience of "doing it my way" when training with Frank Farrelly, the creator of Provocative Therapy. Among the forms of practice used, Michael reviewed videotaped client sessions with Maxime. The process of peer review and scrutiny forced him to examine his style and skill set and helped him use new and more challenging methods. One day, Maxime observed how Michael not only had thrown himself into his practice, experimenting with the latest ideas but had done so with an American accent. Embarrassingly, Michael had become so immersed in what he was doing that he had lost sight of how he was mimicking his teacher. Maxime's feedback helped, provoked him to adjust his practice, and became the scaffolding for his learning and growth as he refined his technique.

How far are you willing to go to learn a new skill or practice a new behavior? How can you genuinely expand your way of being and doing?

17.3.3 Repetition

Learning involves persistently putting yourself in situations that demand more from you, conditions that provide challenge and support. Practice requires repetition and will foster more intentional action while ensuring that new activity becomes more familiar. You will remember how René Jones insisted on weekly practice of a new set of skills in his executive meetings, repeating the same mantra—"use the three rules"—until his team began to operate differently.

Ann, a senior executive we coached, weaned herself off her an old view of herself to a more enabling identity. Much of the coaching built a series of experiments: repeated trials of what she could become, observing and imitating colleagues that she admired; opportunities for her to see herself in action in more vital and compelling ways; and a willingness to enjoy and value the tentativeness of new roles. Her practice involved setbacks, but the challenge also allowed her to reflect deeply and question who she was and whom she was becoming.

Ms. Imperfect was the provocative name Ann gave to her practice persona. This allowed her to challenge her problem. She used a provisional self as a learning frame, with permission to go beyond her usual limits as she experimented. She sought and received feedback, not only from us as coaches but from two colleagues she confided in, thereby creating a supporting structure. Most importantly, Ann also developed a tolerance for being seen as imperfect in the behaviors she practiced.

Earlier (Chapter 8) we met Joel, the senior executive whose career had plateaued. This pressure increased his willingness to try a range of new and riskier experiments, each of which was tentative and uncomfortable. However, as he repeated and practiced, he began to experience himself differently and be seen by his colleagues differently, and his identity began to change. Joel selected a small number of behaviors to grow and practice. His most significant gain, however, was the idea "that I can build different parts of myself and not be bound by how I have been."

17.4 Beginnings and learning

Early in our training as therapists, our supervisors instilled in us that how we began a session, a conversation, or a change initiative, sets the tone for everything that follows. This notion has become one of our mantras. We frequently notice the early patterns of interaction between senior executives in team discussions, patterns that enable and constrain their work.

Equally, when we start something new, we set the tone for what follows by using structured activities and rituals. At the start of a process, rituals are valuable in building a safe transition zone that signals what will follow and allowing people to practice together, publicly demonstrating their growing provocative selves.

The New Zealand All Blacks, consistently one of the leading teams in world rugby, always begin their competitive matches with the haka, a ceremonial Māori dance usually performed to display a tribe's pride, strength, and unity. The All Blacks use the haka to challenge their opponents, as a sign of respect and to show their physical prowess. Traditionally, the haka was used on the battlefield to prepare warriors mentally and physically for battle and, socially, when groups came together in peace.

This sports example shows how starting rituals set the scene and signal to newcomers and the established team how an organization currently expresses its values and beliefs.

As an executive, a coach, or a change agent, you also need to consider how to create rituals and enabling conditions early on, setting the scene for developing provocative capacity.

17.4.1 Start with relationships

Starting rituals orient people to how they do business, how power and authority are used, and for what purpose. Many companies now pay close attention to the beginnings of projects, building strong relationships and establishing conditions that will allow the pressures of change to be felt and dealt with. Strong relationships and trust assist in regulating the disequilibrium that inevitably occurs.

We remember working with a senior team who reported high levels of conflict and disagreement, so we spent considerable time building trust and openness before examining their problems. After the event, the team leader informed us that it was the first time they had ever tried to understand each other as individuals, listening to each other and acknowledging past hurts and mistakes. How we began our workshop with this team provided an example of how they could start their team meetings.

How you begin something, how you set the scene as you start something, is critical. For many, it is the start itself where the provocation happens. Finally, observing the rituals indicates how safe it is to give opinions and question expertise and authority. Do you want to begin by creating specific conditions for safety and trust? Of course, but also to stretch the definition of safety from protecting something to being safe to practice new skills that will help navigate the inevitable challenges and disturbances.

17.4.2 Where shall we begin? Warming up for work

Creating provisional zones through ritual, warm-up, and practice reduces the disturbance in a system and temporarily allows people to learn what is necessary to survive and thrive. There will be plenty of time for provocation and more disruption later. Such explicit processes acknowledge the uncertain context, provide direction, and permit exploration of the ambiguity and anxiety.

As leadership educators, we typically begin sessions with a check-in and a warm-up, transitioning from the outside world to our presence in the workshop while also helping the participants prepare to be learners. Depending on the type of session and its duration, we may also use a more provocative warm-up activity.

Perhaps the best-known introduction to Adaptive Leadership is the "Where Shall We Begin?" exercise. Soon after arriving in the room, sometimes without any introduction or preamble, we ask the group, "Given what we are here to do, where shall we begin?" Then, we remain silent for anywhere between ten and thirty minutes as participants squirm in discomfort, feel disoriented, and begin to develop a means of response. They ask us what we mean, propose the need to clarify our purpose, and suggest we should define leadership. Or they simply tell us that it's our responsibility and that we have control of the agenda. Occasionally, a participant will put themselves forward and take on the role of facilitator.

The exercise, which stems from the work of Ron Heifetz and Marty Linsky at the Harvard Kennedy School of Government, signals to participants that we think differently about leadership and the role of authority. They see that they will have to work together and relate to us in unfamiliar and more engaging ways. We want them to feel these distinctions early and to use them as a point of reference for the learning work that will follow. This approach draws participants' focus and attention into the room, away from outside preoccupations and toward their colleagues. It is a provocative way to begin, a shocking ritual. Still, it usually achieves its purpose, rapidly creating a provisional zone between the outside world and the newly constructed world of learning. It forces people to feel and think deeply and quickly, challenging their expectations of what a facilitator should do.

The exercise reminds us of the shock and disturbance we felt when we learned to scuba dive. After a day of practice in the shallow water, the instructor asked us to sit on the ocean floor in deep water and breathe with our new apparatus for five minutes to acclimatize to the sensation of being underwater. It felt like an hour. But we remembered the training mantra, "Don't hold your breath, breath in for four and hold for four, breath out for four and hold for four." This training saved Maxime's life a day or two later when her equipment failed, and she had to use someone else's oxygen in a technique known as buddy breathing. Controlled breathing was initially designed for people in highly intense situations, such as firefighters, soldiers, and first responders. It offers a fast and effective way to reduce stress and gain mental clarity. Maxime used the breathing ritual to focus and calm down, signaling to her parasympathetic nervous system that she needed to do something different and had the means to save herself.

In his first months as the new school Principal, Chris Sarra faced similar transitional challenges. He had practiced and refined his approach before tackling the big challenge at Cherbourg State School. Because his background was different, Chris needed to reassure the parents that uncertainty was expected and healthy as he began to change the school and that they could rely on him for support and guidance. He did this frequently and incrementally built his credibility as well as their capacity to tolerate challenges.

How you begin a project, a new relationship, a job, or a major life transition will significantly impact how you continue with this new process. Good beginnings, rituals, and structures will temporarily reduce the disequilibrium in the system you are part of and provide a container for orientation and the required controlled breathing. The art is regulating the pressure so that there is just enough provocation to assist you to be at your edge but just enough support that you aren't overwhelmed and risk getting the bends.[1]

How does your team or organization create a provisional environment for newcomers to learn? What rituals and beginnings do you use? What means do you have to provoke people at the beginning to signal something different but do so without overwhelming them?

We have shown how a provisional self provides, like an airlock, a tailored and supported environment for the individual and collective transitions required. It is your job as a leader, facilitator, coach, or change agent to assist people to build their own airlock. This is where they can continue to breathe but make the changes needed to swim successfully in the new oceans. Of course, sitting on the bottom of the ocean is an unnatural thing to do if you haven't practiced. But, once you have mastered this skill, you will have the capacity to tolerate riskier underwater adventures.

The next chapter will examine some of the lessons you can learn about using provocation from the subjects of our ten case studies. The seven key lessons we discuss may be relevant to your own experience.

Note

1 For the uninitiated, the bends, or decompression sickness, are caused when a diver moves from a high pressure environment to one of low pressure too rapidly, causing bubbles to form in their bloodstream. The bends are potentially lethal.

References

Casals, P. (2010). Quoted by Terry King, page 250 in Gregor Piatogorsky: *The Life and Career of the Virtuoso Cellist.* McFarland & Co, Jefferson, NC.

Farrelly, F., & Brandsma, J.M. (1981). *Provocative Therapy.* Meta Publications, California, USA.

Ibarra, H. (1999). Provisional selves: Experimenting with image and identity in professional adaptation. *Administrative Science Quarterly*, *44*(4), pp. 764–791.

Johnstone, M.A. (2018). *Do We Really Learn from Experience? Developing a Provisional Self for Practice and Learning.* LinkedIn, 30 April 2018. https://www.linkedin.com/pulse/do-we-really-learn-experience-developing-provisional-johnstone-phd/. Retrieved 9 October 2020.

Schumpeter, J.A. (1975). *Capitalism, Socialism and Democracy.* Harper-Collins, New York, 3rd Edition.

18 LESSONS IN THE USE OF PROVOCATION

The truth will set you free. But first, it will piss you off.
Gloria Steinem, The Truth Will Set You Free, 2019

18.1 Introduction

Throughout this book, we have provided a range of anecdotes, stories, and case studies illustrating the use of provocation, an activity designed to engage people when change is needed. We have shown how those working on behalf of their business, community or group have stepped forward, taking risks for something that mattered to them. We have also shown how provocative moments require careful diagnosis and a degree of courage, and how it is unusual for others to thank you for unsettling their world. In addition, we have explored provocative strategies used in response to profound external crises across various sectors and the opportunities for change and innovation in each of them.

This chapter will weave the threads of conversation together. We think there are seven key lessons from our case studies. In summary, they are:

1. Provocative action was catalyzed by a profound and disorienting experience, which helped clarify the nature of the challenge they faced;
2. Our protagonists experienced critical disbelief, resistance, and personal attack, as well as reputational risk. This changed them and forged a robust personal and professional identity;
3. They confronted the rigidity of a longstanding paradigm, developed a new philosophy, and established a new set of ethics and values that were more consistent with the aspirations of their community or organization;
4. They persistently raised challenging questions, made hard decisions, and held others accountable;
5. They had to respond to the consequences of the disturbance generated. Among these were significant losses;
6. They created a strong holding environment because of the unusual circumstances they faced; and
7. The people we discussed all cared deeply and held the interests of others above their own. They expressed deep and practical love.

DOI: 10.4324/9781003321200-24

18.2 A disorienting dilemma

While the circumstances described in our case studies were different, they all involved a profound disorienting dilemma, an adaptive challenge. There was no immediate answer, but our protagonists all felt compelled to act. Because it was disorienting and uncertain, our subjects became open and reflective, and saw things differently. They all described how their new experience was not compatible with their prior knowledge or belief systems. They reconsidered their beliefs, had deep conversations with others, asked hard questions, raised unpalatable truths, and persistently rattled the cage. What was clear to them was not obvious to others. Identifying the adaptation required was at the heart of their provocative work.

Charlie Massy and Colin Seis (Chapter 8) felt pushed to their limits by an environmental crisis, by drought and fire, and significant personal trauma. They describe these experiences as "breaking open the cosmic egg." These shocks opened them to new ways of looking at themselves and the world. In addition, they broke away from long-held family and local traditions and practices, many of which put them at odds with parents and neighbors.

Chris Sarra (Chapter 10) built his Stronger and Smarter philosophy on the back of his own experience as an indigenous child invisible to his teachers. He realized that teachers didn't expect him to do well, and he set out change this. His approach was disorienting to others because he would not collude with the idea that indigenous children could not learn like other Australian children.

M&T Bank (Chapter 11) had to navigate a year of grief following the death of several executives, including their legendary CEO. The shock required René Jones, as the new CEO, and his two most senior colleagues, to simultaneously steady the ship and calm people down while reorienting the business to address several emerging challenges. As Kevin Pearson said, "We had become complacent and were resting on our laurels." M&T's disorienting dilemma allowed them to see things as they were rather than as they assumed they were. As a result, they began to pave a way forward.

The central dilemma for Kibbutz Yizrael (Chapter 9) was how could it survive and thrive. As they rode the waves of change, sometimes responding to them and at other times creating them, they relied on three provocative strategies to navigate through the storm of the 1980s.

First, by standing up and speaking out, issuing calls to action in the face of the financial devastation, and with pleas for responsible and shared leadership across the community. Our friends' persistent but measured approach was appropriate even though the solutions were unpalatable to many.

Second, mobilizing their community to reflect deeply on underlying values, attitudes, and behaviors meant confronting what community members couldn't or didn't want to see. Kibbutz life had to evolve, had to become fit for purpose. People needed to recognize that they couldn't continue to operate in isolation from the changing environment around them.

Third, they helped build Kibbutz Yizrael's adaptive muscles—drawing on intrinsic Israeli attitudes of resilience and tolerance of ambiguity, infused with a provocative mindset. For many years, as in a children's playground, life on Yizrael had been a "balagan"—messy, noisy, busy, disorganized, rough, but, ultimately, creative. Israelis are known for their brashness and directness. These were qualities needed to ask hard questions and keep disequilibrium levels productive.

18.3 Strong resistance and pushback

The trailblazers discussed in this book met considerable resistance, including within themselves, as they grappled with transforming not only their communities or organizations but also their internal landscapes. For example, René Jones and Kevin Pearson at M&T Bank revealed how much opposition there was to recruit outsiders to several core roles. Some longstanding staff believed their leaders had broken the bank's unspoken contract to promote loyal staff to senior roles. By changing the "rules of the game," many felt let down and were reticent to support the new recruits.

The pushback against Charlie Massy's ideas was intense and included government pressure. Regenerative farmers all had to learn to live with and respond to a wide range of disbelief, personal attack, and even social rebuke and marginalization. They discovered what happens when your actions threaten a worldview that others hold dear. One of Charlie's colleagues spoke of how his family and friends felt threatened, describing how "family farm inheritance doesn't allow people to take much risk. They've got someone—an older person—looking over their shoulder who's not going to let them. The world revolves around just their one little place."

Being different, standing out is difficult at the best of times, but when your difference is ongoing and persistent, it begins to wear thin for others. Provocation begins to feel like a siege. As such, the changes that early regenerative farmers made were significant and against all odds. Yet, they had few local allies even though they were part of wider holistic networks and communities of practice.

All our subjects discovered that their communities and colleagues didn't applaud them when they began using new and unproven ways or when they acted as if they had uncovered previously hidden truths. They found themselves out on the ice alone. If there was any support or applause, it was usually from a safe distance. The pioneer often suffers the same fate as the prophet or messiah.

When people feel provoked, they push back in different ways. Sometimes these are very personal. For example, Nyadol Nyuon spoke of how her own community attacked her for not being "female enough," breaking traditions, and "bringing shame" because she spoke out as a single mother. Some white Australians attacked her as "ungrateful for everything Australia had done for her" when she raised questions about racism.

Strangely, many of our protagonists felt like members of ultraorthodox religious communities who leave their protected world and enter secular society. Many were shunned and ostracized by those whose traditions they abandoned. They didn't quite fit in with the wider community for some time, partly because they didn't know the game's rules and because they still hadn't developed the requisite skills required to live the new dream. They found themselves in a liminal zone. For example, in the case of our farmers, they lived in between the worlds of mechanical and regenerative farming with all the associated social and relationship confusions. They experienced shame, and many reported psychological upheavals. The costs are high in the short-term, and the gains are only evident over an extended period.

The primary lesson here is that pushback and opposition are inevitable consequences of provocation. You should expect it and know that it will come from various sources and in varied forms, including highly charged emotional outbursts and attacks.

18.4 They poked a stick into a prevailing paradigm

All those we spoke to confronted paradigms whose fundamental elements had not been tested and, therefore, resisted easy modification. Like an outdated computer operating system, the prevailing coding needed revision. In some cases, it took a crisis, an external event, to create a tipping point.

Shimon and Peter started by helping their community avoid collapse. Then, once they had cauterized the wound, they began a long process of helping to question the fundamental beliefs of the settlement. They understood that the prevailing ideology and core beliefs, forged during the hard days of the kibbutz's formation, were essential to all members because they defined what being a kibbutz meant. Therefore, it was hardly surprising that each step Shimon or Peter took was deeply unsettling to many people. Even though their proposals made sense practically, they were hard to reconcile ideologically.

The success of Kibbutz Yizrael was built on finding a pathway between survival and adaptation and between pragmatism and ideology. Shimon's and Peter's contribution was their willingness to ask, even insist, that their colleagues examine the restrictions of the original doctrine. They needed to keep what was essential and find different ways to express their values and aspirations.

We have shown how Charlie Massy's earlier campaigns against the wool industry targeted powerful vested interests. But his and Colin Seis's promotion of regenerative farming confronted a different paradigm, including their own thinking. At least initially, the enemy was within, and Charlie and Colin needed to disturb their own systems. Once these farmers were sufficiently disturbed, they could dismantle and reconstruct their personal theory of how things work. In so doing, they first changed their internal coding and then the rules of agriculture and management. Charlie's and Colin's new philosophy, ethics, and values challenged and unintentionally threatened their peers and locally accepted practice, and even family. It was a high cost to pay that only the committed would choose to bear.

It is no wonder that, as they rejected the old ways, the opposition and criticism they encountered was strong. They became masters of negotiating with the status quo and figuring out when and how to push it, challenge it, harness it, and when to leave it alone. Charlie and Colin discovered that you must get out of the way and create new conditions to foster learning and progress to mobilize change. They faced a typical adaptive paradox. Until your own understanding and perception change, and your mind adapts, you can be blind to what is all around you. Together, they have described the foundations of ecological literacy, encompassing curiosity, observation, pattern recognition, and interpretation, as well as a relentless focus on maladaptive behavior that leads to environmental and human destruction.

The experience of our protagonists highlights two crucial principles of provocation. First, the more rigid and entrenched a system is, the more potent and persistent the provocation needs to be. All our protagonists needed to provoke others for anyone to take heed, and they needed to do so persistently over time. Second, you know that you have unsettled entrenched thinking and beliefs when you begin to get attacked personally. The irrigation industry establishment found it hard to counter the logic of water reform arguments, particularly given the thoroughness of the science, so they attacked government officials personally.

All the stories show us that when a complex system is disturbed, it approaches the edges of chaos, and the disequilibrium becomes visible to people. A drought that denudes a farm of its topsoil, a plague of grasshoppers that destroys a crop, or wild storms that create flooding, are all "edges" of chaos that will attract people's attention. Here, in Australia, as in many other parts of the world, such events have become more frequent, more severe, and sequential, prompting people to action.

David Gruen was determined not to "waste" the crisis created by Covid-19 and set about creating profound culture change. Building on the changes started by his predecessor David Kalisch, in 2020, David Gruen and the ABS quickly changed decades of practice by implementing rapid but less accurate surveys that provided immediate information to the government and the public about the impact of Covid-19. As with many of our protagonists, they began to change the prevailing paradigm, creating new, more flexible structures, and becoming more responsive to the needs of their community.

18.5 Ask hard questions, make difficult decisions

A hallmark of provocative action is the willingness to ask hard questions. But, as our subjects discovered, if you ask questions, some will describe you as a troublemaker, seeing you as impudent or arrogant; others won't even listen.

When Nyadol Nyuon challenges Australians to apply the same standards to South Sudanese youth as to white kids, she is not adopting a neutral position. On the contrary, she is asking the public to examine their own beliefs and biases. This can be provocative to those who want to be reassured that they are not bad rather than forced to confront their racism. Nyadol, who has suffered more than her interlocutors ever will, has not put herself forward to make their lives easier by asking more straightforward questions. Instead, she is a catalyst who is there to shake up the way they see the world.

Sarah, who we first met in Chapter 6, didn't ask direct questions. But her powerful story stimulated her colleagues. For example, she indirectly asked them how they could find other avenues to express their commitment and passion. Her story elicited a process of self-questioning and reflection that opened a significant issue that no one could talk about—grief and the possibility of hope.

Chris Sarra is a master at asking questions. He pushed everyone at the Cherbourg State School into awkward areas that touched on matters of bias, collusion, expectation, and satisfaction. But Chris also asked more profound questions about Australia's attitude to indigenous children and how the education system made these kids invisible. He insisted on confronting unpalatable truths, realities many preferred to avoid. His questions helped the community at Cherbourg articulate their desire for children to receive a better education. They helped loosen an entrenched status quo founded on the assumption that indigenous children are less able to learn because of their external environment, a situation that encouraged these same children to think poorly of themselves.

At the heart of asking provocative questions is the idea that you will bypass the usual reactions, defenses, and habits of mind. Good questions, big questions, can all be provocative because they take people to an unexpected and often uncomfortable place. In so doing, you will allow others to think and explore more deeply. The examples and stories we have outlined show how the protagonists used questions as a powerful means to pierce the armor of established ways of doing things and engaged their communities in meaningful dialogue.

18.6 Hard decisions

Making decisions is one of the most provocative things you can do, particularly when you fulfill an authority role, representing a team or community, and when the decision affects a range of members. Making a ruling is confronting when it forces people to take sides, identify where their loyalties lie and consider how much loss they can tolerate. Provocative decisions place you, as an authority figure, in the spotlight. Inevitably, they will prove unpopular with some people, the impact is uneven, and this will reflect on you.

Peter Pezaro discovered this during his time as the General Manager of Kibbutz Yizrael. In the context of an ailing economy, he saw the need to do what was necessary to avoid collapse, occasionally pushing acceptable boundaries. A hallmark of decision-making in a communal settlement like Yizrael was that even the most senior person was not authorized to make major decisions independently. On a kibbutz, the whole community made big decisions while specialist committees made others. It was tough to act quickly, but there were occasions when speed was precisely what was required, prompting unpredictable responses from other community members.

Some of the decisions Peter made stand out because of the reactions they provoked. For example, at one point, it was clear the citrus orchard was no longer viable. The agriculture committee decided to close the orchard, and Peter offered to be the bearer of the bad news. However, he hadn't expected such a strong reaction even though he understood what a blow it would be to the man who had built this sector. Sadly, it is now thirty years since they have spoken. A few years later, Peter had a similar experience with a younger kibbutz member he had mentored and supported in a new business venture. But after the new business lost NIS 11 million over three years, Peter closed it down.

In René Jones's case, he decided that it was necessary to confront decades of thinking in M&T Bank and take some chances following the CEO's death. His decisions and the questions he asked his staff were not loud or dramatic, but they were provocative because they required people to navigate new terrain away from the well-worn pathways of the past. They took expert bankers, more comfortable with routine and certainty, into the domain of experimentation. For example, René changed the purpose of the Executive Team meetings and insisted on "only three rules," a decision that put pressure on all his seasoned colleagues because they were used to a very different regime. It took six months before this decision bore fruit, and René's stance was vindicated.

The unexpected nature of these difficult decisions, running contrary to what people anticipated, opened to scrutiny the values and beliefs of the affected communities. They enabled change to happen. It takes personal courage and conviction to act against the norms and wishes of your colleagues, especially if you are concerned about letting others down. Turning away from or challenging long-established norms and the wisdom of elders are provocative acts.

18.7 The impact of change is uneven: Expect loss

Provocation is usually unsettling and sometimes profoundly so. When you disturb an existing system with all its habits and traditions, there will be consequences. But the impact will be felt differently across the organization, or community. Moreover, the loss that people experience is deeply personal, often endured for a long time, and can impact livelihoods, positions, and status.

Kibbutz Yizrael confronted existential and practical challenges over several decades, leaving many people disoriented and disillusioned. Large numbers gave up and left the community, and some friendships or professional relationships didn't survive. These are actual losses that many feel to this day. On a kibbutz, personal and formal business relationships become fused. One day you are friends and allies, the next day, as Peter found as General Manager, you decide something on behalf of the community that can affect your friends personally. This is a profound experience to undergo, and Peter felt it deeply.

The culling of the citrus orchard was a blow to the foundation dream of the settlement and the individuals involved. The orchard was a part of the origin story and had many supporters who felt the pain of its loss acutely. A kibbutz is a tight-knit community where most aspects of daily life are on display. However, when there is a problem to solve and significant pressure, the environment can become a hothouse.

It is essential not to distance yourself from the grit and toil of making profound change as a provocateur. Instead, you must get your own boots dirty. When Chris Sarra began to implement his Stronger and Smarter initiative, he did what he required others to do, including having high expectations about what the children could achieve and consider themselves part of the problem. Many of the teachers were insulted. Unable to accept their collusion in a low-performance, low-expectation culture, many resigned.

Ken Henry's speeches about indigenous disadvantage have had the same effect at a national level, but the losses are less visible. They are implicit, hidden from view, in the advantages that white Australians have, allowing them to act as if this issue is not their problem. Many people will need to make complex adjustments about Australia's past relationship with its First Nations people to address the many disparities. But these ideas are hidden in their history and culture but will eventually need to be addressed.

18.8 A strong holding environment

Another common thread in our case-studies is how each needed and created a holding environment that helped the organization or community deal with disruption. Such a container was required for different reasons, including that the provocation came from unexpected people and situations.

On September 11, 2001, we were at the Harvard Kennedy School of Government in Cambridge, Massachusetts, to meet with our colleagues Ron Heifetz and Marty Linksy when we saw the attack on the Twin Towers reported on TV. Within three hours of the assaults, the School's executive body had arranged a gathering in its famous Forum, a tiered open space used for public addresses. The dean, Joseph Nye, spoke to the large crowd of students and faculty. He declared that for as long as people wanted it, the Forum would remain open to discuss what was happening in New York and Washington, examining what it meant for people individually and as a society. There were only two rules: anyone and everyone could speak, and everyone was to listen and respect the feelings and thoughts of all speakers, no matter what they revealed. Jessica Stern, a Harvard specialist in international terror groups, also spoke at this initial gathering, providing background to what drives people to take extreme action.

The Forum's physical space, the authorization by the Dean, his two guiding rules of conduct, and the collective shock, anger, and grief people felt resulted in several hours of far-reaching discussion. The holding environment was sustained over many days and, like a well-managed pressure cooker, allowed discussion on genuine and raw questions relating to US policy, culture, and behavior. Many of the case studies we have explored incorporate the lessons we learned during that period. What is important is that you create a container with boundaries within which the provocative work of adaptation can occur.

Chris Sarra, for example, developed a framework based on his Stronger and Smarter vision to mobilize change at the Cherbourg State School. Whenever there were doubts or criticism, whenever he made errors, the boundaries of his work were evident. The vision was the container, guiding his efforts and helping others know what was in and out of scope in the broader conversation. The concept, with its simple but powerful credo, became the holding environment. Chris added elements to this to make sure it became increasingly safe to have the difficult conversations needed. For example, he insisted at the beginning of meetings with parents that "they wouldn't leave until everything had been thrashed out." He created a ground rule that reassured people that they would be taken seriously and created a safe environment to talk and express fear and anger.

In other situations, your role and position help create a holding environment for the change involved, as we saw with René Jones and how he created a new rhythm for his Executive Team meetings. He gently insisted that people only follow three rules, and they do so until the group began to learn new ways of problem-solving. His three rules, the routine of meeting every Tuesday and the persistent pressure to try new approaches, created an incubator that allowed these seasoned bankers to develop new capacities and apply them to the more complex challenges they faced.

While we may want our political leaders to make change that disturbs the status quo, we don't expect challenge from twelve-year-old children, especially those from disadvantaged circumstances. When it comes from someone unexpected, the surprise acts as a temporary holding environment. But when the shock occurs in a sanctioned location, the container is stronger.

On September 11, 2019, Australians discovered this when Dujuan Hoosan, an Arrernte and Garrwa[1] boy from Central Australia, spoke at the United Nations Human Rights Council in Geneva. Dujuan spoke from the heart about his experience in school and how he had run afoul of the law and nearly gone to jail. He told the Council, "I came here because our government isn't listening. Adults never listen to kids like me. But we have important things to say."

What was disturbing was the disjuncture between Dujuan's articulate comments and his school reports. He speaks three languages, is considered a healer by his people, but has struggled in the mainstream school system. His appearance at the UN, in addition to his poignant and cheeky performance in Maya Newell's 2019 documentary *In My Blood, It Runs*, elevates the importance of education for indigenous children and the unsuitability of what is currently available to them. He asks for the right to receive an education that honors his heritage and traditions while enabling him to navigate the white world. Dujuan provokes mainstream Australia with his simple needs, reminding us that the lofty goals of longstanding public policy are far from being achieved.

Dujuan Hoosan, Chris Sarra, and Charlie Massey provide examples of different types of provocation from unexpected people and unusual places and the importance of creating a holding environment.

18.9 Purpose and deep love for others

Throughout this book, we have spoken of provocation with and for a purpose. We have shown the fundamental human issues that lead managers, teachers, politicians, community members, group facilitators, change agents, and those on the margins of society, such as refugees, to take risks and disturb others. We hope it has become clear that you only take provocative action when you care enough. When your purpose is both clear and shared, and it is about others.

Sometimes, the purpose is about a high-order human value such as authenticity or inclusion. Nyadol Nyuon has shown us how her commitment to being herself, despite the pushback from others, but especially in her South Sudanese community, is driven by the respect she has for her heritage and the care she has for others like her. When she speaks about Australian attitudes to young South Sudanese men, she does so out of love for them and a commitment to build a more connected and compassionate society. Nyadol does not shy away from controversy or from speaking provocatively. Despite the vitriol she has suffered, she continues to stand up, driven by her care for other people of color.

Charlie Massy displays his care for others in a more global manner. In arguing for a new way of farming and adopting a provocative position, he demonstrates his love of humanity and the planet. He is alarmed by what he sees happening to the environment, arguing that there is clear evidence that the systems that define the planet are faltering because of the impact of industrial, fossil-fueled capitalism. Charlie believes that the biggest tragedy is that there is "an absence of a sense of tragedy," even though it is clear that humans are changing the Earth's physical and ecological conditions.

Chris Sarra's love is more direct and immediate. He wants Aboriginal children to have a better life, full of the opportunities he has experienced. He sees his work as a mission to care for children who have been told they aren't worth the effort. Sarra's Stronger and Smarter philosophy has arisen from seeing the effects of neglect and low expectations on children. But his provocative leadership is also intended to encourage people to "connect with their own sense of humanity" and challenge the status quo, including their role in maintaining it.

During our conversation, Chris was clear about our collective responsibility to stand up and speak out when faced with the kind of challenge he met at Cherbourg. He notes that if you walk past inequality or injustice, you become a bystander and risk giving up your own integrity.

> *If you are confronted by a circumstance that lacks integrity. Then, whether you are a schoolteacher, a senior bureaucrat, parent, a child support worker, a doctor, or whatever, the choice is the same for all of us. If we encounter a shitty status quo where people are being sold short or their humanity is being undermined, we choose whether we collude with that or not. It's as simple as that. If we choose not to collude with it, that invokes a whole series of circumstances, which is going to mean a lot of hard work.*

Chris has a moral code and challenges others profoundly by talking about the ways we all collude in letting problems continue by turning away from them. For Chris, collusion is tantamount to giving up on our humanity, a high price to pay for regularly ignoring a problematic situation. Therefore, it is necessary to work at a deeper spiritual level because "it goes beyond the realm of our humanity."

Our protagonists' provocation disturbs some people to their core and, occasionally, turns others away, distracting them from essential work. Yet, despite their occasional mistakes, we can appreciate their purpose, as well as the love and care they demonstrate for people, the community, and the planet. There is much to learn from their passion. Without it, their actions would amount to dangerous indulgences rather than the powerful provocations to change that they are.

Note

1 Arrernte and Garrwa are two of the multitude of Aboriginal tribes and language groups across Australia and live in and around Alice Springs, Central Australia.

References

Newell, M. (2019). *In My Blood It Runs*. Documentary Film. https://www.imdb.com/title/tt8192948/. Retrieved 22 January 2021.

Steinem, G. (2019). *The Truth Will Set You Free, But First It Will Piss You Off! Thoughts on Love, Life and Rebellion*. Murdoch Books, Allan and Unwin, London.

19 EPILOGUE—THE ALBATROSS AND THE CONDUCTOR

19.1 Flight of the albatross

Leaders, like an albatross, need to step out, beyond the known, in order to fly.
Comment during a workshop session 2019

Birdwatchers will describe to you the majesty of the albatross. They are the largest seabirds, with a ten-foot wingspan and the ability to travel great distances. The gray-haired species can circle the earth in forty-six days following the ocean currents. Albatrosses are social creatures and mate for life.

The albatross is used to symbolize both good and bad fortune, becoming familiar through Samuel Taylor Coleridge's poem *The Rime of the Ancient Mariner*. Here the allusion is to a burden as in "an albatross around your neck."

As well as being the subject of western literature, these remarkable birds also have a special place in many spiritual traditions and myths. For example, the Māori of New Zealand hold the albatross in high regard, seeing this bird as a symbol of their own powers of navigation across vast oceans. In Māori lore, and long before Coleridge, their ancestors migrated to New Zealand or Aotearoa in great canoes, one of which was captained by the great chief Toroa. The Māori gave the albatross the name Toroa out of respect for its powers, beauty, and bravery. In addition, in Māori custom, if you want to pay respect to someone, you can use the phrase "te rau o titapu," or titapu's plume: titapu are the fine feathers from the albatross treasured by Māori royalty.

While they are renowned for their prowess in the air, and revered in many cultures, the albatross is not born with the ability to fly and soar; flying is something they have to learn. The ability comes from a combination of genetics, practice, and bravery. Although their wings are designed for sailing, they are a handicap for taking off. As a result, the birds build their nests on the windward side of islands, high up, so they can use the natural advantages of the location to assist, where they can jump off, into the wind, and hope for the best.

Young albatrosses have to learn to undertake an unnatural task: jumping off a cliff. So, they practice, stretching and flapping their wings—a comical sight. At times, they are seen to practice jumping a few centimeters in their air. But in the end, the only way an albatross can actually learn to fly is, like parachutists and base-jumpers, to leap out. Albatrosses have to have the stomach for risk because they learn

DOI: 10.4324/9781003321200-25

by doing, just like you as a practitioner of provocation. To realize the ideal of being an albatross, the young birds must leap, catch a breeze, and only then can they soar. In this manner, a young bird is not really an albatross until it has leapt out and discovered its ability to fly.

19.2 Mastery: Conductor and first violin at the same time

In the high art expression of provocation, in the service of learning and progress, there comes the opportunity to create the music of change and dance within it at the same time. Just as the albatross soars, you as a conductor can orchestrate the work of others.

Any skill or expression of human capability must begin with learning individual elements and putting them together, an awkward, mechanical, and mundane manner. This applies to learning a musical instrument, becoming a carpenter, taking the path to design digital games, or learning to become an albatross who bravely leaps into the unknown. Thus, with diligence, humility, and practice, you move from beginner to competent performer.

When you as a practitioner have learned well, experimented, succeeded, and failed in equal measure, you develop more than adequate and skillful provocation skills. You are confident to step up, steady yourself, hold a group's attention, and raise the baton. As a practitioner, you have learned to manage your ego, be clear on what success will look like, and accept that failure and confusion may well find a way in. You offer at least a moderate risk on behalf of your own and others' learning and growth.

And with any diligently developed skill or gifted natural ability, there comes unbidden, a moment of leaning forward, beyond your individual point of balance, into a shared "here and now" capsule of time. The usual method of steady, scientific noting of the passing of the minutes, hours, and days does not apply, and time as you know it is suspended. The members of the temporary orchestra before you, each playing themselves as instruments to the best of their current ability, join with you as conductor and you with them, to create a piece that has never been heard before and will never be heard in quite that way again.

Others may later describe the event in terms of your courage, but you will know that you had simply allowed yourself to respond to the call of the song the group was singing. You were moved to join your voice with theirs, and something entirely new came to life. Your move was not a stepping down or abdication of all you knew. Instead, you joined them, bringing your authority and knowledge that gave you a place at the front of the room. With the group, you allowed the alchemy that held old understandings in place to become pliable and porous. There was a temporary warp in the field that kept understandings as separate islands, and when the resonance subsided, many, including you, had eyes that glistened with new energy, understanding, and hope. Some would later say there was love involved.

19.3 Your turn

If the routines of your life or the prevailing habits of your family, team, organization, or community are constraining, limiting growth and learning, or disadvantaging those you care about, the albatross and the conductor may show you your next steps. The albatross can help you breathe life into people's hopes, capacities, and willingness to take the risks needed for change. The conductor can inspire by closely observing those gathered to orchestrate something never heard before. The albatross is our totem and the conductor our role model.

This book has invited you to the edge so that you can consider your relationship with provocation, and your willingness to disturb other people. We assume you are committed to something bigger than yourself. You have enough chutzpah and self-belief to ask hard questions of others, comment on things that are not working, and ask others to sit in ambiguous spaces for a prolonged period until some answers or resolution appears.

You also have to think about the reciprocal side of provoking others: your capacity and willingness to be provoked by others or the situations you are in. As we have shown throughout this book, it is tough to get real change without some disturbance to the way things are and some pressure on the status quo.

We have attempted to show you why provocation is needed, how you might use disturbance in different situations, and in so doing, redefine provocation as a resource, a thing of value. The examples we provide and the many people whose stories we told illustrate that provocation, while not without its dangers, can and does help people make progress on what matters.

We hope we have oriented you, shown the pathway to skillfulness, and most of all, helped you have faith. Unlike many other valuable skill sets and ways of thinking, provocation cannot be exercised on your own in front of the mirror. Yes, you can prepare for your next step, even rehearse the options of what you might do or say. But in the end, like the albatross, you have to step out, past the edge of certainty, fueled by your care and aspiration and your sense of what can and should be, and leap out.

We hope you will catch the wind and find yourself having many albatross moments. That you will harness and conduct with skill and care, and in so doing help those around you build the more adaptive and responsive environments you want.

We hope too that you will discover the joys and possibilities of provocation, and that we will see you out of the edge more often or flying the vast expanses of change.

We wish you well in your next flight.

Reference

Coleridge, S.T. (2014). *The Rime of the Ancient Mariner.* Vintage Books Classics, London.

WHAT TO DO NEXT?

Now that you have read *Provocation as Leadership,* you can extend your understanding and practice of provocation by using the materials the authors make available online where you can:

- Participate in virtual webinars and skill sessions that will explore new and experimental tools and techniques;
- Listen directly to the authors—watch their videos, and read their blogs;
- Register for the *Provocation Works* newsletter; and
- Gain access to new material and resources.

To unlock these possibilities, please visit:
www.vantagepoint.net.au
www.theprovocativeleader.com

BIBLIOGRAPHY

ABC (2004). *Good Morning Mr Sarra. Australian Story*, 4 October 2004. https://www.abc.net.au/austory/good-morning-mr-sarra-oct-2-2004/9999366. Retrieved 10 March 2021.

ABC (2017). Comic Hannah Gadsby. *Forcing the audience to look beyond laughter*. Interview with Hannah Gadsby. Leigh Sales, 7.30 Report, *ABC Television*, 14 September 2017. https://www.abc.net.au/7.30/comic-hannah-gadsby,-forcing-the-audience-to-look/8947186. Retrieved 23 August 2020.

ABC (2018). *Nyadol Nyuon Commentary on The Drum. ABC Television*, 2 January 2018. https://www.abc.net.au/news/2018-01-02/the-drum-tuesday-january-2/9299748. Retrieved 10 December 2020.

ABC (2019). *One Plus One: Nyadol Nyuon*. Online Broadcast, *ABC News*, 17 June 2019. https://www.abc.net.au/news/programs/one-plus-one/2019-06-27/one-plus-one:-nyadol-nyuon/11258150?nw=0. Retrieved 15 December 2020.

ABS (2020). *Innovation in a Time of Crisis: The Australian Bureau of Statistics Response to COVID-19*. 29 May 2020. https://www.abs.gov.au/websitedbs/d3310114.nsf/home/innovation+in+a+time+of+crisis. Retrieved 30 April 2021.

ABS (2021). *Household Impacts of COVID-19 Survey*. 16 March 2020. https://www.abs.gov.au/statistics/people/people-and-communities/household-impacts-covid-19-survey/latest-release. Retrieved 7 July 2021.

Accenture (2021). *Purpose: Driving Powerful Transformation for Banks*. Report, 5 May 2021. https://www.accenture.com/us-en/insights/banking/purpose-driven-banking-powerful-digital-transformation. Retrieved 1 August 2021.

AgTech … so what? (2020). *Regen Ag Series #4, 'Greenwashing' … or Good for Business?* AgTech Podcast, 9 September 2020. https://www.agtechsowhat.com/agtechsowhatepisodes/2020/9/9/regen-ag-is-it-greenwashing-or-good-business. Retrieved 10 January 2021.

Andolfi, M., Angelo, C., Menghi, P., & Nicola-Corigliano, A.M. (1983). *Behind the Family Mask: Therapeutic Change in Rigid Family Systems*. Brunner-Mazel, New York.

Architectonics (no date). *What Is a Moment?* Online lectures notes, MIT Architectonics: The Science of Architecture. http://web.mit.edu/4.441/1_lectures/1_lecture5/1_lecture5.html. Retrieved 16 October 2020.

Ashby, R.M. (1956). *An Introduction to Cybernetics*. Methuen, London.

Bateson, G. (1972). *Substance and difference*. In *Steps to an Ecology of Mind: Collected Essays in Anthropology, Psychiatry, Evolution, and Epistemology*. The University of Chicago Press, Chicago.

Barr, B.A. (2021). *The Making of Biblical Womanhood: How the Subjugation of Women Became Biblical Truth*. Brazos Press, Ada, MI.

Bennis, W.G., & Thomas, R.J. (2002). *Geeks & Geezers – How Era, Values and Defining Moments Shape Leaders*. Harvard Business Review Press, Cambridge, MA.

Berne, E. (1964). *Games People Play*. Ballantine Press, New York.

Blake, T. (2001). *A Dumping Ground: A History of the Cherbourg Settlement*. University of Queensland Press, St. Lucia, Qld.

Blount, A. (2018). *Alma Blount and the Art of Teaching Leadership*. Sanford School of Public Policy Online, Duke University. https://sanford.duke.edu/story/alma-blount-and-art-teaching-leadership/. Retrieved 22 July 2021.

Bridgewater Associates (no date). *Principles and Culture*. https://www.bridgewater.com/principles-and-culture. Retrieved 16 October 2020.

Brown, B. (2011). *The Power of Vulnerability*. TED Talk, 3 January 2011. https://www.ted.com/talks/brene_brown_the_power_of_vulnerability/transcript. Retrieved 10 October 2020.

Callahan, S. (2016). *Putting Stories to Work: Mastering Business Storytelling*. Pepperberg Press, Melbourne, Vic.

Cambridge Dictionary (2020). Online Dictionary. https://dictionary.cambridge.org/dictionary/english/provoke. Retrieved 10 August 2019.

Cambridge Dictionary (2020). Online Dictionary. https://dictionary.cambridge.org/dictionary/english/rivalry. Retrieved 10 August 2019.

Capoccia, G., & Kelemen, R.D. (2007). The study of critical junctures. *World Politics, 59* (April), pp. 341–369.

Carroll, L. (2010). *Alice's Adventures in Wonderland*. Penguin Press, London. First published 1865.

Casals, P. (2010). *Quoted by Terry King*, p. 250. In Piatigorsky, Gregor (ed.) *The Life and Career of the Virtuoso Cellist*. McFarland & Co, Jefferson, NC.

Cohan, W.D. (2016). *The Inside Story of Why Arianna Huffington Left the Huffington Post. Vanity Fair*, 8 September 2016. https://www.vanityfair.com/news/2016/09/why-arianna-huffington-left-the-huffington-post. Retrieved 8 July 2020.

Coleridge, S.T. (2014). *The Rime of the Ancient Mariner*. Vintage Books Classics, London.

Csikszentmihalyi, M. (1998). *Flow: The Psychology of Optimal Experience*. Harper Perennial Books, USA.

Dalio, R. (2017). *Principles: Life and Work*. Simon & Schuster, New York.

Darwin, C. (2003). *The Origin of Species*. 150th Anniversary Edition. Penguin Books, USA.

Davis, S. (2015). *Learning to Fly: A Memoir of Hanging On and Letting Go*. Atria Books.

Dunlap, K. (1925). *Old and New Viewpoints in Psychology*. Wolfe Publishing, Mosby Europe.

Eichholz, J.C. (2014). *Adaptive Capacity: How Organizations can Thrive in a Changing World*. LID Publishing, Greenwich, CT.

Edmondson, A. (1999). Psychological safety and learning behavior in work teams. *Administrative Science Quarterly, 44*(2), pp. 350–383.

Erikson, E.H. (1950). *Childhood and Society*. New York: Norton.

Farrelly, F., & Brandsma, J.M. (1981). *Provocative Therapy*. Meta Publications, California, USA.

Foucault, M. (1983). Discourse and Truth: The Problematization of Parrhesia. Six lectures. https://foucault.info/parrhesia/. Retrieved 30 June 2020.

Frankl, V. (1975). Paradoxical intention and dereflection. *Psychotherapy, 12*(3), pp. 226–237.

Gadsby, H. (2018). *Nanette*. Netflix Special. Recorded at Sydney Opera House. https://www.netflix.com/watch/80233611?trackId=14277281&tctx=-97%2C-97%2C%2C%2C%2C. Retrieved 1 June 2021.

Gadsby, H. (2019). *Three Ideas. Three Contradictions. Or Not*. Ted Talk. https://www.ted.com/speakers/hannah_gadsby. Retrieved 30 August 2020.

Ganz, M. (2011). *Public narrative, collective action, and power*. In Odugbemi, S. and Lee, T. (eds.) *Accountability Through Public Opinion: From Inertia to Public Action*. The World Bank, Washington D.C, pp. 273–289. http://nrs.harvard.edu/urn-3:HUL.InstRepos:29314925. Retrieved 20 October 2020.

Gersick, C.J.G. (1991). Revolutionary change theories: A multilevel exploration of the punctuated equilibrium paradigm. *The Academy of Management Review*, *16*(1), pp. 10–36.

Giroux, H. (2010). *Teachers as transformative intellectuals*. In Canestrari, A.S., & Marlowe, B.A. (eds) *Education Foundations: An Anthology of Critical Readings*. Sage Publications, Los Angeles, pp. 197–208.

Google (2015). *Creating a Culture of Innovation: Eight Ideas that Work at Google*, Google workspace, https://workspace.google.com/intl/en_in/learn-more/creating_a_culture_of_innovation.html. Retrieved 10 May 2020.

Haley, J. (1973). *Uncommon Therapy*. W.W. Norton, New York.

Hameiri, B., Bar-Tal, D., & Halperin, E. (2018). Paradoxical thinking interventions: A paradigm for societal change. *Social Issues and Policy Reviews*, *13*(1), pp. 1–17. 10.1111/sipr.12053. Retrieved 12 May 2021.

Hamilton, E., & Cairns. (1963). *Plato: The allegory of the cave*. Republic VII, from *The Collected Dialogues of Plato*, translated by Shorey, P. Random House. https://yale.learningu.org/download/ca778ca3-7e93-4fa6-a03f-471e6f15028f/H2664_Allegory%20of%20the%20Cave%20.pdf. Retrieved 10 June 2021.

Hardin, G. (1968). The tragedy of the commons: The population problem has no technical solution; it requires a fundamental extension in morality. *Science*, *162*(3859), pp. 1243–1248. 10.1126/science.162.3859.1243. Retrieved 1 September 2021.

Harris, R. (2020). *Real Risks*. Podcast. https://podcasts.apple.com/au/podcast/real-risk/id1515258303. Retrieved 20 December 2021.

Hayley, J. (1976). *Problem Solving Therapy*. Jossey Bass, San Francisco, CA.

Heffernan. M. (2020). *Unchartered: How to Navigate the Future*. Avid Reader Press, Simon & Schuster, New York.

Hegarty, R. (2001). Foreword. In Blake, T. *A Dumping Ground: A History of the Cherbourg Settlement*. University of Queensland Press, St. Lucia, Qld.

Heifetz, R. (1994). *Leadership Without Easy Answers*. Harvard University Press, Cambridge, MA.

Heifetz, R., & Linsky, M. (2002). *Leadership on the Line*. Harvard University Press, Cambridge, MA.

Heifetz, R., Grashow, A., & Linsky, M. (2009). *The Practice of Adaptive Leadership: Tools and Tactics for Changing your Organization and the World*. Harvard Business Press, Cambridge, MA.

Heller, J. (1995). *Catch-22*. Simon & Schuster, New York.

Hendry, A., & Kinnison, M. (2017). Perspective: The pace of modern life: Measuring rates of contemporary microevolution. *Evolution: International Journal of Organic Evolution*, Wiley Online, 31 May 2017. 10.1111/j.1558-5646.1999.tb04550.x. Retrieved 1 May 2021.

Henry, K. (2006). *Managing Prosperity. Address to the 2006 Economic and Social Outlook Conference*, Melbourne, 2 November 2006. Australian Government Treasury. https://treasury.gov.au/publication/economic-roundup-spring-2006/managing-prosperity. Retrieved 11 September 2021.

Henry, K. (2007). *Treasury Chief Attacks Welfare, Koori History*, 27 June 2007. http://www.kooriweb.org/foley/resources/pearson/ct27jun2007.html. Retrieved 11 September 2021.

Hoffman, L. (1981). *Foundations of Family Therapy: A Conceptual Framework For Systems Change*. Basic Books, New York.

Houfek, N. (2007). *The Act of Teaching*. Video from Derek Bok Center for Teaching and Learning, Harvard University. https://www.youtube.com/watch?v=6ssHzyVn3HY&feature=emb_logo. Retrieved 20 October 2021.

Ibarra, H. (1999). Provisional selves: Experimenting with image and identity in professional adaptation. *Administrative Science Quarterly, 44*(4), 764–791.

Ibarra, H., & Obodaru, O. (2016). *Betwixt and Between Identities: Liminal Experience in Contemporary Careers*. INSEAD Working Paper No. 2016/79/OBH. 9 November 2016. https://ssrn.com/abstract=2866988 or 10.2139/ssrn.2866988. Retrieved 17 May 2021.

Jaeggi, R. (2015). Towards an immanent critique of forms of life. *Raisons Politiques, 57*(1), pp. 13–29. 10.3917/rai.057.0013. Retrieved 10 June 2021.

Jenkins, R. Editor (2004). *Social Identity*. 2nd edition. Routledge, London. (Professor Sociology at University of Sheffield, UK.)

Johnstone, M.A., and Fern, M. (2017). *Holding on and Letting Go – An Australian Story of Organisational Learning in the Bureau of Statistics*. Unpublished Working Paper, Vantage Point Consulting, Canberra, Australia.

Johnstone, M.A. (2018). *Do we Really Learn from Experience? Developing a Provisional Self for Practice and Learning*. LinkedIn, 30 April 2018. https://www.linkedin.com/pulse/do-we-really-learn-experience-developing-provisional-johnstone-phd/. Retrieved 9 October 2020.

Johnstone, M. (2019). *Diversity, Adaptation, and Leadership: Mangroves and Migrants Can Teach Us a Lot*. LinkedIn, 23 April 2019. https://www.linkedin.com/pulse/diversity-adaptation-leadership-mangroves-immigrants-johnstone-phd/. Retrieved 1 April 2021.

Jones, E. (2020). *My Life and Rugby: The Autobiography*. Pan McMillan, United Kingdom.

Kalla, J.L., & Brockman, D.E. (2020). *Which Narrative Strategies Durably Reduce Prejudice? Evidence from Field and Survey Experiments Supporting the Efficacy of Perspective-Getting*. Open Science Framework Preprint, 28 December 2020. https://osf.io/z2awt. Retrieved 8 July 2021.

Kegan, R. (1994). *In Over Our Heads: The Mental Demands of Modern Life*. Harvard University Press, Boston, MA.

Kegan, R., & Lahey, L.L. (2016). *An Everyone Culture: Becoming a Deliberately Developmental Organization*. Harvard Business Review Press, Cambridge, MA.

Kuhn, T. (1962). *The Structure of Scientific Revolutions*. University of Chicago Press, Chicago.

La Barre, P., & Webber, A.M. (2001). Interview with Arno Penzias in *The Innovation Conversation*. Fast Company. 30 June 2001. https://www.fastcompany.com/43221/fast-talk-innovation-conversation. Retrieved 1 June 2020.

Lewis, M.W. (2000). Exploring paradox: Toward a more comprehensive guide. *Academy of Management Review, 25*, pp. 760–776. 10.5465/amr.2000.3707712. Retrieved 5 November 2020.

Lipsyte, R. (1964). Clay wins title in seventh round upset as Liston is halted by shoulder injury. New York Times on the Web, 26 February 1964. https://archive.nytimes.com/www.nytimes.com/books/98/10/25/specials/ali-upset.html?scp=3&sq=robert%2520lipsyte%2520cassius%2520clay%2520sonny%2520liston&st=cse. Retrieved 29 March 2022.

Martin, P. (2021). *How the ABS Came Our Secret Weapon.* Peter Martin Economics, Online Newsletter, 10 March 2021. https://www.petermartin.com.au/2021/03/you-cant-fix-economy-if-you-cant-see-it.html. Retrieved 10 April 2021.

Massy, C. (2011). *Breaking the Sheep's Back.* Queensland University Press, Brisbane.

Massy, C. (2017). *Call of the Reed Warbler: A New Agriculture, A New Earth.* Queensland University Press, St. Lucia, Qld.

McKinsey (2020). *Innovation in a Crisis: Why it is More Critical than Ever.* Research Paper, McKinsey & Company, 17 June 2020. https://www.mckinsey.com/business-functions/strategy-and-corporate-finance/our-insights/innovation-in-a-crisis-why-it-is-more-critical-than-ever. Retrieved 18 May 2021.

Meadows, D.H. (1999). *Leverage Points: Places to Intervene.* The Sustainability Institute, Hartford, CT. First published in Whole Earth, Winter, 1997.

Meadows, D.H. (2009). *Thinking in System.* Earthscan Publishing, London, UK.

Megginson, L. (1963). Lessons from Europe for American Business. *Southwestern Social Science Quarterly, 44*(1), pp. 3–13.

Merriam-Webster (2020). Online Dictionary. https://www.merriam-webster.com/dictionary/provocateur. Retrieved 16 August 2020.

Mezirow, J. (1991). *Transformative Dimensions of Adult Learning.* John Wiley & Sons, New York.

Minchin, T. (2010). *Prejudice.* (The Ginger Song). Ready for this Live Tour. https://www.youtube.com/watch?v=KVN_0qvuhhw. Retrieved 1 January 2022.

Mindell, A. (2002). *The Deep Democracy of Open Forums.* Hampton Roads Publishing, Newburyport, MA, USA.

Miron-Spektor, E., Ingram, A., Keller, J., Smith, W.K., & Lewis, M.W. (2017). Microfoundations of organizational paradox: The problem is how we think about the problem. *Academy of Management Journal, 61*(1), 2017. Published Online: 16 March 2017. https://www.researchgate.net/publication/315078722_Microfoundations_of_Organizational_Paradox_The_Problem_Is_How_We_Think_about_the_Problem. Retrieved 17 August 2021.

Nesta. (2020). *The Moment We Noticed.* Report from The Relationship Project, Nesta.org. https://relationshipsproject.org/content/uploads/2020/07/The-Moment-We-Noticed_RelationshipsProject_202.pdf. Retrieved 1 May 2021.

Newell, M. (2019). *In My Blood It Runs.* Documentary Film. https://www.imdb.com/title/tt8192948/. Retrieved 22 January 2021.

Ostrom, E. (1998). A behavioral approach to the rational choice theory of collective action presidential address, American Political Science Association, 1997. *American Political Science Review, 92*(1), pp. 1–22.

Ostrom, E. (2009). A general framework for analyzing sustainability of social-ecological systems. *Science*, 325(24), pp. 419–422.

Pascal, B. (1966). Pensées, translated by Krailsheimer, A.J. (Penguin, London. The Thoughts of Blaise Pascal [1669]). https://oll.libertyfund.org/titles/pascal-the-thoughts-of-blaise-pascal. Retrieved 1 May 2021.

Peate, R. (2015). *On Writing*. Self-Published. https://rpeate.wordpress.com/on-writing/. Retrieved 1 July 2019.

Pesala, B. ed (1991). *The Debate of King Milinda*. Motilal Banarsidass Publishing, Delhi.

Polanyi, K. (1944). *The Great Transformation: The Political and Economic Origins of Our Time*. Beacon Press, Boston, MA.

Potok, C. (1967). *The Chosen*. Simon & Schuster, New York.

Potok, C. (1981). Culture confrontation in Urban America: A writer's beginnings. In Jaye, M.C., & Watts, A.C. (eds.) *Literature and the Urban Experience: Essays on the City and Literature*. Manchester University Press, Manchester, UK, pp. 161–168.

Raynor, M.E. (2007). *The Strategy Paradox: Why Committing to Success Leads to Failure and What to do About it*. Crown Business Publishers, New York, NY.

Rehm, J., & Biggs, B. (2021). *The Four Fundamental Forces of Nature*. Space.com. 24 December 2021. https://www.space.com/four-fundamental-forces.html. Retrieved 17 May 2021.

re:Work with Google (2016). *Project Aristotle – Team Effectiveness*. https://rework.withgoogle.com/guides/understanding-team-effectiveness/steps/introduction/. Retrieved 29 March 2021.

Reverso Dictionary. Translation, https://context.reverso.net/translation/german-english/zwischen+Mensch. Retrieved 7 April 2022.

Rosenheim, E., & Golan, G. (1986). Patients' Reactions to Humorous Interventions in Psychotherapy. *American Journal*. PMID: 3963269. 10.1176/appi.psychotherapy.1986.40.1.110. Retrieved 12 November 2020.

Rozovsky, J. (2014). *The Five Keys to a Successful Google Team*. re:Work Google. https://rework.withgoogle.com/blog/five-keys-to-a-successful-google-team/. Retrieved 22 May 2021.

Ruelle, D., & Takens, F. (1971). On the nature of turbulence. *Communications in Mathematical Physics, 20*(3), 167–192. Open Access. https://projecteuclid.org/journals/communications-in-mathematical-physics/volume-20/issue-3/On-the-nature-of-turbulence/cmp/1103857186.full. Retrieved 11 September 2021.

Sanders, S. (1975). *Honda: The Man and His Machine*. Little Brown, Boston, MA.

Sarra, C. (2005). *Strong and Smart: Reinforcing Aboriginal Perceptions of being Aboriginal and Cherbourg State School*. PhD Thesis submitted to Murdoch University, Perth, WA, September 2005.

Sarra, C. (2014). *Beyond Victims: Dr Chris Sarra on the Challenge of Indigenous Leadership*. Speech on ABC Big Ideas with Paul Barclay, 8 September 2014. https://www.abc.net.au/radionational/programs/bigideas/beyond-victims:-the-challenge-of-indigenous-leadership/5727864. Retrieved 12 February 2021.

Scharmer, O., & Kaufer, K. (2013). *Leading from the Emerging Future*. Berrett Koehler, San Francisco.

Scheibe, K.E. (1995). *Self Studies: The Psychology of Self and Identity*. Praeger, Westport, CT.

Schumpeter, J.A. (1975). *Capitalism, Socialism and Democracy*. Harper-Collins, New York, 3rd Edition.

Sevareid, E. (1964). *Eric Sevareid Essays*. McGraw Hill, New York.

Sheehy, G. (1974). *Passages: Predictable Crisis of Adult Life*. Random House Books, New York, NY.

Steinem, G. (2019). *The Truth will Set you Free, But first it will Piss You off! Thoughts on Love, Life and Rebellion*. Murdoch Books, Allan and Unwin, London.

Stronger Smarter Institute. (2017). *Implementing the Stronger Smarter Approach.* Stronger Smarter Institute Position Paper. https://strongersmarter.com.au/wp-content/uploads/2020/08/PUB_Stronger-Smarter-Approach-2017_final-3.pdf. Retrieved 1 February 2021.

Studdert, D.M., Flanders J., & Mello, M.M. (2015). Searching for public health law's sweet spot: The regulation of sugar-sweetened beverages. *PLoS Med, 12*(7), p. e1001848. 10.1371/journal.pmed.1001848. Retrieved 29 October 2021.

Swift, J. (2008). *A Modest Proposal.* A Project Gutenberg ebook. Originally published in 1729. https://www.gutenberg.org/files/1080/1080-h/1080-h.htm. Retrieved 2 October 2017.

Tainter, J. (1990). *The Collapse of Complex Societies.* Cambridge University Press, Cambridge, UK.

Tame, G. (2021). *Grace Tame's Press Club Speech in Full.* National Press Club, Canberra, 3 March 2021. https://www.news.com.au/national/politics/grace-tames-australian-press-club-speech-in-full/news-story/2f641d003254955a25d754a6a59b1926. Retrieved 30 September 2021.

Tetlock, P.E., & Belkin, A. (1997). *Counterfactual thought experiments in world politics.* In Tetlock, P.E., and Belkin, A. (eds.) *Counterfactual Thought Experiments in World Politics.* Princeton University Press, Princeton, New Jersey, pp. 3–38.

Ulrich, W. (1983). *Critical Heuristics of Social Planning, A New Approach to Practical Philosophy.* Revised edition, J. Wiley & Sons, London.

Valentish, J. (2018). *'I Broke the Contract': How Hannah Gadsby's Trauma Transformed Comedy.* Interview, *The Guardian*, 16 July 2018. https://www.theguardian.com/stage/2018/jul/16/hannah-gadsby-trauma-comedy-nanette-standup-netflix. Retrieved 5 November 2020.

Vassolo, R., & Weisz, N. (2022). *Strategy as Leadership.* Stanford University Press, Stanford, CA.

Waldrop, M.M. (1993). *Complexity: The Emerging Science at the Edge of Order and Chaos.* Simon & Schuster, New York.

Watzlawick, P. (1973). *The Language of Change: Elements of Therapeutic Communication.* Basic Books, New York.

Watzlawick, P., Weakland, J.H., & Richard Fisch, R. (1974). *Change – Principles of Problem Formulation and Problem Resolution.* W.W. Norton & Company, Inc., New York, NY.

Weiss, L. (2003). *My Two Lives.* Griffin Press, Sydney, NSW.

Wheatley, M. (2002). *It's an Interconnected World.* Shambhala Sun, April 2002. https://margaretwheatley.com/wp-content/uploads/2014/12/Its-An-Interconnected-World.pdf. Retrieved 15 August 2021.

Whyte, D. (2003). *Crossing the Unknown Sea: Working and the Shaping of Identity.* Penguin Books, USA.

Williams, D. (2005). *Real Leadership: Helping People and Organizations Face Their Toughest Challenges.* Berrett-Koehler Publishing, San Francisco, CA.

Winnicott, D. (1960). The theory of the parent-child relationship. *International Journal of Psychoanalysis, 41*, pp. 585–595.

Xu, L. (2018). *Hannah Gadsby Blasts "Good Men" at Hollywood Reporter Women in Entertainment Event.* Speech to Hollywood Reporters Women in Entertainment Event, 6 December 2018. https://www.hollywoodreporter.com/news/general-news/hannah-gadsby-blasts-good-men-at-hollywood-reporter-women-entertainment-event-1166569/. Retrieved 30 August 2020.

Zak, P.J. (2015). *Why Inspiring Stories Make Us React. The Neuroscience of Narrative.* Cerebrum, February. https://www.ncbi.nlm.nih.gov/pmc/articles/PMC4445577/pdf/cer-02-15.pdf. Retrieved 29 December 2021.

Zak, P.J. (2019). *How Our Brains Decide When to Trust. Harvard Business Review*, 18 July 2019. https://hbr.org/2019/07/how-our-brains-decide-when-to-trust. Retrieved 29 December 2021.

Zander, B., & Zander, R.S. (2000). *The Art of Possibility: Transforming Professional and Personal Life*. Harvard Business School Press, Boston, MA.

Zartman, W.I. (2000). *Ripeness: The hurting stalemate and beyond*. In Stern, P., & Druckman, D. (ed.) *International Conflict Resolution After the Cold War*. The National Academies Press, Washington DC, pp. 225–250. https://nap.nationalacademies.org/read/9897/chapter/7. Retrieved 29 August 2020.

INDEX

For Product Safety Concerns and Information please contact our EU
representative GPSR@taylorandfrancis.com
Taylor & Francis Verlag GmbH, Kaufingerstraße 24, 80331 München, Germany

www.ingramcontent.com/pod-product-compliance
Ingram Content Group UK Ltd.
Pitfield, Milton Keynes, MK11 3LW, UK
UKHW052225190926
475702UK00007B/1202
* 9 7 8 1 0 3 2 3 3 4 7 2 1 *